*Making, Keeping, and Losing Friends*

# Making, Keeping, and Losing Friends

## HOW CAMPUSES SHAPE COLLEGE STUDENTS' NETWORKS

Janice M. McCabe

THE UNIVERSITY OF CHICAGO PRESS
CHICAGO AND LONDON

The University of Chicago Press, Chicago 60637
The University of Chicago Press, Ltd., London
© 2025 by The University of Chicago
All rights reserved. No part of this book may be used or reproduced in any manner whatsoever without written permission, except in the case of brief quotations in critical articles and reviews. For more information, contact the University of Chicago Press, 1427 E. 60th St., Chicago, IL 60637.
Published 2025
Printed in the United States of America

34 33 32 31 30 29 28 27 26 25   1 2 3 4 5

ISBN-13: 978-0-226-84334-6 (cloth)
ISBN-13: 978-0-226-84417-6 (paper)
ISBN-13: 978-0-226-84416-9 (e-book)
DOI: https://doi.org/10.7208/chicago/9780226844169.001.0001

Library of Congress Cataloging-in-Publication Data

Names: McCabe, Janice M., author.
Title: Making, keeping, and losing friends : how campuses shape college students' networks / Janice M. McCabe.
Description: Chicago : The University of Chicago Press, 2025. | Includes bibliographical references and index.
Identifiers: LCCN 2025006447 | ISBN 9780226843346 (cloth) | ISBN 9780226844176 (paperback) | ISBN 9780226844169 (ebook)
Subjects: LCSH: Dartmouth College—Students. | Manchester Community College (Manchester, Conn.)—Students. | University of New Hampshire—Students. | College students—Social networks—United States. | College students—United States—Social life and customs. | Friendship in youth—United States. | Educational sociology—United States.
Classification: LCC LD1441 .M33 2025 | DDC 378.1/980973—dc23/eng/20250225
LC record available at https://lccn.loc.gov/2025006447

♾ This paper meets the requirements of ANSI/NISO Z39.48-1992 (Permanence of Paper).

*To Kallen and Cole*

# Contents

*List of Illustrations* ix

INTRODUCTION
Friendships in College · 1

## Part One
PROCESSES OF MAKING, KEEPING, AND LOSING FRIENDS · 23

CHAPTER ONE
Making Friends: Initial and Secondary Friendship Markets · 25

CHAPTER TWO
Keeping Friends: The Friendship Funnel and Friendship Expansion · 70

CHAPTER THREE
Losing Friends: Breaking Up and Fading Away · 107

## Part Two
HOW INSTITUTIONS AND IDENTITIES SHAPE THESE PROCESSES · 135

CHAPTER FOUR
College Characteristics: How Networks Differ by Institution Type · 137

CHAPTER FIVE
Student Identities: How Race, Class, and Gender Shape Networks · 172

CONCLUSION
Points of Intervention · 200

*Acknowledgments 211*
*Appendix A: Researching Students' Networks
on Three Campuses 215*
*Appendix B: Tables Describing Study Participants
and the Campuses 225*
*Notes 235*
*Bibliography 255*
*Index 265*

# Illustrations

## Figures

I.1 Ideal types of friendship networks: samplers, compartmentalizers, and tight-knitters 5
1.1 Melanie's friendship networks, Dartmouth year two and at graduation 28
1.2 Grace's friendship network, UNH year two 34
1.3 Safiya's friendship network, Dartmouth year two 38
1.4 Morgan's friendship network, UNH year one 40
1.5 Tom's friendship network, Dartmouth year three 54
2.1 Robbie's friendship network, UNH year three 71
2.2 Otto's friendship networks, UNH year three 92
2.3 Troy's friendship networks, Dartmouth year two and at graduation 96
2.4 Kira's friendship networks, Dartmouth year two and at graduation 98
2.5 Layla's friendship networks, Dartmouth year two and at graduation 100
3.1 Bill's friendship networks, Dartmouth year two and at graduation 108
4.1 Terrence's friendship network, MCC year two 148
4.2 Yusef's friendship network, UNH year three 155
4.3 Rachel's friendship network, UNH year three 161
5.1 Danica's friendship networks, Dartmouth year two and at graduation 176
5.2 Jennifer's friendship networks, Dartmouth year two and at graduation 180
5.3 Patrice's friendship network, MCC year two 188

# Tables

| | | |
|---|---|---|
| 1.1 | Friendship Network Characteristics by Campus: Comparing Dartmouth College, University of New Hampshire, Manchester Community College, and a Midwest University | 16 |
| 2.1 | Change during College for Dartmouth College Respondents | 94 |
| 4.1 | Friendship Network Type by Campus | 140 |
| 4.2 | Friendship Network Characteristics by Campus | 141 |
| 6.1 | Points of Intervention for Students and Colleges | 202 |
| B.1 | Characteristics of College Friends | 225 |
| B.2 | Characteristics of Sample by Campus | 226 |
| B.3 | Characteristics of the Three Institutions | 228 |
| B.4 | Participant Key Characteristics | 230 |

[ INTRODUCTION ]

# Friendships in College

"At times, I could find myself being alone in college. Especially my first two weeks. I felt like, how could I be so alone with like 15,000 people around me? You can really feel that way at times." Yusef's[1] sense of loneliness was something I heard often from the college students I interviewed. These feelings, however, surprised Yusef, who said he knew he "was gonna have a good time" at college and felt at ease attending one that was only an hour from his hometown. Throughout his first two years at the University of New Hampshire (UNH), Yusef felt lonely at times. He felt less so as he found his place with his tight-knit group of friends. By the time I spoke with him in his third year at UNH, Yusef had seventeen close friends. Over half of them were students he had met at UNH, and most of them were Black students, like him.

Two hours away, at a smaller college, Uma also felt "really lonely" in her first fall at Dartmouth. She explained, "I first fell in love with Dartmouth when my older brother visited," and was "really excited" for her first term there. Once she arrived on campus, however, Uma found it to be "a hard time." Her difficulties did not lie in the academic work, despite being a pre-med student at an Ivy League school. Rather, it was Uma's social life that was "really hard." She reported feeling lonely due in large part to a "really, really stressful" situation with her two first-year roommates, who were "crazy partiers" and "would lock me out of the room sometimes." Uma joined a sorority "mainly because everybody else was going through rush," but she "absolutely hated rush," noting that her sorority "never really felt like a comfortable place for me." She described her feelings of discomfort and not belonging as "amplified when I'm around fifty girls who I just don't know that well," as she was in this sorority. Neither her first-year dorm nor joining a sorority helped Uma to feel less lonely. When another campus organization, the orchestra, went on tour, Uma got "really close" to another member, Ellie, who became one of her best friends. Ellie also introduced Uma to her other friends, leading to the development of a more meaningful circle of friends. Uma is multiracial as are her two closest friends, Ellie and Isabel, and sharing this experience brought them closer. Uma summed up the difference it made to be in college with "real friends": "I feel so much happier now that I have really close friends. And I think that's a lot more important than the grades on my transcript."

Like those at four-year residential campuses, students at a two-year community college spoke about both their feelings of loneliness and the important role that friendships played in their college experience. Erin, a White woman and a thirty-four-year-old student in her second year at Manchester Community College (MCC), explained, "I've never had a lot of close friends," noting, "I like my own company. I like my girlfriend's company. I like my dog's company." And yet she also told me:

> I feel like the friendships I've made are what turned it [community college] into an experience. They're what turned it into a chapter of life. They bring a lot of things to life that may seem like mundane things, like coffee becomes a whole new thing [with a friend beside you]. They renew my energy. They inspire me and help me figure things out and learn new things about myself and them. I definitely feel like they have an enormous impact on my educational experience and on my ability to keep refocusing and keep going forward even when I'm starting to get tired.

During our interview, Erin emphasized that she is not someone who spends a lot of time with friends, and she only considered three people to be close friends (including her girlfriend, who is not a student), so I was a bit surprised by her passionate appreciation of her college friends. Erin noted, "It makes a big difference when you see other people who are fighting the same fight and going for the same thing . . . It's a constant reminder of why you're here." Erin's experience makes clear that friendships hold much potential. Their potential is not only for helping students feel socially connected, but also for providing academic support and motivation.

Despite vastly different college experiences, Yusef, Uma, and Erin all experienced loneliness, and they all experienced the benefits of meaningful friendships. Study after study shows that social connection, specifically having high-quality relationships, increases people's health and happiness.[2] Uma experienced this, for example, when she developed a meaningful circle of "real friends." Research also demonstrates that relationships matter for psychological well-being in the first year of college.[3] On college campuses, students are surrounded by potential friends, often by thousands of same-age peers, as Yusef explained. College students sit beside their peers in class, often walk to and from activities with many other people, live in close quarters in residential campuses, and cross paths in dining halls, student organizations, and libraries. They also use social media and other technology to connect with people on campus and at home in ways that were not possible in previous generations.

College campuses thus contain a paradox: students are surrounded by potential friends, yet they also feel lonely. Over people's lifetimes, young adulthood stands out as the time when friendships are most important.[4] It also stands out as the point in the life course when people report the highest levels of loneliness, with ages eighteen to nineteen as the peak of loneliness in several recent studies.[5] College campuses are facing the highest rates of anxiety, depression, and suicidal ideation on record, with seemingly constant headlines about the mental health crisis on college campuses.[6] In 2023, the US surgeon general declared that the United States has an "epidemic of loneliness and isolation," one that is "more widespread than many of the other major health issues of our day," such as smoking, diabetes, and obesity.[7] While rates of loneliness and isolation have been climbing over time, they became more acute during the COVID-19 pandemic when students were engaged in remote learning and experienced physical isolation.[8]

All of the ninety-five students that I spoke with on three campuses reported having friends, yet having friends did not always keep them from feeling lonely. Why? What features of friendships keep us feeling lonely and what helps us feel supported? National survey data showing that 43 percent of college students feel isolated from others "some of the time" and another 23 percent "often" feel isolated[9] point to the need for research not just on friendships, but on meaningful and supportive ones. Focusing on these meaningful friendships, I ask which features of colleges help them form and which get in the way of them forming as well as remaining in students' lives.

In this book, I trace students' experiences of making, keeping, and losing friends on three different types of college campuses. Building on recent works such as *Platonic*, *Modern Friendship*, and *Big Friendship* that celebrate friendship and give advice for strengthening adult friendships, I focus on a specific age group and context, and take a network and institutional approach to the topic.[10] I find that students' experiences with feelings of loneliness and belonging are tied more to the relationships among their friends—that is, the structure of their friendship network—than to the number of friends they have.[11] In other words, the loneliness epidemic on college campuses is less about the problems individual students have making friends and more about the structure of their networks, the structure of the institutions they attend, and how their identities matter in each of these places. Meaningful friendships are crucial to thriving in college and combating loneliness. However, meaningful friendships are not automatic; they are achieved as students work at making, keeping, and losing friends. Learning how these processes operate during college can not only help while they are students, but also help ward off loneliness beyond graduation.

During the interviews, the systematic questions I asked students about their friends and the relationships among them allowed me to construct sociograms—or network diagrams—of students' friendships. Using social network techniques, I place students into a typology: samplers, compartmentalizers, and tight-knitters. These three network types are shown visually in figure I.1. Samplers make a friend or two from a variety of places, but their friends remain unconnected to each other. Compartmentalizers have friends belonging to two to four clusters, with friends knowing each other within the clusters but not across them. And tight-knitters have friends who form one densely woven friendship group where nearly all of their friends are connected. Tight-knitters have the most dense connections between their friends, and samplers the least dense.[12] Institutional structures at each college shape the types of networks students form. Each of these three network types has advantages and disadvantages.[13] Importantly, students experience both loneliness and meaningful friendships differently depending on their friendship network type. In each type, however, experiencing meaningful friendships embedded within a network helps students feel socially connected.

While it may seem random whether students make friends and where they make friends on campus, friendship networks are patterned in ways that are shaped by institutional features of the colleges that students attend as well as by students' identities. Students often expect to make friends when they first arrive on campus, but neither Yusef, Uma, nor Erin made meaningful friendships during this initial "friendship market" period. Students' comparisons of themselves to others, specifically their perceptions that "everyone else has already made friends," contribute to feelings of loneliness and isolation. There are, however, multiple opportunities to make friends, and the sociological concepts of propinquity, homophily, and the friendship market explain the patterns in these seemingly random formations.

Yusef, Uma, and Erin all made friends later in college. During what I call the "secondary friendship market," they formed friendships in clubs, which helped them meet people they had things in common with and saw often. In this way, their secondary friendship market experiences draw on homophily (that is, similarities in interests or identities) and propinquity (that is, regularly coming into contact with someone). Yusef made his closest friends at UNH on the football team and in a club for Black engineers. The time the football team spent together training, practicing, and playing

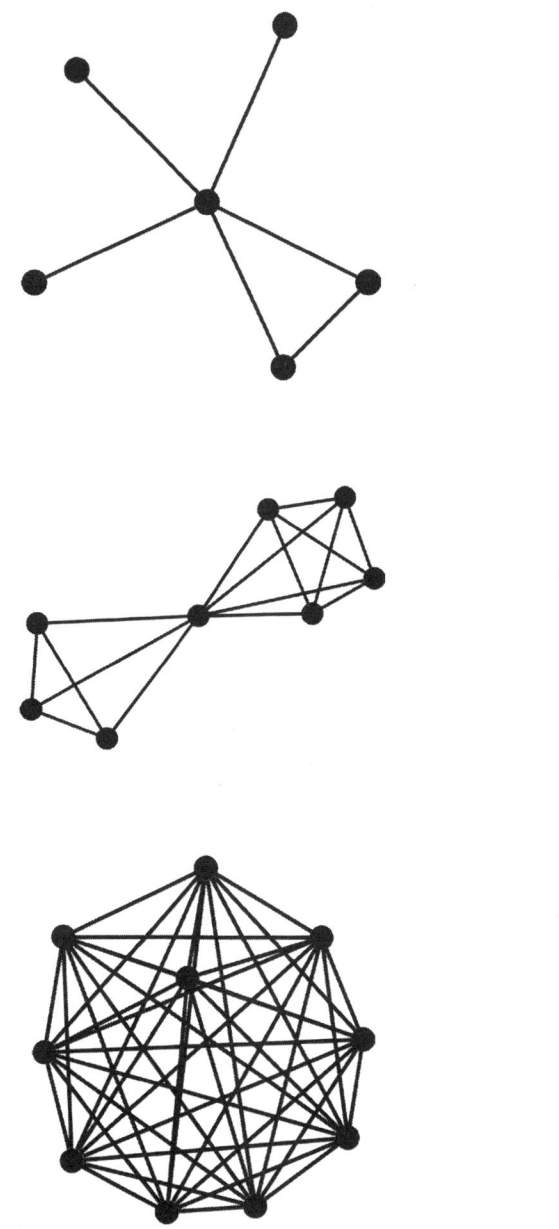

FIGURE I.1. Ideal types of friendship networks: samplers, compartmentalizers, and tight-knitters.

enabled propinquity to craft strong bonds. In the Black engineers club, the commonalities of being a Black student on a predominantly White campus and in a predominantly White major bonded them together and provided Yusef with social and academic support. Similarly, Uma met one of her closest friends in orchestra, and they bonded not only over music but also over being pre-med students: "we have so much in common . . . there are certain things that I don't have to explain to her." They also discussed their shared identity of being multiracial and appearing White, and how that gave them "a lot of privileges." Erin met her closest friend at MCC through the Pride club, both seeking to support and connect with others with marginalized sexual identities.

The institutional patterns of Dartmouth made restarts easier for Uma, but they also made keeping friends a challenge because they are not physically together on campus all four years. At Dartmouth, students take classes during the full year (fall, winter, and spring terms) during their first and fourth years, but during their second and third years they are required to take two of these terms away from campus.[14] Uma talked about the difficulties that came with being away from campus while on an internship in spring term, when her two closest friends were both at Dartmouth: "It's really worried me [because] it becomes very difficult to stay in touch and have the same deep closeness when you're physically very far apart." For Erin, the commuter structure of MCC and the age gap between herself and other students made it more challenging to make and keep friendships over time. Each campus has institutional features that make it easier and harder for friendships to form, to stay, and to support students, as I explain throughout this book.

Moreover, through talking with students and analyzing what they shared with me, I discovered ways that students, their parents and supporters, and colleges themselves can shape the way that students make friends, keep friends, and lose friends during college. I share these insights throughout this book, summarizing them at the end of each chapter.

## What Researchers Know about College Friendships

When adults tell young people that "college is the best time of your life," they are usually referring to their interactions with peers and their time outside of the classroom. Educational researchers have also recognized the importance of peers in students' college experiences, including their sense of belonging and success. In the most widely used theories within education, including those focused on involvement, integration, engagement, and belonging, peers are considered crucial for college student success on a range of measures, including grades, persisting rather than dropping out, and graduating.[15] For example, in what has been described as the "definitive study of how students change and develop in college,"[16] Alexander Astin points to students' peer groups as the "single most potent source" of this change and development.[17]

Although education researchers have long recognized the power of peers, the focus on friendship, as a specific type of peer relationship, has been uneven, and many gaps remain.[18] Much of the research on college friendships has appeared in the past decade, and has largely focused on establishing the importance of friends and describing those whom friendship ties happen between. For example, a sociological book on students' experiences at a liberal arts college emphasized that students need "at least one or two friends . . . for psychic survival at college," but that their "feeling of being 'at home,' as if this is 'my campus,'" is strengthened by having a "broader network of acquaintances."[19] Similarly, researchers, arguing for a "relationship-rich education," asserted that students' relationships with peers "are likely to be the most significant" relationships they have in college.[20] The support and information that students get from their relationships, including their friendships, serve as social capital.[21] My prior work, particularly my book *Connecting in College*, based on research at one large public Midwestern university, showed how friendship networks both help and hinder academic and social success during and after college. By identifying the three network types shown in figure I.1—tight-knitters, samplers, and compartmentalizers—I demonstrated how racial, gender, and class disadvantages lead students to form different types of networks for support. Moreover, the support students experienced differed according to the connections between their friends. In other words, it is not just friends that matter for academic and social success, but also friendship networks.[22]

Two main processes shape who people become friends with: homophily and propinquity. Homophily, or similarity, forms the basis of many friendships, such as the same-race bonds that provide important support and emotional connection for Black students or others from minoritized backgrounds and for women students.[23] Propinquity, or coming into regular contact, shapes the friendships that students form and makes it feel easy to keep particular friends as well. Clubs play a big role in this.[24] Numerous studies note that students make friends in clubs.[25] Friends also can be "connectors" by providing information about clubs and making the involvement more comfortable. Having a friend in a club, however, was not always enough to make it sufficiently comfortable to join, particularly for students from less advantaged backgrounds joining exclusive spaces like sororities.[26]

Social network analysis, which involves mapping connections to measure network structure, is useful in describing students' friendships. Quantitative studies of friendship networks have assessed their racial composition in college[27] and how friends' academic achievement and resources affect students' academic achievement.[28] This research finds that students of color are more likely to have interracial friendships than are White students. The results of one study of 800 first-year college students illustrate the general patterns, finding the highest rates of same-race friendships among White students (85 percent), followed by Black (69 percent), Asian (48 percent), and Latinx (20 percent) students.[29] However, once structural diversity on campus is considered, friendship patterns reveal that students of color are friends with same-race others more often than would be randomly expected and more often than White students. Network analysis also maps the connections between students' friends, resulting in the network typology of tight-knitters, compartmentalizers, and samplers, described above. As I developed this typology in *Connecting in College*, I became curious about how these types worked on different campuses. Although sociologists for more than a decade have been calling for more network research, noting "rich possibilities for scholars to map precisely the dynamics of undergraduate social networks," many gaps remain in our current knowledge.[30] I take up this call, uniquely pairing quantitative measures of network structure (such as density, centrality, and modularity) with qualitative measures of students' experiences of friendship across three postsecondary institutions.

The ways that we can keep in touch with friends have changed dramatically over the past generation. Today's college students need not leave messages for each other on whiteboards outside their dorm rooms. Instead, phones allow people to feel both more connected and lonelier.[31] Numerous experts have noted how social media and smartphone use often contribute to loneliness despite the possibilities for connections.[32] One study of 1,649 adults in several countries found that spending more time on social media was associated with more loneliness, and that people who use this time "with the motive of maintaining their relationships feel lonelier than those who spend the same amount of time on social media for other reasons."[33] While social media are not the focus of this book and I did not systematically measure students' use of them, social media come into students' stories of how they make, keep, and lose friends. Students' experiences do not point to social media alone as the cause for feelings of loneliness and isolation. Some of my suggestions to students and their supporters involve how to be more meaningful in their use of technology in their friendships.

Along with making friends, another important task of young adulthood is identity development.[34] These two tasks are linked: we see ourselves through our friends. Friends contribute to students' identity development through developing an identity that is similar to a friend based on interests or aspirational goals, as well as through distancing from a friend seen as having negative traits.[35] Put simply, we craft our identities in ways that draw out similarities to particular friends and stark differences from others. An ethnography of how students become socially involved at a large public university stresses that students often end up with "cookie-cutter identities" rather than complex and dynamic ones.[36] Even the higher status roles of "educators" and "managers" occupied by White men limited students' feelings of belonging. Many women ended up as "caregivers" and "associates" and men of color as "associates" and "entertainers," feeling overlooked for their contributions yet staying in these roles to maintain approval and avoid ostracism from peers. Throughout their identity development, students refine who they are not just internally but also in relation to their friends and peers.

Colleges, particularly residential campuses, are organized to help students make friends. Student affairs staff spend much time and energy helping students transition to college and to have a good college experience. Most colleges have an orientation that involves not only academic information about the college but also icebreakers and other opportunities to meet peers. Many colleges require students to live in residence halls in their first year, noting that it increases connections to the campus and to other students. As students and their families consider where they will attend college, the quality of the classes is not the only important factor. The COVID-19 pandemic brought to the fore "the idea that students don't go to college simply to gain knowledge but also to connect with others,"[37] thus emphasizing the importance of friendship ties.

Students experience college differently according to their different social identities and backgrounds. Despite gains in access to higher education in the past forty years, racial and class inequalities remain in the types of institutions students attend, their experiences there, and whether they graduate.[38] White and Asian students disproportionately attend four-year colleges, particularly selective ones, and graduate at higher rates than do Latinx, Black, and Native American students.[39] A growing body of research documents how students from marginalized backgrounds experience college differently and unequally.[40] While these works touch on friendship, there is much we do not know about how social identities impact friendship processes and networks.

Community colleges are a particularly important site, given their promise of social mobility through open access and lower costs,[41] but sociologists have mostly neglected what happens there.[42] Given that more than 1 million students graduate from US community colleges each year[43] and that students' experiences there are different from those of students at four-year residential campuses,[44] students' experiences with friendships are likely different as well. Hints of this appear in studies of the experiences of community college students, including a finding that stronger connections with friends on campus "made academic life 'fun'" and "meaningful."[45] Researchers have yet to study friendship network structure or how friendships influence student success at community colleges. Important gaps, therefore, remain in our understanding of friendship networks across a range of institutions, particularly at two-year colleges. An institutional perspective is well positioned to shine light on processes at community colleges, filling gaps in what we know about friendships in these settings.

Along with a social network approach, I use an institutional approach throughout this book to illuminate how features of colleges impact students' experiences. Past research on college life shows ways that such features matter. For example, a case study of Bowdoin, using interviews with students as well as archival research, demonstrates how the "core structures and practices" of the college "are essential to the enactment and entrenchment of racial ignorance and structural White supremacy."[46] Researchers using this institutional approach acknowledge the different resources (such as cultural, social, and economic capital) students bring to college, but focus on colleges as "generative systems of meaning and action."[47] An incisive book about sexual assault on campus develops the notion of "sexual geographies" to examine how "particularly in college settings—sexual outcomes are intimately tied to the physical spaces where they unfold." Institutional decisions involving roommates, dorm furniture, and access to and control of common spaces, including where parties involving alcohol can happen, all influence students' options and experiences.[48] Drawing on this approach, I investigate how features of institutions drive students' friendships in terms of their structure and content. Combining an institutional and social network approach enables attention to campus structures and structural inequalities as well as individuals' agency.[49]

## The Three Campuses

Many studies of higher education focus on four-year colleges, particularly elite ones,[50] which means we know less about the types of colleges most students attend. As of 2021, there were 18.7 million college students in the United States, including about 5 million at two-year institutions and 9 million at public four-year institutions.[51] Research studies with cross-campus comparisons of other aspects of students' experiences in the "experiential core" of college[52] note how campus structures influence students' experiences,[53] so it seemed likely that friendships matter in different ways for students' success on campuses depending on their structures. I was intrigued and wanted to better understand how campus structures influence friendships, particularly at nonresidential two-year colleges.

Thus, I knew that I wanted to study students' friendships on multiple campuses, including two-year as well as four-year institutions. I decided to choose three institutions in similar locations that differ in size, selectivity, residential life, and campus racial culture, to allow me to leverage strengths of case study design. *Making, Keeping, and Losing Friends* builds on my prior work to examine previously overlooked institutions and individuals. Using a mixed-methods longitudinal approach and a comparative case study of students' friendships at three types of postsecondary institutions—a small elite private college (Dartmouth College), a large public university (University of New Hampshire, [UNH]), and a nonresidential community college (Manchester Community College [MCC])—I examine how institutions matter for students' friendships. This book focuses on ninety-five participants—thirty-five at Dartmouth, thirty-four at UNH, and twenty-six at MCC—who completed a semi-structured, in-depth interview, survey, and egocentric network data with me about halfway through college.

In line with a case study approach, my focus is on identifying patterns within and across institutions, rather than being generalizable to specific populations.[54] New Hampshire is an interesting location, as it is one of the least diverse states, yet has high levels of growth among racial minorities, concentrated in areas around these three institutions.[55] Dartmouth has a rich and troubled history of racial inclusion, beginning with its founding mission to educate Indian youth, yet only graduating nineteen Native American students in its first two hundred years. UNH has fewer academic resources and cultural programs than Dartmouth, but more than MCC, which offers no academic resources or student clubs specifically for students of color. As I recruited students, I sought to obtain the most diverse sample I could, including a range of race, class, and gender backgrounds, majors, and hometowns.[56] Thus, I relied heavily on flyers that I posted on each campus, and I also recruited through campus clubs, where I would attend to explain the study or they would forward an email invitation to participate. I also asked the students I interviewed for suggestions of others to talk with, particularly peers with different experiences. Aware of my identity as a middle-aged White woman and a professor at Dartmouth, and how these identities might be seen differently by students depending on their own identities, I approached each interview with kindness and curiosity about the particular window into campus life provided by that participant. In constructing each case, I draw on multiple sources of evidence,[57] specifically field notes from my observations in public spaces (libraries, cafeterias, and so on), archival documents written by and about the institutions (in local papers, *Princeton Review*, and so on), student surveys and interviews, and network data on students' friendships. I sought to interview students when they were halfway through college, at graduation, and every five years after that.[58]

While these three campuses were chosen because they fit a common type of institution of higher education, it is not just the type but also the specific campus structures that influence students' experiences making, keeping, and losing friends on each campus. Thus, before I go into those specific experiences, I provide snapshots here of each campus, drawn from my field notes.

On a chilly New England day, I drove an hour to my first meeting at Manchester Community College (MCC) to decide if it would be a good site as one of the three campuses where I would be interviewing college students about their friendships. There were no tours offered of MCC, and it held an "open house" once a year, which occurred about a month before I began exploring campuses. As I pulled into the driveway where my GPS directed me, I saw a large, square gray building ahead, surrounded by an equally large parking lot that resembled what you might find at an office building or hospital.

I arrived around 9:40 a.m. for a 10:00 a.m. meeting, which gave me plenty of time to find a parking spot and the meeting room. As I stepped inside the front door, a White middle-aged woman sitting at a small desk looked directly at me and said, "Hello, good morning," in a very friendly voice. I got the impression that she warmly greeted everyone who entered the building. I signed in at the sheet on her desk, which noted my name, the reason for my visit, and my car make, model, and license plate number.

The building reminded me of a high school, with long and wide hallways, lots of classrooms, and a central lobby, which students called "the pit." As I headed to my meeting, I wandered down the long, white hallway, where there were mostly empty classrooms. One held eight or nine students seated at desks with an older White man at the front of the room, presumably the instructor. When I reached the end of the hall, I headed upstairs because the office where I was meeting was number 303. I continued to walk down several long, white, quiet hallways. After two turns, I ended up in a deserted hallway filled with large, overstuffed chairs in bright geometric patterns. Off to the left, I could see an empty basketball court. As I kept walking, I noticed four offices that resembled large cubicles, fully enclosed in glass and in the middle of an otherwise open area. Looking at the signs outside, I saw that one of these offices belonged to the person I was meeting. Another was the head of clubs, whom I planned to meet with on my next visit.

I ended up returning several times to meet with different staff and administrators, including two meetings with the president of MCC to gain access. It was clear to me that the institution did not get many requests from researchers wanting to understand their campus or their students. I returned to post flyers and to recruit at a club fair, where I had a table next to student clubs and four-year colleges to which students could transfer. I also returned to attend some club meetings and classes, to recruit for my study and when I had an interview scheduled. Each time I went to MCC, I spent some time in the common spaces on campus, such as the cafeteria and library, to better understand student life there. I was able to reserve "study rooms" in the library for my interviews as well as two conference rooms on campus, so that interviews would be private. In the end, I interviewed twenty-six students.

The week after I first visited MCC, I drove two hours to Durham, where the University of New Hampshire (UNH) is located. Once I exited from the highway, I drove past a sprawling horse farm at the edge of campus and then the football stadium. Parking was much more complicated than at MCC, so it took time to find an open spot of on-street parking where I could pay for two hours of parking, which is how long I expected to need for the tour. By the time I parked and found the admissions building, it was just two minutes until the tour was set to start. The admissions building resembled a small house, and a young woman, whom I assume was a student, was seated at the desk right inside the door. She told me that the program was just starting, in the back room. I walked through the doorway she pointed to and found a large room with fifty or sixty chairs set up in rows, all facing two students and an admissions officer who began by explaining the mechanics of applying to UNH.

We spent about ten minutes in that room, and then the group split into two smaller groups, each led by a student. The students mentioned that each hour they did two separate tours. We went first to a dorm, then to the athletic facilities (including the hockey arena, which sparked excitement among many of those on the tour),[59] an academic building, the library, the study abroad facility, and the student union to end. The campus had a lot of green space and trees, and many types of buildings, including brick Romanesque Revival architecture as well as colonial and more modern construction. Most of the tour was about clubs, social life, and the dorms. It did, however, include bits about academics: all students do research and almost all classes are taught by faculty, who love for students to attend office hours. Although the campus was much bigger than MCC, I left with the impression that it would be easy to navigate the campus and to be a student at UNH.

As I did at MCC, when I traveled to UNH for interviews, I would also spend time in common spaces on campus, particularly the student union, where I would also repost flyers advertising the study, and I attended a couple of club meetings to recruit for my study. I interviewed thirty-four students at UNH. (The appendixes include more details about the participants and the campuses.)

Back at Dartmouth, where I am a faculty member in sociology, I also took a campus tour to see Dartmouth through more of the student lens. As had been the case at UNH, students led the tour. We met on the second floor of an ornate and distinguished old building with an expansive view of the green, the central grassy space on campus. The admissions building was one that I had never entered in the five years I had been a faculty member. There were parents and high-school-age students sitting and standing in small clusters in the big open lobby on the second floor. When it was time for our tour, a student called us over, and about a dozen of us set off across campus. The only building we went inside was the library, which is impressive in its stately beauty[60] and its range of types of study spaces. The rest of the tour involved walking past many academic buildings where classes are held and one where students might live. Like UNH, Dartmouth is located in a college town, and the campus is picturesque. Unlike the tour at UNH, the Dartmouth tour did not take us inside a dorm, and we did not see the athletic facilities. I had been inside Dartmouth's gym and knew it was older and smaller than the expansive complex at UNH. The tour highlighted the range of classes that Dartmouth offered, access to faculty who are "just waiting in their office for you to stop by," research opportunities with faculty even for first-year students, many study abroad programs, and numerous campus clubs and organizations to join. In sum, it focused considerably more on the academic aspects of campus than did the tour at UNH.

Because I work at Dartmouth, it was easier to schedule interviews there. As I had done on the other campuses, I used flyers and outreach to clubs and organizations to recruit as diverse a sample as possible. I ended up interviewing thirty-five Dartmouth students.

Although all three campuses are located in New Hampshire and are within two hours' drive of each other, they looked and felt quite different from each other. As my field notes suggest, some of these differences were apparent even in my introduction to each campus. They also came through in my interviews with students. One big difference between campuses is the intensity of academic and social life. Both were particularly intense at Dartmouth, such that Jennifer told me, "The academics at Dartmouth make it impossible for anyone to survive without having close friends." Jennifer had observed that if students were not equipped to handle the academic rigor of Dartmouth, there was little room for error, and they would have to take time off. Jennifer's friends encouraged her to "survive" Dartmouth, but they also seemed to make it something special for her. Also reflecting the intensity, Safiya explained how she needed to be selective with friends, because every friendship was a time commitment and her schedule felt full already due to the "strenuous academics." In contrast, no students at UNH referred to their campus as strenuous or intense.[61]

Despite these differences, the two residential campuses have more of a peer-centered environment than does the nonresidential community college. At UNH and Dartmouth, students not only take classes together but spend most of their time with peers, including in clubs, dining halls, and residence halls. Studies that ask students to track their time show that they spend nearly all their time with peers, whether socializing, attending class, or in clubs.[62] Renata, a Dartmouth student, told me that "it's getting to the point where like if I'm alone, I feel strange." Like most students at UNH and Dartmouth, Renata was often around friends: eating, studying, or hanging out. At MCC, most students noted that they rarely saw each other outside of class. Exceptions were programs with cohorts taking classes together, such as nursing and HVAC, and some project-focused clubs, but even there the frequency and regularity was less than on the residential campuses. Indeed, the residential campuses had large student affairs departments that worked to support students' residential and extracurricular lives, whereas MCC had two full-time staff members devoted to these tasks. The peer-centered environment at the residential campuses worked so seamlessly for some students that they did not experience making friends to be a challenge. During our interview, I asked Tom, as I did each participant, about the biggest obstacle for him socially on campus at Dartmouth. Tom responded, "Socially? Um, I don't know. To be honest, I never thought of any hindrances. Yeah, I don't know." Tom had found friendship easily at Dartmouth, and his friends formed a tight-knit group. This was not the case for all students on campus.[63] Far more common than Tom's experience are those of students like Yusef, Uma, and Erin, who have "hindrances" and times when they feel lonely, even in the peer-centered environment of the residential campuses. This book identifies aspects of college campuses that make friendships feel easy and those that serve as barriers to making and keeping friends.

## Students' Friendship Networks at Each Campus

From the network data I collected from each of the ninety-five students I interviewed, I found all three friendship network types at each of the campuses.[64] I also identified features of each campus that shaped students' networks. As shown in Table 1, Compartmentalizers are the most common type at each campus, as they were at the large public Midwestern university that I studied in *Connecting in College*.[65] Tight-knitters and samplers are present on all campuses as well, although tight-knitters are more common at UNH and samplers at MCC. Chapter 4 provides a detailed discussion of differences across campuses.

Students' stories show how friendship experiences and strategies differ by network type. Tight-knitters often do not feel comfortable joining something alone. One tight-knitter, Jennifer, told me that she does not even like walking into class alone, so she'll text a friend, "Where are you? Let's walk in together and sit together." Jennifer explained that when she has class with friends, "usually we meet right outside the class, and then walk in together. And we sit together." She noted, "I like to do that. I would much rather go with a friend. I feel less awkward walking into a big room full of people." In contrast, samplers are not surrounded by a close-knit group of friends, but instead often have friends who are very different from each other and

TABLE 1.1. Friendship Network Characteristics by Campus: Comparing Dartmouth College (DC), University of New Hampshire (UNH), Manchester Community College (MCC), and a Midwest University ("MU")

|  | DC (N=35) | UNH (N=34) | MCC (N=26) | Overall Sample (N=95) | "MU" (N=67)[a] |
|---|---|---|---|---|---|
| Density of friendship ties (mean) | 0.53 | 0.58 | 0.43 | 0.52 | 0.56 |
| % Samplers | 14 | 21 | 35 | 22 | 18 |
| % Compartmentalizers | 63 | 44 | 46 | 52 | 49 |
| % Tight-knitters | 23 | 35 | 19 | 26 | 33 |
| Number of friends | 11.9 | 12.3 | 8.2 | 11.0 | 18 |
| % Friends at their college | 72 | 75 | 44 | 65 | 65 |
| % Friends from home | 29 | 32 | 67 | 40 | 38 |
| % Friends from home who also attend their college | 1 | 7 | 9 | 5 | 12 |

[a] McCabe, *Connecting in College*.

can fulfill different needs or interests. One sampler, Danica, explained, "My communities and my friendships are not what I thought they would be and not what I wanted them to be, but, I think, they're exactly what I need them to be. Everyone in my life fulfills a different role in a different aspect of my personality." Unlike Jennifer, Danica attended classes and club meetings by herself. She often had a friend or two in each of these settings, and they might sit together, but she would show up on her own. Compartmentalizers often have different groups of friends focused on these different identities or interests; for example, a social group and an academic group, or groups organized around their biology major and their interest in orchestra. Compartmentalizers might have one group that operates more like that of a tight-knitter and others where they show up alone, like samplers.

In line with research on US adults, which finds that network size is shrinking over the past couple of decades,[66] I also find that students' friendship networks have gotten smaller. My measures are based on students' self-reported "closer friends," relationships they not only listed but discussed with me throughout our interviews. In *Connecting in College*, the students I spoke with in 2004–5 named eighteen friends, on average, with most reporting between six and twenty-five friends. In 2016–17, at UNH and Dartmouth, students named twelve friends, and this number is only eight for students at MCC, as shown in Table I.1. When I interviewed Dartmouth students the second time, it was within weeks of their college graduation, and the number they reported was virtually unchanged at 11.5 (compared to 11.9). These numbers of "closer friends" all resemble the third level in psychologist Robin Dunbar's work on the circles of friendship, namely, that people have approximately fifteen "best friends." My findings differ, however, in exploring the ways these friends are connected to each other. Dunbar's fifteen ties as three groups of five friends[67] characterize the compartmentalizers but look different for samplers and tight-knitters.

Given the current availability of technology for people to stay connected across physical distance, I expected students to have more close friends from home than they did a decade ago. My data, however, do not show this pattern. Of the friends that students at UNH and Dartmouth told me about, 72–75 percent attended their college, more than the 65 percent in my previous study, and 29–32 percent were friends from home, fewer than the 38 percent in my previous study. These are shown in the middle rows of Table I.1. Compared to the research I collected a decade earlier at MU, students at the residential campuses kept fewer friends from home in the network of people they considered close friends. This occurred despite the increased ease that technology (such as the more widespread use of cell phones, video calls, and group chats) and social media allow in staying connected with friends from home.[68] This suggests two clear patterns. First, students do not have more friends from home than in the past, despite the ease with which technology allows these relationships to be maintained. Second, friends who attend the same college clearly play a central role in students' friendship networks.

In this book, I frequently discuss meaningful friendships. By combining in-depth interviews with quantitative network analysis, I am able to look not only at numeric features of students' friendship networks but at how they experience them. Students noted that having friends did not protect them from loneliness or isolation, but meaningful friendships did, especially when embedded in a network. Not all students I spoke with reported having meaningful friendships. At the end of chapter 1, I explain the barriers that students experienced to forming these meaningful friendships. They are experienced differently by students with different types of networks. They are mostly in one-on-one relationships for samplers. Compartmentalizers seem particularly protected against loneliness when they have meaningful friendships in more than one of their groups. Tight-knitters most often experience meaningful friendships, but the effects can be more negative if they unravel. Features of colleges campuses also encourage meaningful friendships. In brief, they do so through structuring repeated contact, conversations that go beyond surface-level concerns, and multiple opportunities to make friends throughout college through strong secondary friendship markets.

## Outline of the Book

This book is organized into two parts, focused on the processes of making, keeping, and losing friends (chapters 1–3) and how institutions and identities shape these processes (chapters 4–6).

Chapter 1 is devoted to how students make friends on campus. I highlight three features that shape how student make friends: the friendship market, perceived similarity (homophily), and proximity (propinquity). Students make friends through the regular and close contact that happens when they live in the same dorm, participate in clubs or student organizations together, or engage in other shared activities. On all three campuses, the first few weeks of college are a "friendship market," where students make friends most easily because they are particularly open as both "buyers" and "sellers" of new friendships. This *initial friendship market*, as I refer to it, happens on all three campuses, as do *secondary friendship markets*, where later in college students are again particularly open to making friends, but the intensity and rhythms of the friendship market differ by campus. This chapter finds that worries about young people being able to make friends are present; however, they seem misplaced. It is not that they are not able to make friends, but their timing may be off. Understanding how the initial and secondary friendship markets work can ease this process for students and for colleges.

In chapter 2, I investigate processes relating to keeping friends and deepening these relationships. Maintaining friendships is easier when students see each other regularly and when they have things in common. In other words, homophily and propinquity work not only to form friendships but also to maintain them. Even so, friendships take work. Most students recognize that they are "worth the work," at least the meaningful and supportive ones. In this chapter, I focus on the identity work that happens within friendships, as people's friends may shift as they discover or alter their identities. I also discuss how students know that a friendship is meaningful or "deep" compared to surface-level. This chapter delves into the benefits of friendships, including emotional support and having fun, along with instrumental support like academic help and advice on relationships. Friendship networks change during college, and I depict students who become more selective over time in whom they consider a friend—a strategy I call *friendship funneling*—and those who add a cluster or two of friends—in what I call *friendship expansion*.

Friendships also end. Chapter 3 focuses on why students lose friendships and how this impacts their network, noting that while there is a stigma to friendships ending, it is a common phenomenon. In my data on networks during college, less than half of friendships (43 percent) remained over the final two years of college. Most friendships fade away rather than breaking up. In other words, most friendships end because one or both participants keep in touch less frequently. Less often, friendships end through a conflict or an intentional break in the relationship. Recognizing that losing friendships can be challenging, yet it also can be beneficial in increasing the friendship support that students feel and the ability to craft their identities, can help students navigate these challenges.

While each chapter explains differences across the three campuses, chapter 4 spotlights key features of each campus that facilitate particular network types or friendship characteristics. In this chapter, I focus on how friendships differ by campus and how the physical space, policies, and practices on the three campuses shape how students form, keep, and lose friends. Many MCC students noted that it was hard to make friends at the community college, yet all but three of the twenty-six MCC students I spoke with made at least one friend. On average, students at the community college made fewer friends than did students on the residential campuses. They also viewed their friendships differently. While MCC students' friendships were important to them, students tended to accept that they might be temporary and focused on a particular class or club rather than wide-ranging and long-lasting.

At the residential campuses, dorms and clubs are two main places that students make friends. Features of each campus, however, influence these processes. The University of New Hampshire provides the option to live in mixed-year dorms, which did not have an active friendship market, so students were not able to make friends here as easily as in first-year dorms. Dartmouth's quarter system and flexible scheduling plan also shapes students' friendships. Compared to UNH, where students are on a regular semester system, at Dartmouth students more frequently make new friends after the initial friendship market because more Dartmouth students are looking for friends in their second and third years when their existing friends might be off campus. These structures, however, make it more challenging to keep friends because propinquity does not keep friends physically together. They also make it easier to lose friends, which can be good if the friendship is not working well, but can be bad if the friendship is one that is meaningful but takes more work than the participants are willing or able to put into it. Understanding how these campus structures shape the ease with which students make, keep, and lose friends will help students through these processes and help campuses to support them.

In chapter 5, I focus on how students' identities impact their friendship networks. Students' intersectional identities shape making, keeping, and losing friends, and these friendship processes involve navigating race, class, and other identities. Students from marginalized groups, including students of color, often found support for microaggressions in other friendships that shared that identity. Yet, students are not defined by just one of their identities. They are individuals composed of multiple identities that vary in their salience over time and in different contexts. Bonding with peers based on a marginalized identity can be a source of belonging, yet it also is not a panacea. Indeed, it can bring its own challenges. At each campus, students from marginalized backgrounds formed dense friendship networks, which served as bonding social capital. The tension is that in doing so, they could find themselves in a supportive but insular network, without bridging social capital that would connect them to new ideas and opportunities; and, when they did not do so, they often experienced isolation and a lack of belonging. I also discuss identity-related challenges within friendship networks, including hostile ignorance from friends and how gender shapes experiences of friendships and network structures.

I conclude the book by discussing practical, theoretical, and policy implications of my arguments. The conclusion details the ways this research provides important insights into neglected social and relational dynamics of college students. Offering four points of intervention, I demonstrate how students and colleges can both benefit from a deeper understanding of processes of making, keeping, and losing friends. By understanding these processes, students and college administrators can intervene at strategic times to maximize success and wellness, and minimize loneliness, isolation, and mental distress. This work also has implications for scholarship on friendship and social capital. The solution to our loneliness epidemic is not just encouraging students to have more friends, but crafting a supportive network for them to do so. Institutions of higher education need to act in strategic ways to support students as they make, keep, and lose friends throughout college and beyond.

Part One
# PROCESSES OF MAKING, KEEPING, AND LOSING FRIENDS

[ CHAPTER ONE ]

# Making Friends: Initial and Secondary Friendship Markets

"I like to feel comfortable and feel like I have lots of friends around me. But at the same time, I only have a few close relationships that really make a difference." Melanie[1] said this to me at the end of her second year at Dartmouth, explaining that she likes "to know the people around" her.

A White woman with a big and contagious smile, wide eyes, and dark lashes, Melanie talked about getting to know other Dartmouth students in many places, including the outdoor orientation program, her dorm[2] floor, her sorority, and clubs, especially the Dartmouth Coffee Club. Her journey through these places to make friends illustrates how this happens on a college campus, including the glitches students experience along the way. Making friends is not something that happens just once, but a process throughout college, as students spend time in different places, as their interests evolve, and as the identities that are salient in their current settings shift. Comparing students' experiences across three campuses reveals that the college a student attends shapes the times and places they most often form friendships.

If you ask students where they met their first friends on campus, many will point to orientation. Melanie did not meet her close friends in orientation, yet she saw it as beneficial in helping her feel "comfortable" on campus. At Dartmouth, orientation occurs right before fall term begins and lasts for approximately ten days for most students, with half that time spent away from campus in an outdoor program, such as hiking, canoeing, or mountain biking, and the other half on campus attending programs and activities to help with academics and community life.[3] Like most Dartmouth students, Melanie participated in the outdoor orientation program referred to as "Trips," spending several days and nights camping and hiking with ten peers. She told me, "I really liked Trips. For me, it's really hard for me to walk up to a group of people I entirely don't know. But if there is one familiar face, I feel much more comfortable. So, just having ten people that I would occasionally see around was very comforting." She said, "It made a difference," although "I don't think any of us became super, super close."

Dorms are another place where students often make their first friends on campus, and Melanie found lots of "friendly" people on her dorm floor, including one of her "really close friends." This deep connection, however, took months to develop. Although Melanie felt like she could easily meet people, she saw making a true connection as more challenging. As we continued to talk about what it was like to make friends at Dartmouth, Melanie paused and let out a big sigh, then told me: "I didn't connect with a lot of people. There are a lot of people who I felt like I could reach out to for a meal or something, but I think the mark of true friendship is not feeling like you have to, like, 'be on' where you're around somebody, you can just kind of relax. And I didn't necessarily find anybody like that till end of winter, early spring term."

When I asked how she made that friend, she explained:

> It was actually one of my freshmen floormates. This girl and I had strangely similar interests. I wanted people to go with me to these funny things that I would find, and nobody would go to. Coffee club, or some concerts, or slam poetry, or just weird things that, on average, people don't really wanna go to except for me. And this one person would go with me. It was really exciting. Over time, it became pretty clear that we were really close friends. We stayed in touch over summer. And now she's definitely one of my best friends, not only on campus but in life.

Melanie leaned back in her chair and smiled as she was talking about this friend, Ryley, her best friend on campus. Although their common interests were clear early on, it took time for their connection to develop into a meaningful friendship.

Melanie continued to make friends throughout college, and common interests and identities continued to facilitate how her friendships formed. Which interests and identities these friendships were based on changed, however, as Melanie's interests developed and her identities evolved over the years. In her second year, which is when Dartmouth students are eligible to join Greek organizations, Melanie joined one. Consequently, her sorority became another place where she made friends at Dartmouth. Melanie told me:

> The way that Dartmouth is structured, it's much easier to meet upperclassmen men than it is to meet upperclassmen women, and I really

wanted to make a female group of friends that I had never had in high school, and I really wanted to meet upperclassmen women, because I wasn't even sure if they existed on campus. So it was important to me to go through [sorority] rush just for the sake of meeting people. Honestly when I thought about it before, I didn't actually see myself affiliated at the end of it, I just saw myself with fifteen people that I could like smile at and hear from, from a mentorship standpoint. But, ultimately, I am lucky that I didn't just feel comfortable in one house, I felt comfortable in every house and, when it came down to it, there were three that I had a really hard time choosing between.

As a White woman from an upper-class background with a "cute" appearance, Melanie found herself with options in sorority rush. She could have chosen to join any of the three "top houses" in terms of status at Dartmouth, and she ended up in one of them.[4]

Similar to Ana Martinez Alemán's findings from two decades ago about the safe space in women's same-gender friendships,[5] Melanie emphasized the importance of women's friendships, particularly given the male-dominated social space on campus.[6] As Melanie talked about the women in her sorority, several of whom she included as friends in her second interview, she told me: "I feel so lucky to be part of that group. They are so much smarter than me and so much more insightful than me. That's something really important for me to find." She referenced something she had heard said, which she said she thought of often: "If you're spending time with people and you feel you're the smartest person in the room, you're not doing it right. . . . I feel really good that I joined that group." Melanie described how it made her "a better person intellectually" to be part of discussions, whether about the US presidential election or about sexual assault, with her group of friends. A shared identity as "smart women" who are interested in the fraternity party scene and in intellectual discussions was something that brought them together.

Friendship is a process; consequently, Melanie, like other students, made friendships not just once, but again and again. The friends Melanie made on campus continued to shift as her identity and her interests continued to change. As Melanie talked more about her experience making friends on campus, she referenced how her idea of "college fun" changed over time. "Coming here, I wanted to know a lot of people, and absolutely got into that very typical freshman craze to want to go to all the frats and get in the basements. It is something I think a lot of freshmen get sucked into, the idea that, in order to go out, I have to go party in frat basements. Eventually, I just realized that can be fun, but not all the time." She contrasted this early

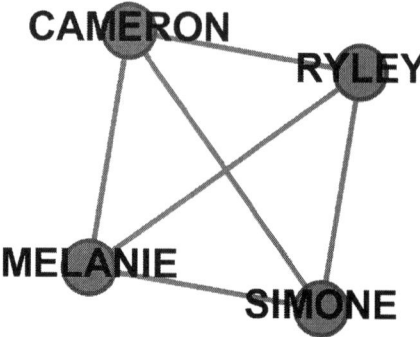

FIGURE 1.1. Melanie's friendship networks, Dartmouth year two (above) and at graduation (on the next page).

Note: In the network diagrams (sociograms), each dot (node) is a person, and those include the student I interviewed and all the "closer friends" they named. Lines represent ties. The respondent is tied to each friend, and the other ties are present when the respondent told me that those two friends know each other. A tie is absent if the respondent's perspective is that those two friends do not know each other. The size of nodes and labels represents centrality in the network. See Appendix A for more detail.

experience of "fun" with her current one: "The thing that makes frat basements fun at this point is the fact that I now have friends in them." Melanie is no longer going to fraternity basements to make friends, but to spend time with friends who are members of fraternities and sororities. She said that "when it comes down to it, a really fun night for me" now involves "hanging out" with a friend. This could include "sipping on a cup of tea and chatting for a while" or going to the climbing gym with her roommate.

Melanie had a tight-knit friendship group that grew over time as she encountered new people in college who shared her interests. At the end of her second year, she named three people as closer friends, as shown above in figure 1.1 Melanie explained, "I tend to develop that big outer circle, tiny inner circle friends structure." Her "inner circle" shown in figure 1.1 was her best friend from high school, Simone, whom she describes as "the other half of my brain. She's an incredible person." They had been friends for eleven years.[7] She also included Ryley, her best friend from Dartmouth, and her boyfriend Cameron, whom she had been dating for about a year at the time.[8] Melanie's inner circle was a tight-knit group, where her friends all knew each other.

As she joined new clubs, Melanie expanded her friendship network from three close friends to seventeen, as shown in the two panels of figure 1.1. Melanie told me that her friendships changed "pretty dramatically" during the two years between our interviews because she is "friends with people in my activities" and "what I was doing on campus changed." She described:

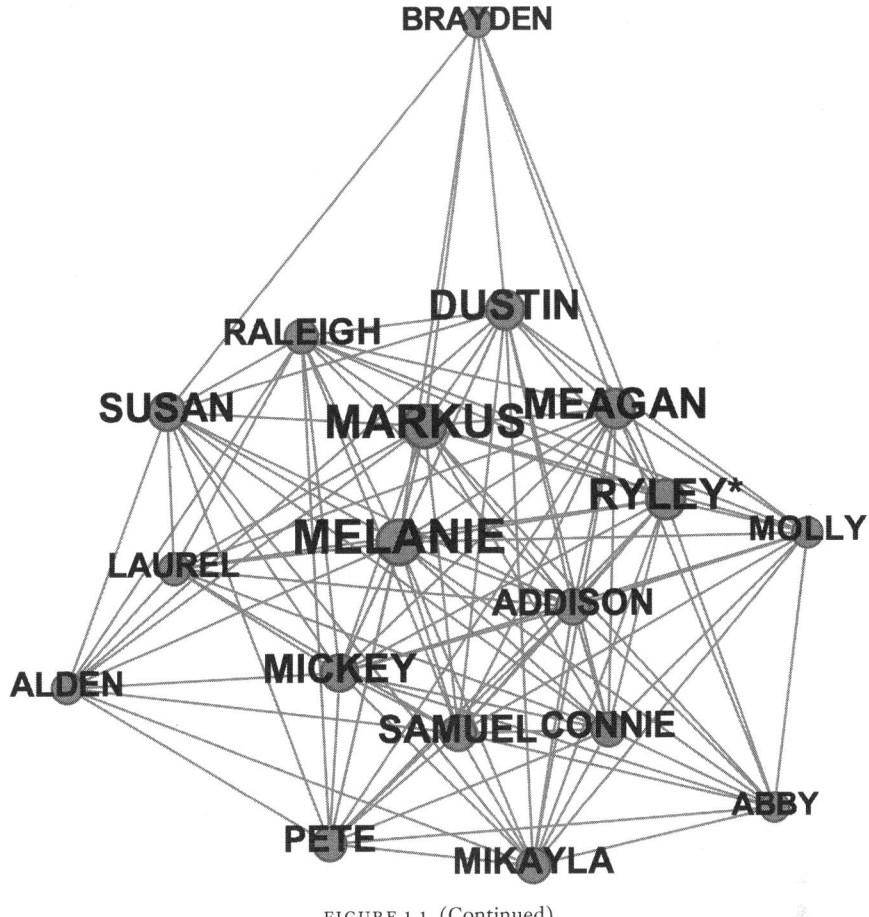

FIGURE 1.1. (Continued)

I entirely stopped attending the Women in Mathematics meeting. I also stopped being so involved in [my sorority] and got really involved in Dartmouth Coffee Club. I became the president of the Dartmouth Coffee Club my sophomore summer and have been since. And it's been really fun to build it into a social space that I wanted to see on campus.[9] Everyone always talks about how Greek life is dominant and everyone complains about the alternative social spaces that exist. So, it was fun to have a little pet project that was curating the alternative social space that I thought was best.

In that space, "we just made coffee every week" and introduced people to each other. They met in the same room in the student union every Friday afternoon, from 3:30 to 5:00 p.m. Melanie explained:

When you abstract things, people bond over things that we do in common. Everybody drinks coffee, no matter what their background is. And, not even coffee, we also have tea and hot chocolate. It's almost like a variable that you can use to leverage connections. I watched one of my friends who's in Dartmouth EMS [Emergency Medical Services]—and that's really about all he does—meet somebody who's very involved in [my sorority], and they had never even seen each other before. They're both seniors, this happened over winter. They both like coffee. It felt awesome to see that happen.

Melanie often introduced her friends to each other. Both times I interviewed her, she had a tight-knit network, which means that most of her friends knew each other, as shown in figure 1.1. Although Melanie's number of close friends expanded, she maintained a tight-knit network.

Another important feature of how Melanie made friends was space.[10] Having space for "hanging out" helped students form friendships and have fun together. While this came up in many students' experiences, most did not notice and discuss it as directly as Melanie did. She told me that the outdoor club "does provide those alternate friendships, but it doesn't provide safe party environments." Her coffee club provided good friends and a regular space, which Melanie (above) referred to as an "alternative social space"; however, she also recognized that it was not the late-night party space that many students were looking for. This lack of consistent "owned" space gave her friendships in clubs less opportunity to develop than those in her sorority, where they would hang out in the sorority house or go together to a fraternity basement. Implied in Melanie's comment about "safe party environments" was the fact that the fraternities held their parties in basements, which were widely seen as not safe.[11]

Being intentional about what they were looking for in new friends helped students form meaningful friendships. Students who were not intentional could find themselves "trapped in [their] friendships," as Melanie put it. She told me, "I know from talking to people who I'm acquainted with but not close with, that many of their close friends are people that they don't really like. That they just felt like they had to stay friends with." This experience of feeling "trapped" is particularly true of tight-knitters, who are surrounded by their friendship group because most, if not all, of their friends know each other, so they do not have other friends (outside of the group) to fall back on. Melanie's advice to first-year students is a good way to combat that feeling of being trapped:

Be comfortable with vulnerability and nontransactional friendships and relationships with people where, someone described it to me recently, "where I was afraid to show love because I was worried it wouldn't be reciprocated or something." But, that's the thing, it never doesn't feel great to have someone be like, "You're cool. I want to be your friend," even if you don't want to be their friend. So, swallow your pride and accept that things maybe aren't going to be reciprocated and that is not a net reducer on your life. That's actually, in many ways, net neutral or net positive for you. So, be comfortable with that vulnerability and rejection, and take it in stride.

Students usually did not start making friends in college by being comfortable with vulnerability. Melanie, for instance, started by looking for fun and friendship in fraternity basements. She ended up finding friends through shared activities with people in the spaces she frequented, particularly her dorm and clubs. Being intentional about whom she considered a closer friend and being open to showing love in her friendships, Melanie made not just friends but meaningful ones—ones who support her. And sociological processes underlie what may seem like Melanie's good fortune.

## Three Dimensions of Making Friends in College

Most college students arrive on campus with the expectation—if not the explicit goal—to make friends during their college years. A student I spoke to recently told me that it felt "both urgent and terrifying" to make friends in college. And, as Melanie's experience also shows, residential campuses are designed to help students form friendships and get to know other students, particularly during orientation programming and in first-year dorms.

Across the three campuses, I find that the structure and rhythms of each college, such as where students live, shape how students make friends there. Yet, there are some overarching features that shape how my participants, including Melanie, make friends.

One important dimension is when friendships form. The first few weeks of college are a *friendship market*[12] where friendships are made most easily because students are particularly open as both "buyers" and "sellers" of new friendships. This *initial friendship market*, as I refer to it, happens on all three campuses. *Secondary friendship markets*, where later in college students are again particularly open to making friends, also appear at each college. Yet, the intensity and rhythms of the friendship market differ by campus. At UNH, the friendship market is most constrained to the initial friendship market, particularly during orientation and in first-year dorms. At Dartmouth, there is both a strong initial friendship market and relatively strong secondary friendship markets, given that students are shifting off campus and on campus each term more than at UNH. Secondary friendship markets happen when new members join sororities, fraternities, and other clubs, as Melanie's story shows, as well as on study abroad. At MCC, there is a less intense version of the friendship market operating each semester. Students at MCC also viewed friendships as more practical and more fleeting overall.[13] On all three campuses, failing to recognize that friendship markets open throughout their time in college, students may feel "trapped in your friendships," as Melanie put it. Differences in how the friendship markets operate by campus make students less "trapped" at Dartmouth and MCC than at UNH. Forming friendships in secondary friendship markets and at other times in college typically takes more effort and intention than it does in the initial friendship market.

A second important driver of friendships is that students make friends most frequently with people they encounter regularly. *Propinquity* is the term researchers use to capture how coming into contact with someone regularly increases the likelihood that those individuals will strike up a friendship. For example, Melanie's best friend on campus was someone who lived on her dorm floor. As described in the following chapters, propinquity also facilitates the continuation of existing friendship ties (see chapter 2) and the lack of it can strain relationships (see chapter 3).

The third important driver of friendships is *homophily*, or similarities between people, including both identity-based homophily, such as same-race and same-gender friendships, and interest-based homophily, such as sports or coffee. As the interviews I did with students show, the opportunities and patterns of friendship formation with similar peers are shaped by and experienced differently on these three campuses. Students themselves sometimes noted these effects, as Melanie did when she talked about wanting to form friendships with other women students. Melanie also noted the importance of a shared love of coffee, slam poetry, and climbing as helping her form friendships because, as she put it, "we bond over things that we do in common."

## When Friendships Form: The Initial Friendship Market

There is clearly something to the temporal aspects of college life. Students' narratives show that they had a much easier time making friendships at the very beginning of their first year. In their longitudinal exploration of 250 students attending 7 liberal arts colleges in New England, Lee Cuba and colleagues refer to this time as the "friendship market." They describe the friendship market as the few weeks at the beginning of college where new students are highly motivated "buyers and sellers of friendships."[14] While this makes forming friendships easier during this window, it also makes social restarts more challenging later in college.[15] Through comparing three types of campuses, I refine this concept into two aspects, discussing this initial friendship market period separately from the secondary markets that happen later in college.

Grace's experiences, including on her first day at UNH, demonstrate the workings of the initial friendship market and students' emotions as they go through it. I met Grace on a chilly November day in the student union, which the students referred to as the MUB. Grace, a white woman with long, straight blonde hair, greeted me with a bright smile, wearing a black warm-up jacket with dark red leggings. She mentioned that she had been a cheerleader since she was six years old, and this was reflected in her bubbly demeanor throughout the interview. When I asked what it was like to make friends when she first arrived on campus, Grace paused and looked down. When she spoke again, her tone was more somber:

> It was difficult. It was very difficult because I knew that all of my friends that I've had for years were going to different places [to different colleges]. And then I was telling myself [Grace takes a deep breath], "Put your big girl panties on and really do it yourself." I was just walking around, just seeing people [and] looking around, like, "Do I approach them? Do I say something to them?" It made me feel very weird, but I knew that I had to get involved around here, and I had to do stuff for myself.

Given her bubbly answers, I was a bit surprised by her description of making friends as "very difficult." However, Grace described how she overcame her apprehension and put her own advice about approaching people into action: "The first day I moved in my freshman[16] year, I saw this girl waiting in front of me to check in and I really liked her shorts, and I was like, 'Oh my God, I want to know where she got those.' So I asked her, I was, like, 'Hey, where'd you get your shorts?' . . . It's a simple question, and then come to find out she was living next door to me. So we were neighbors and also best friends. And it was really cool 'cause we live right next to each other, so that was definitely a plus." During the friendship market period, Grace expressed needing to use all her courage to approach Francis, a stranger at the time. Without Grace realizing it, propinquity kept them in each other's orbit, making it easier to connect since they were neighbors in the dorm. Grace shared this advice with other students: "I always tell people, I'm like, 'Don't be afraid to ask questions and don't be afraid to introduce yourself.' It sounds weird

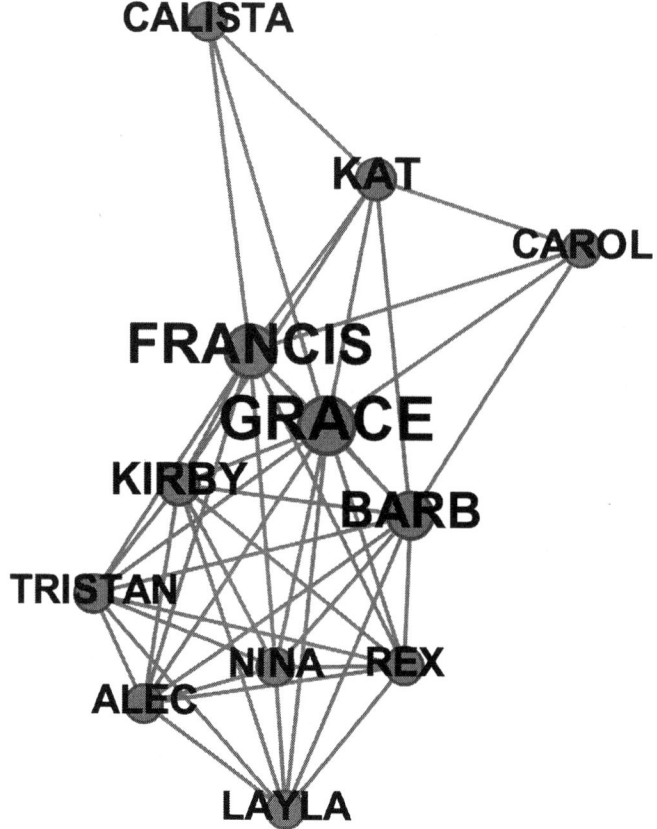

FIGURE 1.2. Grace's friendship network, UNH year two.

sometimes, but that's how you're gonna make your friends and that's how you're gonna make a life for yourself in college. It can be difficult for a lot of people." While it may have seemed like luck that Grace met her friends, her proactive and intentional strategies[17] also played a role in making the group of friends shown in figure 1.2. Her friend Francis, whom she met on the first day, is connected to most of Grace's friends, including her friends from home.

In orientation programs, dorms, and clubs, students are particularly open to making friends during this initial friendship period, yet students need to participate to reap these benefits. As a tour guide at UNH, Grace got many opportunities to give advice to prospective students and said that she encouraged them to join clubs: "That's what I tell people on my tours now. I'm like, 'Get involved. Literally, that's the most important thing you could do for yourself when you get here.'" Joining clubs during the initial friendship market was a good way to make friends.

The initial friendship market, however, does not shield students from feelings of loneliness. Even Grace, who had friends and made a good friend on move-in day, reported feeling lonely and found that making friends was not as stress-free as she would have liked. Part of the stress is how quickly friendships can change during this period. The rapidity of friendship change during the initial transition to college has been noted in research on campus life since the 1950s.[18]

While students want and expect to make friends, also widespread is the perception that everyone else already has friends. This can make campus life lonely, even during the initial friendship market period. As discussed in the introduction, students contemplated, "How could I be so alone with like, 15,000 people around me? And you can really feel that way at times too," as UNH student Yusef put it.

The initial friendship market opens quickly, forms friendships quickly, and ends quickly. Emotions are often strong. Students are excited to meet new friends, and they can quickly feel bonded to each other even when they have known each other for just a few days. It can feel intense to many students and outsiders, including students' advisors and parents. Part of the loneliness that Yusef referred to is related to the intensity of these early friendships. The intense displays of bonding, as with one student who told me she was "immediately best friends with everyone on my floor," could magnify feelings of loneliness for those who did not have this experience, particularly when they expected immediate feelings of closeness. Students typically felt internalized pressure to participate in and succeed in the initial friendship market and, consequently, feelings of loneliness and isolation when they did not live up to these expectations.

There were differences in the intensity of the friendship market across the three campuses and how unique this one period was in students' college careers. The initial friendship market is particularly intense and open the first few weeks of the first year at residential campuses like Dartmouth and UNH. For example, Natalie recognized how quickly she not only made friends but a new best friend at UNH, explaining that "within two weeks, I was like, 'You're my best friend, I love you.'" At UNH, this time is most markedly different from other times in its openness. Because Dartmouth has more shuffling of students (different people on campus and off each term because of the D-Plan),[19] it has smaller friendship market windows (that is, secondary friendship markets) each term, but still the main one is first term of students' first year. MCC has less strong friendship markets overall because it has different rhythms. Many MCC students enroll part time, and they may also take a class or two, then take a break, then return to MCC or transfer elsewhere. Friends made on campus are seen as more temporary at MCC, but still important.[20] Whether in the dorms, in orientation programs, or in clubs, students are particularly open to making friends and becoming friends during the initial friendship market period.

## Initial Friendship Market: Orientation Programs

The first place many students encountered other students (that is, potential friends) physically on campus was in orientation or pre-orientation programs. Students often expressed some worries about making friends at a new school. Orientation and pre-orientation programs are designed to respond to these worries by helping students get to know their peers and serving as a pathway to friendship formation. When I asked Daisy, a UNH student with an outgoing and chipper personality, what was most helpful for her socially on campus, she replied, "Doing the pre-orientation thing, just 'cause I was so nervous about making friends." Her experience was not unique.

Many students at the two residential campuses described friendships formed in orientation programs. This particularly stood out at Dartmouth, where most interviewees mentioned orientation friendships, likely because orientation was longer and involved small groups. At Dartmouth, nearly all students (roughly 90 percent)[21] participate in first-year Trips,[22] an outdoors-focused orientation program in which students spend a few days in a small group with other first-year students and a more experienced student leader doing activities ranging from "strenuous hiking" to museum exploration. Students at Dartmouth and UNH also mentioned identity-based and interest-based orientation and pre-orientation programs as important places where they made friends.

At Dartmouth, pre-orientation programs connected first-generation and low-income students (through FYSEP)[23] and international students (through ISPOP),[24] facilitating friendships during the friendship market period. During my initial interviews, both programs were a few days long and occurred before students went on Trips; FYSEP was five days and ISPOP, two days. Thanks to alumni donations in 2020, FYSEP expanded to a four-week program, which seems as if it would only make these friendships stronger. More time together provides more opportunities to bond. Every student I interviewed who participated in FYSEP described the important role it played in helping them make friends on campus. For these low-income and first-generation students enrolled at a private elite college, it felt comforting[25] to have friendship ties before entering Trips, general orientation, and classes. Even when they made new friends in these places, who replaced those at FYSEP as the main friends they hung out with, students referred to these FYSEP ties as important. Knowing they could make friends, that they were not alone, and that they belonged on campus was facilitated through FYSEP friendship ties, even when these ties themselves did not last.

This experience of making friends in orientation programs also came through in my interviews with Troy. A Black man at Dartmouth, Troy arrived at my campus office for our first interview wearing a navy V-neck sweater over a button-up dress shirt. He shook my hand firmly when we met, and throughout the interview, I was struck by his calm demeanor. Troy had a close-knit group of friends, mostly made up of other Black men whom he met during FYSEP orientation.[26] Troy considered himself introverted and slow at making friends, but the FYSEP program made the friend-making process quite smooth. In Troy's words, there was something "automatic" about their connections. Their shared experiences brought them together. For example, Troy explained how it would take ten times longer to tell a story to someone who came from a different background than to one of his friends from FYSEP because within FYSEP there was a shared understanding of certain, unspoken things. Troy commented, "That quickness to pick up on each other's positive stories and narratives allowed us to blend together really well."

International student orientation was another identity-based program where students made friends before classes started. Like others I spoke with, Safiya made friends quickly during international orientation. Safiya, a Black woman from Africa,[27] arrived at our interview wearing a white button-up shirt with a small black diamond pattern over her thin frame and a white wrap over her short natural hair. Speaking softly and with a slight accent, she commented on how "it was easy to meet people" during orientation and on the comfort and ease of not needing to explain things that pertained to being Black and from Africa. She described these as her closest friends because of the "support" and "loyalty" they provide, "not having to question whether someone has your best interests at heart." As figure 1.3 shows, Safiya had two groups of friends: at the top of the sociogram are her friends at Dartmouth and at the bottom are her friends from home. Brianna bridges the two groups because "I've known her since first grade, but we weren't really close friends until freshman year." She described how they became friends at college, both seeking "someone to relate to." Safiya noted that "I think that's what happens" because of "being out of the country and the commonality." Homophily brought them together once their identity as an African student, particularly one from the same country, became salient at Dartmouth, despite having attended school together for a decade.

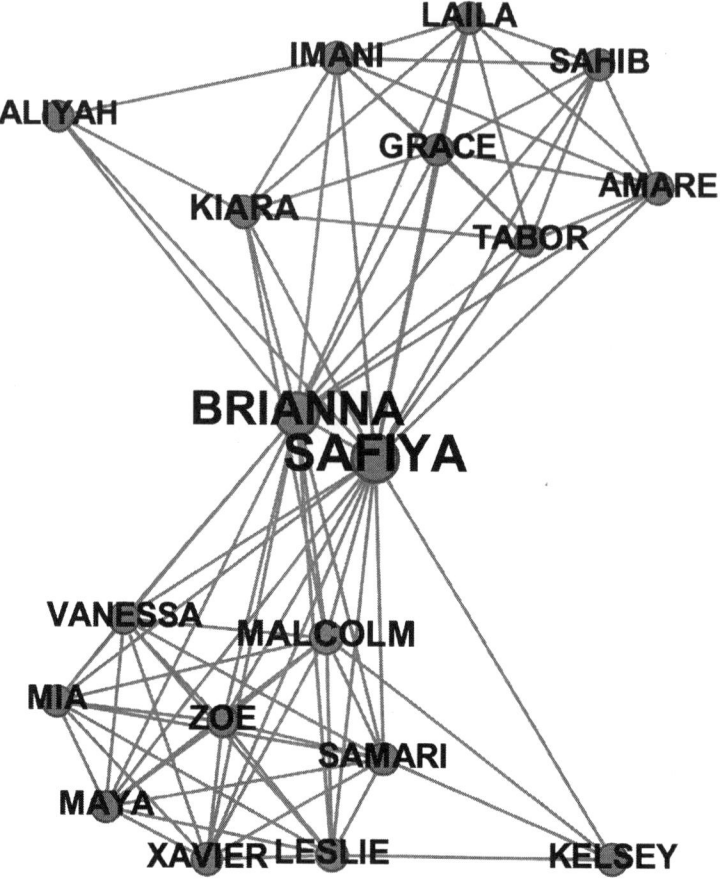

FIGURE 1.3. Safiya's friendship network, Dartmouth year two.

For both Troy and Safiya, identity-based orientation programs served as the foundation of their college friendship networks because of both homophily and propinquity.[28] The term *homophily* was proposed by sociologists Paul Lazarsfeld and Robert Merton in the mid-twentieth century to refer to the tendency for friendships to form among people who are similar.[29] As a racialized space, campus is not experienced in the same way by all students. Rather than students of color wishing to segregate themselves, they are often seeking (and receiving) support from those with common experiences, which they often find among same-race friends.[30] Some students of color, moreover, pursue racially homophilous friendships, while others prefer racially diverse friendships.[31] These preferences also may change over the college years.

Interest-based pre-orientation programs, like those based on outdoor activities or service work, also bring students together based on common interests. One example involves Timothy, a White UNH student who differed from most respondents in choosing UNH because of a specific academic program. Forestry is what drew Timothy to UNH. Timothy was tall and lanky, with dark, wavy hair, a chiseled jawline, and thick-framed glasses. When I asked Timothy how he made friends at UNH, he explained: "I did a pre-orientation backpacking trip, and I got really close with the people in my backpacking groups. And we still hang out like every day. We live near each other too, which helps. I have other friends who I met at orientation and in my classes who I hang out with, but not as much as my backpacking friends." Living nearby allows propinquity to bring them naturally together and eases the burden of logistically figuring out when and how to meet.

Common activities, such as finding joy in hiking, can draw people together, forming the basis of a budding friendship. Although she was just a first-year student when I interviewed her at the dairy bar at UNH, Morgan had a quiet and serious demeanor as she told me about her academic goal to be a genetics counselor and her two-night trip to Acadia National Park over the upcoming weekend with a campus group—and not with any of her friends. Morgan made friends through the outdoor adventure pre-orientation program, PAWS, shown in the top cluster in figure 1.4.[32] When I asked for her advice for a new UNH student, Morgan replied: "Just get yourself to meet people, and then you can become friends with some of their friends. Then your circle of friends can just expand throughout the year. So, join things that interest you, even if your friends don't do them." An activity that students both enjoy can not only bring them together as friends, but also keep the friendship together, as described in the next chapter.

Homophily works in general orientation programs, not only in identity- or interest-based ones. For example, UNH student Lindsay said she met some friends at orientation, particularly one friend who connected because they are both from New Jersey. Jennifer made friends at Dartmouth even earlier than orientation, at admitted students day, explaining that she became friends with her host: "It was really easy for us to become friends because we have a lot of similar interests, and we were both from LA. We grew up in the same-ish type of neighborhood." Although it was not a specific program for her identity group, Jennifer was still able to bond on that homophilous identity. Similarly, Dartmouth student Sydney described making her first friends at the end of Trips, when all the groups met at Moosilauke Ravine Lodge for dinner and socializing. She said, "That ended up being my group for the entire term. To be honest, all of us are Black, and

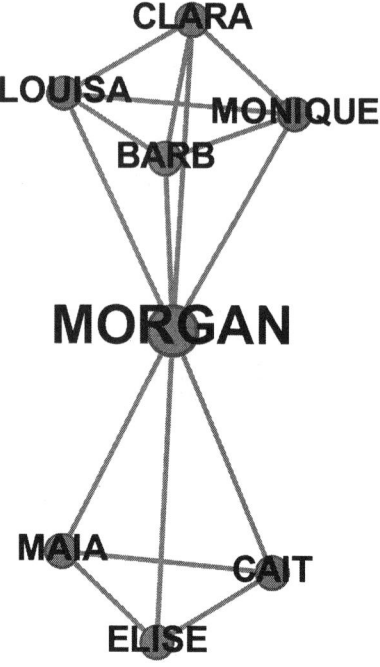

FIGURE 1.4. Morgan's friendship network, UNH year one.

we kind of flocked to each other because, especially at the Lodge, there were just so few of us." The sense of familiarity that comes from being from the same state or the same racial group is a way that friendships form. Homophily bonds similar people together, creating bonding social capital.

As this section has shown, propinquity and homophily bring friends together during orientation programming in the initial friendship market to form students' original friendships on campus.

## Initial Friendship Market: First-Year Dorms

Many students talked about becoming friends with their roommate, their next-door neighbor, or someone on their floor or in their building. Sometimes these friendships were formed during resident advisor–led activities, like icebreakers, where students discovered a similar interest (for example, "we both really like coffee") or hobby ("we're both dancers") or that they are from the same place ("she's also from New Jersey"). Other times, the layout of the building facilitates these connections, for instance, by including lounges, and students signify their openness to making friends by being in these spaces and by keeping their doors open. Notably, as these examples show, commonalities need not be big or meaningful to form the basis for a friendship.

Propinquity, or the repeated encounters between people propelled by proximity, is a powerful force shaping friendship formation. Students make friends through the regular and close contact that happens when they take classes together, live in the same dorm or residence, participate in clubs or student organizations together, or engage in other shared activities.[33] Researchers have documented this tendency among a range of groups, including among college students for those who share rooms, floors, and houses or buildings.[34] The students I interviewed talked about it as well, although they did not refer to it as "propinquity." Tom, for example, a fourth-year Dartmouth student, told me, "I've always been a big believer in that friends are primarily just a geographic moment." Indeed, propinquity demonstrates that friendships are made when geography brings people together repeatedly.

Most students on the residential campuses had at least one student from their first-year dorm on their friend list when I first interviewed them, which was usually at the end of their second year. When I asked how friends met, students would frequently reply that they were their roommate or floormate or met in their dorm. At Dartmouth, roommates are assigned based on matches to some key questions about tidiness and study habits, then randomly. At UNH, most students choose a roommate, either someone they knew from high school or from brief chats in the Facebook group for incoming students. For example, Heidi described how, after she posted in this group, a "girl who was from a couple towns over from me commented on" her post, they found out they played the same sports, "so we started talking and we met up and decided to be roommates based on that. We got along well."[35] Roommates chosen in this way were usually based on homophily.[36]

When I pressed students about how they met in their dorm, if they were not roommates, I noticed how the physical layout of the building mattered. For example, in dorms with floor bathrooms, sometimes students recognized each other from those spaces and would eventually start up a conversation in the hallway. Others talked about conversations that started because someone had their door open. For example, Sophia told me that she struck up a friendship with one of her roommates at UNH right away, they "started chatting and we had our door open and the girls across the hall from us did too, and we just went in and talked to them and went out to dinner with them for the first time. That's how we all became friends, really. That's where our friendship blossomed."

Hanging out in dorm lounges and keeping your dorm door open signify a particular openness to friendships, making it easier to meet others active in the friendship market. UNH student Timothy explained: "On nights and weekends, if you want to hang out with somebody, there's usually somebody out in the lounge, or with their door open, or music playing." Similarly, Cindy advised UNH students: "If you're a freshman, definitely leave your door open if you're living in the dorms. And live in a freshman dorm, the specified freshman dorms, because most people won't know each other, so they're gonna be wanting to make those connections." Cindy's advice draws on both propinquity and the initial friendship market concepts. Ethnographies of college life also observe the power of an open door on a dorm floor to invite conversations and getting to know each other.[37]

Another common place to make friends was in the lounges in dorms. Students would walk by the lounges on their way in and out of the building, seeing who is in there studying or hanging out. For example, Amanda talked about how "spatially the way the Choates [dorm at Dartmouth] are set up, it facilitates more running into each other and friendship, in my opinion." Amanda noted the common spaces where two buildings meet, and that the students are in doubles rather than triples so that "you just have you and your roommate versus [with] three people in your room where you were kinda your own little group." Students usually did not become friends the first time they crossed paths in a lounge, but rather over the course of days or weeks of seeing each other, often when they discovered a shared interest. Discovering this shared interest, however, requires that they engage in some sort of interaction or conversation, such as commenting on a sticker on a laptop or liking someone's shorts, as we saw with Grace.

The opposite features can lead to negative experiences in dorms. Consider, for example, Kylie's experience as the fourth person in a suite with three friends at UNH. "A lot of times, with suites, they're planned with friends. So, I got paired with friends and, in my head, I was just, like, this is either going to be a really great experience or a really crappy one. It ended up being a really crappy one." Kylie made friends elsewhere, including in her classes and group therapy. Suites also do less to facilitate the running into each other of propinquity than do traditional dorms because students do not cross paths with potential friends in floor bathrooms or lounges since these are private amenities inside each suite. Kylie's situation with her suitemates shows that for the friendship market to be operating, both buyers and sellers must be present; Kylie sensed her suitemates to no longer be "buyers" of friendship.

Jennifer's experience was more extreme. A Latina at Dartmouth, Jennifer described herself as "really shy." When she was talking about her friends at Dartmouth, I noticed that she did not mention her first-year floor. Once I asked about it, she told me, "I really hated my whole freshman floor. They're not really friendly. They all got along really well, and I was just that one person who was just living there. . . . Most of my floor was White. I think there was one other woman of color on my floor, but I never got to know her." She mentioned, "I'd go to floor meetings and sit there quietly, and I tried a couple of times to go when they were all hanging out in the hallway, but I just didn't feel comfortable." Fortunately, she had come to Dartmouth having friends already on campus. As mentioned earlier in this chapter, Jennifer had clicked with her roommate at the admitted students day,[38] and then became friends with her friend group. Like Kylie, Jennifer relied on other options besides dorms where she was able to make friends.

Dorms housing only first-year students had the most open and intense friendship markets. The structures behind this varied by campus. At Dartmouth, students live in dorms with other first-year students unless they apply to live in a Living-Learning Community (LLC), which are either interest- or identity-based. At UNH, students choose to either live in a first-year dorm or learning community, or be assigned to a general dorm or themed community. While it might seem useful to make cross-year friendships in general dorms, the friendship market operates in first-year dorms, but rarely in other dorms on campus. Amanda, who was a resident advisor (RA)[39] in the dorms, described that second-year students were less open to making friends than were first-year students because by their second year "they've already found their place here." Although they did not use this term, students' experiences show that the friendship market was not operating in general dorms on campus. The initial friendship market operates strongly in first-year dorms.

## Initial Friendship Market: Clubs and Organizations

The preceding two sections only drew on students' experiences from the residential campuses because Dartmouth and UNH had dorms and orientation programs, while MCC did not. On all three campuses, however, clubs and organizations served as important sites of friendship formation early in college, while the initial friendship market was in operation. Clubs and organizations were also part of the secondary friendship market, as discussed later in this chapter.

Students themselves often saw these benefits of joining a club and doing so early in college, during the initial friendship market period. Ciara, who was in her first year at MCC, told me that it would be good to join a club "to meet new people that have the same interests as me." Another MCC student, Skip, told me he viewed joining a club early in college as "a chance to meet new people" on campus.

At each campus, students made friends early in the year through clubs, and clubs had an initial period where they were explicitly looking for new members. At MCC, many students formed friends in clubs or organizations, including the nursing club, the Campus Activities Board, and a group for single mothers. The community college helped students to find these clubs through its annual club fair, where it allowed me to have a table to recruit for this study. Dozens of students walked past the twenty to twenty-five tables highlighting clubs, colleges they might want to transfer to, and other campus opportunities, such as my study. These tables were located centrally on campus, in the main walkway and lounge, where no one could miss seeing the tables and posters. Students could sign up to indicate interest in attending future meetings or joining the mailing list. Similar events occurred on the central quad or green at Dartmouth and UNH during the first week of fall term.

During the initial friendship market, students joined a range of clubs, often based on both an interest in the activity and a desire to meet people. Violet transferred to MCC after a year at a private four-year college, attending MCC classes online for a term before attending in person. When she first came to the community college campus, Violet sought out clubs. In her words, "So, I remember coming here, and the first thing I thought was, I need to join a club or I'm just going to die, socially. So, I showed up to my first CAB [Campus Activities Board] meeting." Violet explained that "it's really my clubs that bring me into these friendships." She compares the friends she makes in clubs to the "acquaintances" she meets in classes: "in a class, you'll meet usually once a week, maybe twice, and you'll see each other for a small amount of time. Usually, your teacher's lecturing, and then you'll leave and text each other and say, hey, what was the homework? And then you'll help each other out, maybe." She contrasts this to the deeper interaction in clubs and organizations:

> With the club, once you have an event planned, now you need everyone's [phone] number, you need everyone's email, you need everyone's schedule. You're gonna be meeting up constantly. In between meeting up constantly, you're just going to go meet up and say, hey, can you believe that happened in the meeting. Then, once you get to the event, you're going to be working the event together the whole time. Clubs are just so more involved than the classroom setting, especially something like CAB, where it's all events, all the time.

Like the structure of a dorm facilitating connections, the structure of the club's meetings allows for repeated encounters.

When they meet regularly and allow for interaction, clubs facilitate friendship formation. Working on a project together can bring friends together more easily. Therefore, students deciding which clubs to join and administrators deciding how to structure clubs would do well to prioritize those with a project that students work on together.

Time is the main barrier blocking students' participation in clubs. At the community college, students' schedules make it hard to attend club meetings. These students typically only come to campus when they have class, and often leave afterward to go back home or to work. In contrast, on the residential campuses, most students stay nearby after class and are not far away even on days when they do not have class. Of course, work schedules can also get in the way of club attendance, particularly for those working long hours, including low-income students or those who do not have parental support or financial aid to pay for tuition and other expenses.[40] Class schedules, sports practices and games, and other club meetings also compete for students' time.

Sometimes students remained with the first club they joined, like Violet; however, they often joined several during the initial friendship market. During this time, they were trying out clubs and seeing if they clicked with their members. For example, UNH student Natalie described what was most helpful socially as "getting involved. I am part of a few different orgs on campus: the sorority, work, volunteer, and a church club. . . . That helped me find my group of people, my friends."

When students did not make "good friends" at orientation programming or their dorms, they often found them in organizations. At Dartmouth, Renata made her first group of friends through the first-generation orientation program, FYSEP, but they were not her permanent group. From her first weeks on campus, Renata was involved in several clubs, including those related to sustainability, divestment, Latinos, and the outdoors. She explained that by "making friends with people I meet through organizations, we have that common thing." Through organizations, Renata made friends with shared interests, friends she felt she had more in common with than those she met in orientation or in her dorm.

Homophily shaped both the clubs that students joined and who they made friends with in the clubs. Early her first year at Dartmouth, Sydney, a Black woman, made friends with other Black women she met participating in clubs and programs not tied to race. Students also bonded on homophily based on the clubs they joined, like the group for single mothers at MCC, mentioned earlier.

Research into the process of how students form homophilous ties finds that it involves intentionality. In a study focused on Black students, Tamara Gilkes Borr concludes that Black students strategically build same-race friendships through regularly coming into contact with other Black students in the African American culture-themed residence hall and in Black clubs and activities, such as the Black Student Union.[41] Many other qualitative studies provide examples of students meeting same-race friends in racial- or ethnic-based clubs, organizations, and activities.[42] Importantly, students also make interracial friendships in student organizations.[43]

Joining a club was not always effective in making friends. While I list it here as an initial friendship market, it differs from orientation programs and first-year dorms in that not everyone in the club or organization is participating in the initial friendship market. Not everyone attending club meetings and events is open to making friends, and it can be hard to tell who is and who is not. Clubs operate as initial friendship markets at the beginning of the year and when it is structured that new members join. A second, related barrier is that because clubs are sites of friendship formation and maintenance, friendships already exist in these spaces. While new people coming by themselves may be looking for new friends, it can be harder to break into an existing group, particularly when a tight-knit friendship group dominates the club. Joining a club later in college is discussed later in this chapter as a secondary friendship market.

Summing up why to explore organizations during the friendship market, UNH student Daisy offers this advice to first-year students: "Finding a corner. It's such a big university, and I love it that way because there's so many things to do. But finding little niches where you fit in, whether it's a club or a group. For me it was work, or living in a small freshman dorm, or being on a small RA staff. Finding a small setting where I fit in was super helpful." Daisy's advice fits with educational research showing that clubs and other extracurriculars facilitate a sense of belonging, which contributes to staying in school and graduating.[44] Those "little niches" are even more powerful in forming friendships when they have a project that students work on together and help students "in the market" identify each other as open to new friendships.

## Initial Friendship Market: Sports Teams

Another important place that students made friends as they transitioned to college was through varsity sports teams. Although I only interviewed one varsity athlete at UNH, his experience on the football team resonates with the eight varsity athletes I interviewed at Dartmouth. At Dartmouth

20 percent of students were on varsity sports teams,[45] so it is a relatively common experience there, much different from at larger institutions. It is even more common, however, at other small liberal arts colleges.[46] Student athletes noted the importance of having a ready-made group of friends they could rely on through their sports team. Automatically, interest-based homophily was at play because they share love of a sport, and often teams are also similar in terms of race, class, and gender characteristics.[47] Moreover, propinquity was also in play because students spent time together daily; in season, they might see each other multiple times a day at practice, lifting, and conditioning, as well as spending days together when traveling for games. Because of their practice schedules, students often had similar class schedules to those of their teammates, which also made it easy to spend time together before and after class, as well as grabbing meals together between practice, class, and studying.

Nearly every athlete I interviewed described the important role their team played as an instant friendship group when they arrived, even if they later became distanced from these friendships.[48] Jenna, for example, told me how she found a home on her swim team. When she visited Dartmouth, Jenna "liked that the swim team was really close-knit," which felt like a welcoming community she wanted to be part of. Jenna commented that she did not make friends in her dorm, and "I wish I did." She explained, "I didn't spend that much time in my dorm, just based on swimming. I spent more time with the swim team. But that's one group of people that I really wish I spent more time with."

Similarly, Ella grew up having close-knit ties through athletics and summer camp, and when she arrived on Dartmouth's campus, she quickly bonded with her crew (rowing) team. As she talked about her friends, Ella pushed back her long blonde hair with her hands and rolled a thin silver chain between her fingers. Her ruddy fair skin, no make-up look, and gray short-sleeve "Dartmouth CREW" t-shirt and jeans gave her a New England athletic appearance. Ella described crew as a "family," made up of people you do not choose, but who become closely bonded because of the time they spend together. She said, "It's funny 'cause usually if you just put us in a room together, I probably would never interact with them." Through the power of propinquity, finding themselves on a team together, they ended up bonding and becoming friends.

A theme throughout Austin's interview was how being part of a large team shaped his experience at a small school. Austin described himself as grateful to have "130 instant friends" through the football team at Dartmouth. He recounted, "The second I got on campus, I was surrounded by over 100 guys that all had the same interest and same opportunities as me. . . . I quickly made friends." He enjoyed spending time with them at practice, studying together, hanging out, and grabbing a meal. He mentioned that it was rare to walk across campus and not see one of them or another familiar face. The large team on a small campus had the advantage of usually turning up a teammate in class or in the dining hall when Austin showed up, as well as having closer ties with those he spent more time with. Austin was closest to several of the guys who played the same position he did, describing them as "like minded," and they "get along so well."

Victoria made friends both in her dorm and through volleyball, even though she described herself as "pretty introverted" and "reserved and quiet" in her first fall at Dartmouth. Volleyball was a fall sport, which meant they started practice before the fall quarter began. Victoria described how "we were here a month before classes started, so I was very close to my teammates and especially my classmates on the team." Victoria commented that going through the same "process" with other first-year volleyball players helped them bond as a unit. There were five of them, who all had a similar class schedule and lived in the "River" dorm cluster together. Victoria also made friends on her dorm floor, describing it as "the strangest thing, our floor was just so close." She noted that the distance from central campus and the perception that it was the "worst" dorm on campus facilitated a "real sense of community" among residents (I heard this from other interviewees as well). Propinquity and interest homophily work together here to bring Victoria and her teammates and floormates into friendships.

Because they had their teammates as an automatic friend group, it was less consequential if they did not click with their orientation group or dorm floor. However, disruptions through injuries, changes in their commitment to the sports, or disagreements with teammates caused larger disruptions in their friendships than was the case for students who formed friends in other ways (more on this in the next chapters on keeping and losing friends). Students such as Jenna, who stuck only with their teammates during the initial friendship market, missed out on the ease with which nonteammate friends could be made in college. In contrast, some varsity athletes also formed nonteammate friendships during the friendship market, often ending up with compartmentalized networks.

Overall, students find it easiest to make friendships during the first few weeks of their first year. This is because they often occupy spaces on campus where other first-year students are also open to making friends, providing an open friendship market. I refer to this period as the *initial friendship market*. Once this period ends, *secondary friendship markets* open up, with intervals varying by campus. Because there is often a stigma or, at minimum, a feeling of discomfort attached to not having friends, students may latch onto the first friends they encounter, rather than remaining open to new friends. Students' experiences, however, show the value of remaining open both during and after this initial friendship market period when students experience the easiest time expanding their network.

## When Friendships Form: The Secondary Friendship Market

After the early weeks of students' first year, the initial friendship market closes; however, there are smaller "pop up" markets that operate at other points. I refer to these as *secondary friendship markets*. Like the initial friendship markets, the details of these secondary markets differ by campus. They operate more strongly when there is more shifting of who is on campus each term. At Dartmouth this happens because of students' pathways off campus and back on each quarter, according to the D-Plan, and at MCC because students may not take classes each semester or the same number at the same time each semester. These secondary friendship markets include study abroad programs, sororities and fraternities, other clubs, and classes. While making friends in secondary friendship markets is not as frequent or seamless as doing so in the first weeks, it happens. Students need not feel stuck with the friends they make during the initial friendship market. Making friends in the secondary market is easier when students are intentional, which involves both being open to new connections and doing things to facilitate them.

As mentioned earlier, students noted the pressure or expectation to make friends immediately. When they did not, they tended to feel ashamed or as if something must be wrong with them, which itself served as a barrier to making friends after the initial friendship market. For example, UNH student Rachel noted, "As a freshman, I feel like I shut myself down to meeting more people because I didn't make connections with people right away. Going into my Spring semester was kind of awkward where people already formed their friend groups and stuff." Referring to this expectation, Kevin advises UNH students: "Don't be discouraged if you don't make as many friends freshman year, because sometimes the friends you make freshman year, you won't even keep them all throughout college." Underlying Kevin's comment is the expectation that everyone does—and should—make friends right away. When students do not, it can become easy to "shut down," as Rachel put it.

Trying to make friends in mixed-year or upper-year dorms is much more challenging for students than in first-year dorms, even during that beginning-of-year time, because it is not their "friendship market." The lack of propinquity that occurred as students hunkered down during the early stages of the COVID-19 pandemic similarly meant that new friendships were rarely formed. In a study of the networks of students at a large public Midwestern university in the beginning of the pandemic in 2020, the friendships students maintained were "reactivations of old friendships or intentional maintenance of current friendships."[49] New friendships were more challenging to form, as in the period after the initial market.

To make friends after the initial friendship market, students often felt they were lucky; however, more than luck, it was typically because of the effort they were putting in. For example, Troy, a Dartmouth student, heard a rumor that his friend group was cliquey and "exclusive," so they worked to specifically be open to meeting people and making friends. Troy described his friend group's approach: "now if we walk into a room with people we don't know, the first thing we do, we introduce the other person or introduce ourselves and try to incorporate the other person into whatever we're talking about or whatever we're doing." This intentional approach to making friends is also reflected in Troy's response to my question about advice for other students: "Branch out. Branch out, learn the people you want to be friends with, learn the people you don't want to be friends with. You don't want to find out end of junior year [or] senior year, that, 'Oh my God. I really hate my friends.' I think that's an unfortunate situation. Better to explore what's out there and realize what you want [and] what you don't want. What you like [and] what you don't like. That way, when you do find what you want and what you need, you'll value it that much more." Rather than falling into a groove of keeping existing friendships without reflection, Troy advises students to "explore what's out there" and to be intentional in the connections they make.

The effort to make friends in the secondary friendship market often included talking to people you do not know and overcoming the desire to retreat into your phone or your room. UNH student Melinda told me that she made friends by following the advice to "put yourself out there and talk to the person in your class." Dartmouth student Melvin succinctly advised his peers to "just be much more intentional as opposed to letting social life just come about as it presented itself." What being "intentional" entailed differed across contexts, but it often meant talking with people you did not know well or inviting them to something. Dartmouth student Melanie mentioned how fear of "rejection" or worry that feelings "wouldn't be reciprocated" was often what held people back, yet it always feels positive, "even if you don't want to be their friend," when someone says, 'You're cool. I want to be your friend.' As discussed earlier, remembering this helped her keep being intentional.

Students' intentional strategies were not always successful. For example, UNH student Kylie told me how she decided she would ask a new person to have dinner together in the dining hall right after learning their name. She said that most people did not go to dinner with her. I suspect this strategy would have been successful during the initial friendship market period. But this worked less well when others had already been here for two years and had friends. It probably came across as awkward, perhaps desperate.

Because students do not know who among them are actively "buyers" of friendship, being in places where they could be approached was another useful strategy. Figuring out where these spaces were on campus took some inside knowledge. These spaces, however, and this pattern happened on all three campuses. At MCC, students did not have orientation, sororities and fraternities, and study abroad where they could make friends, but hanging out in common spaces facilitated friendship formation in a more universal way. In these spaces, students took initiative, either approaching another student or being receptive when an invitation to connect came to them. For example, Violet made a friend when another young woman asked if she could sketch Violet. Violet agreed and struck up a conversation with her. Dory made a friend by bonding with another student about their hair, which was different in color but similar in style. Both had these initial discussions in "the pit," which is the largest lounge at MCC, an open area in the center of the building, with a large TV screen and lots of windows.

Renata, a student at Dartmouth, summarized how propinquity enabled students to make friends: "I understand how friendships here are. They kind of like are sporadic. You meet once and then you say hi, hi, hi, hi, hi, 'til you have another chance crossing. And then you actually hang out." Propinquity enabled students to make friends by seeing others regularly. Even if these connections seemed "sporadic," they were patterned by propinquity.

Along with the importance of propinquity, homophily, and intentionality, I found a few specific "pop up" locations where friendships formed after the initial friendship market. These secondary friendship markets, such as study abroad programs, sororities and fraternities, other clubs, and classes, were important places where students made friends and felt a sense of belonging. In her exploration of belonging on college campuses, sociologist Lisa Nunn also notes that some college students experience social belonging right away, whereas for others this develops over time, and for some this social belonging is never experienced.[50] Similarly, I find that some students make friends right way and keep those friends, whereas more often students' friendships develop over time. And some students fail to develop meaningful ties in college, as I discuss at the end of this chapter.

# Secondary Friendship Markets: Study Abroad and Off-Campus Programs

Most students who studied abroad and in domestic off-campus programs described friends they made there. Indeed, many of them raved about it. In her second year at UNH, May did a "semester in the city program" and made what she called "my first group of best friends here" with the three other women she shared an apartment with. "We got super, super close and I just realized how important it was to have such a close-knit group."

Students' desires—and their need—to form friendships makes study abroad programs secondary markets. Like the initial friendship market at the beginning of college, they have a cohort of students who are all new at the same time, looking for friends, both as "buyers" and "sellers." UNH student Lori explained how she was unsure socially about going abroad because she felt like "I had to start over and make new friends again." While she had friends at UNH, none of them was going on her program. In our second interview, two of her closest friends were those she had met while studying abroad nearly four years ago. Similarly, Dartmouth student Sydney described feeling hesitant about going abroad without a friend. She did not know anyone on the program and wondered: "At first, I was like, what are we going to talk about for this long? But I feel like we all just got to know each other so much better" through spending so much time together. Sydney made close friends from her study abroad program, two of whom remained close friends, including one who became her roommate when they returned to campus.

As with other friendship markets, making meaningful friendships in this space is not automatic. They take time to develop. This time together can be encouraged through students' own intentional actions and through propinquity bringing students together regularly. Given Dartmouth's intense academic schedule, Dani felt like the lower demands of classes abroad allowed more time for friendships to blossom. She explained, "My abroad experience was great in that, because you didn't really have strenuous academics, so I had a lot of time to invest in friends. I think that's one of the reasons I came back from abroad with such strong friendships. So, I try and carry that over to here." Students who felt they did not have the time to invest in their friendships, like Dani, often left their study abroad experience not only with new friends but also with a new appreciation for the value of friendship ties.

## Secondary Friendship Markets: Greek Letter Organizations

Greek letter organizations also have a built-in time when students are open to making new friends. That is, they operate as a secondary friendship market because when students first join, they are perceived to be open to making friends, and members (both new and existing) are open to becoming friends with new members. Indeed, many students noted that they joined the organization to make friends. At some campuses, this coincides with the initial friendship market, when students join Greek organizations at the start of their first year. Other campuses, such as Dartmouth, do not allow students to join until their second year. Other structural factors include the number and percentage of Greek students; for example, 10 percent of UNH students (1,800) are members, compared to 70 percent of eligible (that is, non–first year) students at Dartmouth (2,200).[51]

I asked students why they joined each student organization, and the most common response for joining a sorority or fraternity was to make friends. UNH student Amber told me her sorority is "how I made my friends," and she advised, "Don't be worried about other people thinking you're weird for pursuing friendships because it's really not weird. Everyone's thinking the same thing." Sororities and fraternities are a pop-up friendship market. In response to my question about what had been most helpful for him socially at Dartmouth, Tom replied: "Frankly, my fraternity. Just having that extra, I don't know what the word is, but that extra layer of connectivity." Tom's tightly connected friendship network is shown in figure 1.5. Dustin viewed joining a fraternity at Dartmouth as a way to make friends easily after seeing this in action when he was in high school and visited his older brother who was a student at Dartmouth. "I ended up spending one night at his fraternity, getting to know brothers and hanging out and playing [beer] pong, and I was sold. I was like, yes, I will definitely join a fraternity when I come to Dartmouth." Dustin told me, "Most of my guy friends on campus are in my fraternity. Not all of them, but the ones I'm closest with. And that's not a coincidence." At UNH, Jane noted that through her sorority, "I've definitely made a whole bunch of new friends that I wouldn't know without being in it." Kevin told me, "I joined a fraternity [at UNH] last semester. That was really cool because I'm meeting like sixty new guys and growing friendships with them. That's definitely a positive for me because I didn't have as many close friends freshman year." He felt that having more friends is something "that's going to help me." Although he did not join with

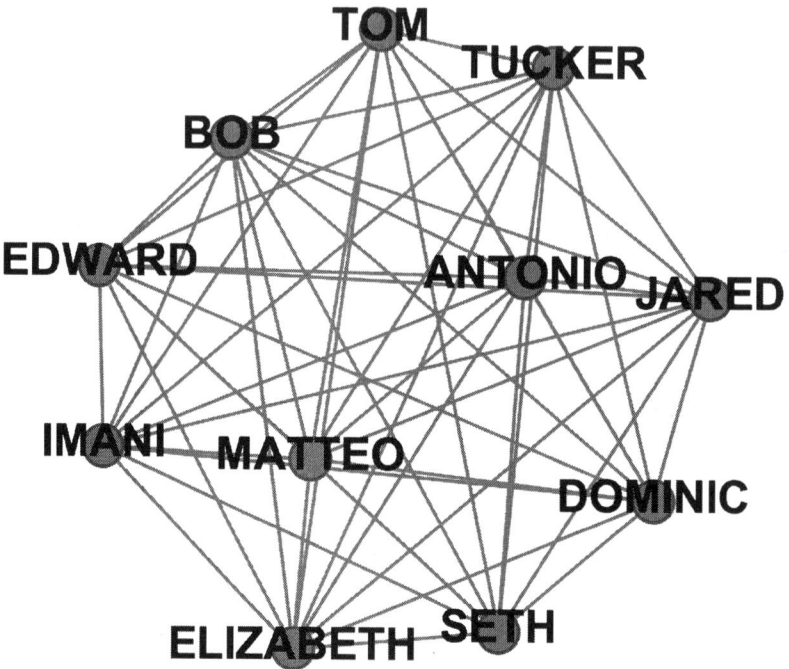

FIGURE 1.5. Tom's friendship network, Dartmouth year three.

friends, he became particularly close to "a couple people that were on my [dorm] floor" who are "now in the same fraternity as me." Propinquity in dorms can also operate to bond friendships within another space—that of Greek organizations. Living in their fraternity or sorority house also draws on propinquity to help form friendships when students see each other where they live and at events.

Not all students who joined Greek organizations to make friends were successful in doing so. When they join to make friends, sometimes it works and other times it does not. For example, about a year after she joined her Dartmouth sorority, Victoria told me, "I still know one person in the house" and that her friendship network since joining "hasn't changed a whole lot, but I am hopeful that maybe it will." Victoria did not participate in a second interview, so I am not sure whether she made friends in her sorority. Dartmouth student Sasha remarked, "I don't really go to anyone in my sorority for any type of emotional support," explaining that "I am not that close to anyone there." When students did not make friends in their house, they often noted that it was because they were not "super involved," as Victoria put it, or "super invested in it," as Savannah phrased it. Savannah also noted that there are "some weird friendship dynamics that are happening just because some people are dealing with drama. I'm not in that. I'm on the outside." She also told me that "it's not so important" because she has friends elsewhere at Dartmouth.

Students explained that their friends' decisions to join influenced them to rush. When students' friends were all joining Greek organizations, students often noted a direct or indirect pressure on them to rush and to join the same house. For example, Sophia at UNH described how "I didn't rush freshman year because I wanted to make friends. I didn't just want my sisters to be my friends. So I decided against it. Then, sophomore year, I was teeter-tottering on the fence about it, but all my friends decided to join . . . so I decided to join." She had only been a member for about two months when I interviewed her, but she remarked, "I'm happy and I like everyone." Not only did Sophia join with friends, she noticed, "I'm excited to meet a lot of new people and I've gotten two really close friends out of it so far."

Making friends by joining a Greek organization can also strain existing friendships. In chapter 3, I talk about students who lost friendships after they or a friend joined a sorority. One such student is Libby, who told me how she and her "good friend" Callie, "drifted apart after Callie joined a sorority." When I asked why, she said Callie "changed a lot" and ended up getting "super involved" in the sorority, which did not leave much time for their friendship. Another example was Sydney. In the first interview, most of Sydney's friends were other Black students whom she met through two race-based student organizations at Dartmouth, which at the second interview changed to mostly friends met through her historically White sorority. She talked about having "a very rough patch" with her existing friends after joining her sorority. Sydney explained, "I was going to every single event because I wanted to meet new people. And I wasn't spending much time with them." She "tried to resolve it" by talking with them, "but it ended up actually getting worse." Sydney described how she was excited to join this new organization, yet "it was a very trying time and I was just really in a very bad place . . . I had all these peripheral friends [new friends in my sorority], but I was losing my really close friends." Students also discussed strains on their relationships when friends get into different houses, particularly when one friend does not get a bid in a house. By definition, Greek organizations are exclusive. Greek organizations also strain friendships in that they take time, and students invest time in the organization rather than in friendships outside the organization.

## Secondary Friendship Markets: Clubs and Organizations

Jennifer's advice to other Dartmouth students is to "do what you're interested in and find other people who are also interested in that." In line with this advice, clubs and organizations are one of the most important sites for friendship formation after the initial friendship market period, and important sources of social capital.[52] Most interviews included at least one friendship that had formed in clubs and organizations. While some formed during the initial friendship market, most friendships through clubs formed later in college. Sometimes the clubs themselves were ones that students joined later in college. Others were clubs students joined right away, but did not make friendships in, or a particular friendship in, until they had participated for a while. Both are ways that the secondary friendship market works in campus clubs.

Bill's path at Dartmouth illustrates these patterns. As a low-income, queer, international, and Asian student, Bill felt he did not fit in with his peers. His first year, he described joining multiple organizations to find a place on campus. One of those organizations was an activist Asian organization. Bill explained how after hearing about it at the activities fair, "in freshman fall, I just attended a meeting, but it turned out I had a conflict during that meeting time, so I never really got involved." In winter term, he was able to attend regularly and found his place. Right before our interview, he was hanging out with four friends, all members, in one of their dorm rooms.

Many students recognized the importance of interest-based homophily in making friends. These included religious organizations as well as those focused on the outdoors, improv, gaming, and writing, among others. For example, Layla grew up Christian and "very religious," and the community and friendships that were most central to her at Dartmouth were those she formed in the Christian Union. Although Layla did not find this group immediately, the students in the Christian Union helped remind her who she was and what mattered in her life. She described experiences with this group that had strengthened her spiritually, emotionally, and physically. Ella explored many different things on campus, filling her outdoorsy void through the Dartmouth Outing Club, noting that she enjoyed both the people and the "summer camp vibe" of the group. Layla's and Ella's experiences echo those reported in other research, including Blake Silver's ethnography of a large public university, where he spends time with students in the Cardio Club and Volunteer Collective as they seek belonging on campus.[53] Similarly, UNH student May explained:

The people you make connections with, you make connections over your mutual interests. If you guys are both really interested in that, it kind of starts you off the bat with, oh, I'm really interested in this, maybe let's go get food and talk about it or something like that. Then you just get closer from there because you always have that baseline to kind of connect on and talk to and grow off of. Where if it's just someone random that you're like, "Hey like let's just get food, let's be friends," it's like, okay, well, do you really have anything in common?

May's advice to students starting out at UNH is to join clubs that you are passionate about because "getting involved with something that you actually have a true interest in, and something you'd maybe want to care about, that you could see yourself into that club all the way until your senior year." In other words, these common interests help solidify friendships.

Clubs are typically better at facilitating friendships when members are not just passively sitting in meetings together but are actively working on projects together. For example, Will talked about how his friendship group "quadrupled in size" because "I joined a club and that is like instant friends basically." The Programming Board club that Will joined at UNH was similar to the Campus Activities Board that Violet joined at MCC during the initial friendship market. Will explained how the format of the club helped friendships form: "There was built-in socialization with the club too, 'cause we'd host a band and then once all that's figured out, we're just hanging out at a concert together. They're really small concerts, so it was mostly just us hanging out at concerts every few weeks." Will noted that they "spent a lot of time together. We'd go to the dining halls together. We'd go to parties. Do random college stuff." Both working on a common project and spending time together helped solidify their friendship bonds.

While clubs are a great place to meet friends, this may not always be easy. During my interviews, several students noted the difficulties of making friends in clubs, specifically noting that this takes initiative. In May's advice to UNH students, she highlights "being able to continue pushing outside of your comfort zone" by going to different campus organizations, "continuing to put yourself out there," even when "I don't want to." Realizing that "I don't want to close off friendships" from forming, she also gave the advice to others to not be too set in "my group," but instead willing to expand it. While it can be challenging to go to a meeting by yourself and easier to go with a friend, in doing so you are less open to making friends. As Troy was talking about his experience at Dartmouth, he told me: "Everything's always better with a friend. But this has limited a lot of my decisions. A lot of times there have been this one club I wanted to try out or [other activity] I didn't do because none of my friends were going. I should've gone, and I could've met new people." The first part is powerful: "everything's always better with a friend." And so is the second part: existing friendships can stop someone from expanding their network, yet if you go by yourself, you could make a new friend!

## Secondary Friendship Markets: Classes

While some friendships form in classes during the first few weeks of school, these ties are not facilitated by the initial friendship market, unless they are classes specifically for first-year students. Friendships in classes can form anytime during college, and one survey shows students' closest friend from college was as likely to be someone that they met in class as someone they met in a dorm.[54] More often than I expected, however, friendships made in class are more acquaintances or short-term friends than they are close, meaningful, or longer term ties. From students' narratives and sociograms, three elements help students form friendships in classes:

1. Propinquity, when students see the same person in multiple classes or their class along with their dorm or club,
2. Spending more time together and getting to know each other more closely, which often happens through class projects, and
3. Bonding through difficulty, either because of the subject or the format of the class.

These three elements drive the secondary friendship markets in classes.

First, propinquity helps friendships form in classes when students see each other in multiple classes or over multiple terms. In this way, they continue to have opportunities to come together. Propinquity propels them together when they see each other in class after class—or in class as well as in their dorm or a club.

Students may sit near each other in class, and then end up in participating in small group discussions together. Or they may be in the same sorority but not know each other until they start sharing notes because they are in the same lecture class. Other times, students may be more intentional in their strategies, like Kylie. A UNH student who realized she felt lonely after not making friends in the dorms, Kylie found class to be a welcome source of friendship. She described how she met one of her closest friends: "She's usually slow to get out of class, so I feel like this is the perfect opportunity, so I asked her to dinner [in the dining hall]. We went, and she's the sweetest girl ever. We got along great, and I met her roommate, and we got along great. And those two were my best friends at UNH and really get along well."

Another way classes mattered was that students would sometimes strike up a conversation with a fellow student (sometimes years later) and felt more comfortable to do so because they had once shared a class together. May, for instance, noted that she got "really close to" a friend after they worked together in the student union, but "I knew who she was since my freshman year because we had a course together, [though I] never really talked to her." Having seen each other in class in the past seemed to have reduced the barrier to getting to know each other when later they found themselves working together.

Importantly, having classes with another person is not sufficient to form a lasting friendship together. It may not be until after the class ends that they realize that propinquity was what was driving their friendship rather than a deeper connection. Alexa described this experience at MCC. In response to my question about whether she had made friends at MCC, Alexa replied: "Not for more than a semester because we never really seem to have the same classes or people leave to go to other schools and or do other things. We'll go out for a couple of drinks together and hang out after class or before class or whatever for that semester. And then they just never make the effort, so I don't really make any extra effort. I try a couple times and then if they don't respond then it's just, like, 'Okay. Have a good life.'" Friendship is a voluntary and reciprocal relationship. While it seems that everyone has equal opportunity to develop it, opportunities are patterned, including in the classroom. In a study of an engineering college, Anthony Johnson shows that privileged students find collaborating with peers to be a much easier experience than do those from less privileged backgrounds. While privileged students exhibit a sense of entitlement to get help from peers, those from less privileged backgrounds exhibit a sense of constraint and often did not seek or accept help.[55] The students I interviewed expressed class-based differences in how comfortable they were in social and academic spaces in classrooms, so these differences may compound into fewer friends made in class.

Second, friendships in classes form through spending time interacting and working together. Mira did not make many friends at MCC, but two of these were through group projects. Austin told me how his passion for engineering came through when he worked through problems, and he bonded with classmates in his engineering and science classes at Dartmouth, becoming friends with a few of them.[56] It was not just the shared interest that brought them together, though; friendship was facilitated by the regular time they spent together. Austin described the process of making these friends in his classes as involving "talking to people after class, getting to know people through doing homework or studying together, that kind of thing."

Time spent together can also be through giving or receiving academic help. One piece of advice that Safiya had for other Dartmouth students is to "be one of the people that ask questions in class and understands the problems so that you can start helping other people, because I've actually made a lot of friends tutoring or just helping classmates." As students helped each other with classwork, they often struck up other conversations and got to know each other.[57] If they do not strike up these conversations or interact much, but simply sit alongside each other, they are likely to consider each other acquaintances rather than friends.

Third, students make not just acquaintances but friends when difficult experiences bring them together. As Dartmouth student Libby explained, "Engineering has prompted a lot more friendships than I expected, because it's kind of the mutual suffering, everyone kind of joins together." In nursing at MCC, Mindy explained: "If you ask people who have been in nursing school, it's very challenging, it's demanding, it's very stressful. So having the friendships within nursing school is very important to me right now since this is a priority in my life, it's a huge focus. So having people who I can count on in school is very important." Students in the nursing program had to pass an exam to progress, which elevated the difficulty and, consequently, the bonding that happened in peer ties. This echoes research on team building, which emphasizes bonding that develops through working toward a common goal.[58]

When students experience stress or isolation in the classroom and share that experience with each other, they can form friendships. Dartmouth student Sasha observed how bonding through difficulty occurs through complaining: "I think they [friendships] arise more from, like, complaining, which is a weird thing. I feel like it's a weirdly drama thing, where if you complain about academics enough with someone, you will become friends with them."

Homophily can come into play when students bond over the isolation or microaggressions based on a common identity. Layla became friends with the only other woman of color in one of her classes at Dartmouth: "I met her in my economics class my last spring. She was standing next to me, and I said, 'Hello, we both look like we need friends in this class. We should be friends.' And she agreed. And now we're gonna be roommates this fall." After graduation, they will be moving to the same city, where they both have jobs.

Without propinquity, deeper interactions, or bonding through difficulty, the connections made in class are likely to be "fleeting friendships" or more acquaintances than friends. As MCC student Violet puts it, "Those people that utilize each other until the semester ends and then, if you're lucky, you say hi in the hallway sometimes, but they're not really your friends." Will, for example, talked about meeting friends in chemistry class at UNH in the first interview, but by the second interview, none of those friends remained.

## Secondary Friendship Markets: Getting to Know Friends of Friends

One common way that students made friends later in college was through becoming friends with their friends' other friends. Sometimes these are friends from home that students will not often encounter in person but will see when they video-chat with a friend or their friend comes to visit. Other times, they are people they encounter often at the dining hall, study sessions, and social gatherings. On occasion, they even become closer friends than the original friend who introduced them.

As the study of social networks makes clear, people are not just connected one on one, but also through a web of connections. This means that when we make a new friend, we have the potential to expand or transform our own network, when we gain access beyond that one node. The impact goes beyond structure to influence as well. The book *Connected: How Your Friends' Friends' Friends Affect Everything You Feel, Think, and Do* delves into this topic, as the subtitle suggests.[59]

Meeting friends through other friends was common on all three campuses. For example, UNH student Kylie made a friend and then met that friend's roommate, and they became a best friend trio. Earlier in this chapter, I discussed how Jennifer expanded her network immediately through clicking with the friends of her host at Dartmouth's admitted students day, which meant that she arrived on the campus in fall with a friendship group already in place. Students' networks could expand even faster when they were exposed to the friendship groups of several friends. This happened to Timothy in the backpacking orientation trip he attended at UNH. He discussed this in response to my question about what he found most helpful socially at UNH, which he named as that trip. Through the trip, Timothy's network expanded twice. In his words: "I started with a small group of friends who all have their own friends, who I've met, and made friends with. So, I've never felt alone, and I've rarely ever had nothing to do. So, that was a good starter."

## Making Weak Tie Friendships

Throughout this book, I focus on the "closer friendships" that students have. These "strong ties," as they are sometimes called, help with social bonding. These are the friendships shown in the sociograms, and those that I asked students to describe in detail.

People's networks, however, go beyond just these closer friendships. Sociologists looking at a range of outcomes—from jobs to disclosure and advice-seeking—find that "weak ties" also play an important role.[60] In fact, sometimes the social bridging that happens through the ties that are not our closest can be the ones that bring valuable new resources and new ideas.[61]

Although I did not systematically collect names of students' weak ties, I asked them to tell me how many people would be in their next level of "less close" friends. In other words, I asked them to name their closer friends, and then I asked how many friends they had in that next level. Overall, the number of "less close" friends is larger at Dartmouth (twenty-six) than at MCC and UNH, which were similar to each other (fifteen and seventeen, respectively). Only two MCC students had relatively high numbers, Violet with thirty and Ruben with forty friends in that next level. In contrast, there were a handful of students at both UNH and Dartmouth who had fifty to sixty friends in that next level, with one student (Amanda) reporting one hundred close friends in addition to her six closer friends. In other words, students varied in terms of their bridging social capital, and bridging social capital was higher overall at Dartmouth than at the other campuses.

Students' connections with others vary not only by friendship network type, then, but also by whether they are relatively limited to that network or if they have a broader range of ties to draw on. For example, Troy, the tight-knitter discussed above, who was finishing up his second year at Dartmouth, reported sixty friends in that next level, which gives him an amazing range of people to reach out to socially, academically, and in other ways. Compare that to Layla, another Dartmouth student with a tight-knit network of eleven friends, who said that she had four friends in that next level of weak ties. Layla is relatively isolated within her tight-knit networks, whereas Troy has connections to many different groups on campus and in other aspects of his life.

Weak tie friendships also came up throughout the interviews, so I include discussions of these throughout this book. Students made these weak tie friends during the same initial and secondary friendship markets where they made their closer friends. Thus, as Melanie's experience at the beginning of this chapter shows, friendship markets are sites for the formation of close friendships as well as weak ties. Students make both types of connections in their dorms, in clubs, at orientation, and at other places on campus. As discussed later, strong tie friendships are less frequent and harder to maintain at the community college than at the residential campuses, so I particularly focus on weak tie friendships for community college students.

## Loneliness: College Life without Friends

While some students had an easy time making friends, others described lonely and hard times. Most students fell somewhere in the middle, experiencing both ease and difficulty through this process. Nearly every student I interviewed had made at least one friend at college. The community college students, overall, had fewer friends and fewer meaningful relationships than the students on the two residential campuses, as I explain in more detail in chapter 4. Overall, the data presented in this chapter show that worries about young people being able to make friends are present; however, they seem overblown.

Some students, however, experienced significant barriers to making friends and experienced loneliness. I refer to this loneliness in extreme levels as isolation. Looking at experiences of students who were lonely or did not make meaningful friendships can help us understand these patterns. Students themselves often reported rather matter-of-factly about these experiences, such as MCC student Paige, who told me: "You become acquaintances, you're friendly with each other, but I haven't really made any lasting friendships at community college. Maybe it's different at a different school, but that's been the main thing for me."

Students with sampler networks reported more lasting loneliness. The lack of connection between friends makes it so that students themselves often had to initiate getting together, rather than relying on someone else in the group for the contact or the support. UNH student Kylie revealed: "I get prone to loneliness, especially during weekends. I think that's the biggest obstacle to [my] academic success." Kylie reported twelve friends, so it was not just the number of friends that mattered, but the depth of these relationships and the lack of ties between her friends. As a sampler, Kylie found it challenging for her friendships to provide her with the social support she needed. MCC student Ciara was another sampler who described "moments where I'm like, 'Wow, I'm really lonely.' But I'm really not." At several points in the interview, she made comments about feeling "sad" or "I don't really have a lot of friends." Ciara included six friends, including her boyfriend whom "I can literally say anything" to, but she mentioned that the last time she had spent with a group of friends was "a couple of years ago at the carnival that they do in Manchester." Like Kylie, loneliness came not just from lack of meaningful friendships but also from the lack of connections between friends in a sampler network.

Four general barriers came up to students forming meaningful friendships on campus. I later discuss additional institutional barriers (chapter 4) and identity-related ones (chapter 5) to making meaningful friendships. These are the four barriers:

1. Not "clicking" with a group during the initial friendship market, such as their roommate or their orientation group,
2. Lacking practice making friends,
3. Not highly valuing friendships or not intentionally doing things to make new friendships, and
4. Being present on campus when their friends were not, as when their friends graduated and they themselves were still taking classes.

The first barrier was not feeling like you fit in with a group during the initial friendship market, such as their roommate, floormates, or their orientation group, which could lead students to feel isolated, if not lonely. For example, Dartmouth student Danica explained how she did not feel like she fit in well with her teammates on her varsity team, her floormates, or her Trips orientation group. As she explained it, "I don't click with a lot of them." Danica described feeling like "life has forced me to grow up" in ways that made her "different" from these peers. Echoing Danica's language, students often referred to this rather vaguely as "not clicking" or "not fitting" in with others or as having "personality differences" or other ways of being different from others.

Students described the hope and then the disappointment of not fitting in with roommates or floormates. Dartmouth student Uma remembered, "I had been so excited to have roommates. You know, you hear all these great stories about people who have roommates who end up being their best friends. And, obviously, I wasn't quite that naive. But I had been hopeful that we could at least be friends. And then this was clear that we were definitely not going to be [laughs]." The extent of Uma's roommate troubles was not typical. She described her two roommates as "crazy partiers. They also just weren't very nice people." They locked her out of her room and used and moved her belongings without permission. For Uma, these challenges with her roommates were compounded by difficulties at other places on campus, where she also tried to make friends. As discussed in the introduction, Uma eventually made a friend in the orchestra but experienced much loneliness until then. For Uma as well as Danica, students reached out by joining clubs and activities, but even with actively seeking multiple opportunities to make friends on different corners of campus, they struggled to find friends who matched their interests.

A second factor is whether students had experience making friends. Some students had a lot of practice making friends—either because they moved around a lot growing up, or they met new people at summer camps or sports teams or other activities—and others attended the same school their whole life so had no need to make new friends.

Students without practice reported challenges making friends on campus. For example, Savannah had a sampler network when I first interviewed her at Dartmouth, and she came from a small town: "I've known all my friends from birth, basically," she said, so "I don't know how to make friends. I've never had to make friends before because my small town was just like everyone knows each other basically." Similarly, because his closest friends had previously been his cousins or siblings, Calvin felt like making friends at Dartmouth was foreign. Given the lack of experience Savannah and Calvin had making friends, it is not surprising that they had a more difficult experience than did many other students.

Compare their experiences to that of another Dartmouth student, Dawn, who had more experience making friends. Dawn told me, "I moved around... my twelve years of grade school, I went to eight different schools, I think. So, I was always meeting new people." She noted that in college, "it's so much easier to make friends from the beginning of the term when you are a freshman, because everybody is trying to make friends." She also realized that later in college, you may find yourself "stuck with that group" and "still the same core group now two years later." Dawn seemed to have a good understanding of, as well as practice in, making new friends.

The third factor that appeared associated with students' lack of meaningful friendships is that they did not seem to highly value friendships or do the work to seek them out. For example, Erin, an MCC student, talked about how "I don't have a lot of friends" because "it's not really a priority for me. It's, I mean, I—This is going to sound a little cynical, but I don't like most people." She went on to explain, "I know enough about them to be friendly, but I feel like, most people, if I go past that amount of knowledge, I don't like a lot of people." Another MCC student, Shirley, told me she does not have time for friends because she is "super super busy all the time." Over the two interviews, she had lost many friends and had not made new ones that lasted, keeping only her boyfriend as a friend over this period. Shirley did not describe efforts to make new friends or a desire to do so. Lacking intentional strategies to make new friends and not placing value on meaningful friendships limited her ability to make and keep these relationships.

Valuing friendship does not mean sacrificing school for friends or being vulnerable all the time. It does mean making space for friends in your schedule and considering making connections as an important part of college, goals that were more common for those at the residential campuses than at the community college.

A fourth factor that led to loneliness was being on campus when your friends were not. Most often this happened when students' friends graduated before them. However, it also happened when students' friends were not on campus because they were taking a leave, which occurred on all three campuses, or an off-term or internship off campus, which was more common at Dartmouth.

This happened to Will when he switched his major in his third year at UNH, which required an extra year of classes to finish his new major whereas his friends graduated on time. He described the experience: "It was tough. The last year of school was pretty lonely. I was looking forward to it because I thought it was gonna be a fun kind of way to just branch off on my own, go to the bars that no one else wanted to go to, or meet some people in classes. But pandemic. So, none of that happened. I just stayed in my apartment. I lived alone. I lived in a studio, so it was extra isolating." While Will blamed the COVID-19 pandemic, his friends graduated in spring 2019, so he had all fall term of 2019 and two months of 2020 to be able to make these new friendship ties. He did not. Even before the stresses of the pandemic, making new friends after the initial friendship market was "tough."

All four of these factors connect to ways that adults find it challenging to make friends, such as taking initiative to make new friends.[62] Thus, while my findings point to these as barriers to meaningful connections on these three college campuses, they are not unique to the college years. Put differently, loneliness is not unique to college students; it is a public health problem.[63]

To wrap up this discussion of making friends, I turn to advice from students. Lindsay, a White first-generation college student, advised other UNH students to "not waste time just trying to fit in, especially the first couple of weeks. That's what a lot of people do to try to find friend groups. Everyone was really concerned with finding friend groups." Lindsay recognized that she and other people will "find friends when I find them" by being "generally nice," and believed that was a better strategy than "trying to push myself onto people or being fake and trying to be something I'm not." Outside of the friendship market, however, friendships do not just happen, they continue to be shaped by homophily, propinquity, and intention. Many students' advice included being intentional in reaching out to others to make friends, which also involves taking a risk and making yourself vulnerable. Danica, a Dartmouth student who struggled to make friends,[64] told me that her advice to "build a friendship here" is "go for it. Ask people to go eat. Ask people to do things with you and hope they say yes."

## Takeaways

For students:

1. Capitalize on the initial friendship market by meeting lots of people. For example, attend orientation events, dorm floor meetings, and other activities. If you want to signify openness to new friends, strike up conversations with people (see Takeaway 7 below) and consider spending time in dorm lounges and with your room door open into the hallway—and know that when others do this, they are likely open to making new friends.
2. As you make friends during the first few weeks of college, reflect on which friends you enjoy spending time with. Rather than focusing on the number of friends, consider the quality of your friendships. Chapter 2 offers advice on keeping those friends and developing meaningful ties.
3. Know that there will be "pop up" markets later. Do not put too much pressure on yourself to make lifelong friends in these first weeks.
4. Participate in secondary friendship markets by being open to making new friends and intentional in the connections you create. Talk to others at these activities, even if you attend with existing friends. Making connections, whether meaningful friendships or weak ties, will help you thrive in college.
5. Throughout college, participate in clubs and activities that interest you, particularly those that meet regularly, and involve a project or some sort of collaborative work. They will develop your knowledge and skills, and expand your connections and social capital.
6. In classes, know that these three things help friendships form: seeing each other frequently and regularly, spending time interacting, and sharing difficult experiences. Engaging in these in your classes will help friendships form.
7. Be willing to "put yourself out there." For example, strike up a conversation with people you don't know. Give them a genuine compliment on something they said, a sticker on their water bottle, or their shorts (remember how Grace met her best friend this way!). Say hi when you see

people whom you've met—for example, if you see someone in the dining hall whom you met at orientation, in class, or in a club. Both require that you are not glued to your phone but instead are present and willing to interact with people rather than only listening to music or scrolling.
8. Do not take it as a failure if they do not reciprocate or if the relationship stops at "hi." They might not be in the friendship market or might just be having a bad day.

For parents and other supporters:

1. Know that the transition to college involves your child making new friends. They may wish these friends happened automatically, but friendships can take some time.
2. Support your child spending time with friends. Clearly, attending classes and doing homework are important for success in college, but so is making meaningful connections.
3. Encourage your child to participate in clubs and activities that interest them, particularly those that meet regularly, and involve a project or some sort of collaborative work.
4. Support your child in taking risks by talking with peers they do not know, particularly those they see often or have something in common with. These actions draw on the power of propinquity and homophily to form friendships.

For colleges:

1. At both residential and nonresidential campuses, making friends helps students feel like they belong. Making friends can support students' academic success as well. Put simply, making connections is central to students' ability to not just survive but thrive in college.
2. Create and support orientation programs that help students get to know not only the campus and its policies, but also each other. Encourage students to attend orientation programs and other activities during the initial friendship market, even after they have made friends. Meeting more people during the initial friendship market expands students' friendship options and gives them a range of weak ties.
3. Also support dorms that encourage students to get to know each other, both through activities where students are regularly seeing each other and getting a chance to interact (like floor meetings and social activities) and through the physical layout, where students have shared spaces to hang out and to pass by each other regularly. Encourage students to at-

tend events in their dorms, both directly by highlighting the benefits of connecting with their floormates and indirectly by training RAs to be engaging and lead meetings that students want to attend.
4. Support a range of clubs and activities, so that students with varied interests can find one that appeals to them. Encourage clubs to meet regularly (to draw on propinquity), and to involve a project or collaborative work. In conversations with students, discuss not only the common interests that may bring them to a club but the features of the club that may encourage these deeper connections, so that students attend regularly and engage in projects to gain the full benefits.
5. Encourage faculty to help students get to know each other in classes, spend time interacting, and do collaborative work. These three elements help students form friendship in classes. Connections could become meaningful friendships or useful weak ties. Along with attending class and doing homework, making connections is central to thriving in college.
6. Support students in taking risks by talking with peers they do not know, particularly those they see often or have something in common with, such as a peer in their dorm, class, or club. These actions draw on the power of propinquity and homophily to form friendships. This can be a powerful way for students at both residential and nonresidential campuses to turn weak ties into closer friendships.
7. When students lack meaningful friendships, staff can help them recognize whether they have experienced any of these four barriers: (1) not "clicking" with a group during the initial friendship market, such as their roommate or their orientation group; (2) lacking practice making friends prior to college; (3) not highly valuing friendships or not intentionally doing things to make new friendships; and (4) being present on campus when their friends were not, such as when their friends graduated and they still take classes. If they have experienced one of these barriers, name it. Then, encourage them to try one (or more) of the takeaways above or in the next chapter on deepening friendships to make new friends and turn weak ties into meaningful friendships.

[ CHAPTER TWO ]

# Keeping Friends: The Friendship Funnel and Friendship Expansion

I first talked with Robbie when he was starting his third year at UNH. Robbie's close friends, (see figure 2.1) all attended UNH, and they formed a tight-knit network where almost all of them knew each other. Only four, however, were friends Robbie had met in college. Two of the others (Tyler and Abraham) were friends from high school, and the other was his brother Kayshav, who was two years older. Robbie entered college interested in mechanical engineering, describing how "growing up with Indian parents, a lot of my family . . . are engineers or doctors, and my parents expected me to be one or the other."

Most of his friends were engineering majors, and sharing a major helped Robbie maintain these friendships, as propinquity and homophily facilitated spending time together. Robbie told me how sharing classes made it easy to spend time together: "We walk together to class. And then after class we'll just grab a meal." Robbie explained, "I hang out with them most of my time. Most of them are in the same major. We also study together, and they help me out a lot 'cause they're smarter than me." He described how they spent time studying different material in the same space, whether the library or one of their rooms, and his friends also "spend time teaching me" because "they learn it quicker than I would." Robbie recognized that because his "friends are also ME [mechanical engineering] majors, we can hang out and do work at the same time," activities also made easier by his tight-knit friendship network. He says, "Doing homework alone is boring, so when I'm there with my friends, it makes it more fun."

The semester I interviewed him, they only took one class together, meaning that propinquity operated less strongly, and intention became more important. Robbie explained, "All of last year, we had all of our classes together." He preferred that because "it was easier that way 'cause we would hang out more." That alignment of their schedules changed when he failed

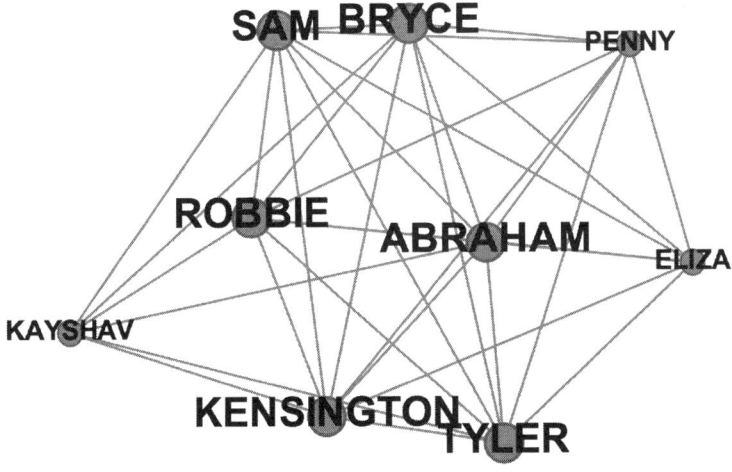

FIGURE 2.1. Robbie's friendship network, UNH year three.

a class and "had to repeat" it, and now "we only have one class together." Because the class he had to retake "was a prerequisite for the other three," Robbie could not take those classes with his friends.

Robbie now makes sure to do other activities with his friends so that they spend time together. For example, Robbie told me how his friend Bryce will "help me with homework, or we'll hang out and watch TV together, or we'll run. Like, yesterday morning, we went for a six-mile run." With another friend he met in class, Penny, he explained that "now we do other things besides classes, like we're watching *Stranger Things* [TV show], and we went apple picking and baked apple pie. So, really a lot of our hanging out is non–academic-related now, as opposed to before." With his friend Abraham, he's found "we have different things we like to watch" on TV, and "he's more adventurous so we go on hikes together as opposed to sitting around, cooking or baking." He also shifted his social time from "freshman and sophomore years I partied a lot" to now "I stopped drinking, I went out less, and if I did go out I would go with friends and it would be better because I'd just tell them I don't drink and they're fine with it. I'd still play beer pong, I just wouldn't drink, so my partner had to drink twice as much." Robbie told me, "I like hanging out with my friends" and "I do care about my grades, I would like to do better, but . . . I like to hang out, spend more time with my friends."

The strategy of being intentional worked for most of the friends he previously spent time with in classes, but not with all of them. Robbie told me that without sharing classes, he was finding it hard to spend much time with Tyler, one of his friends from high school. Robbie described how Tyler "crams so much in, I don't even see him." Tyler has three jobs, "a few clubs," a girlfriend, and a full load of classes. Tyler tells Robbie, "Oh, we should hang out," but Tyler's schedule makes it hard to find the time. "And when we do, he's falling asleep."

With Robbie's friend Sam, who is a computer science major, shared interests and propinquity in where they live facilitates time together. Robbie and Sam go to the gym "almost every day," and they also like watching TV together. *Breaking Bad* was the show they were watching together most nights. Robbie described how earlier on the day of our interview, Sam "texted me and we got a meal together." The day before, "we went to the gym, we usually always go to the gym to do workouts together." After their workout, they "grab food." Robbie noted that "it's nice that he lives in the same building" because that makes it easier to meet up to work out, eat, and watch TV together.

The multiple ways that Robbie connects with his friends make these "multiplex ties," which are easier to maintain and more likely to last across the two interviews. Multiplex ties are those that are connected in multiple ways.[1] Robbie's friends engage in social activities together (watching TV, playing pong, and going to the gym), as well as a range of academic activities. Robbie's friends study together, both alongside each other and quizzing each other for exams. They spend time together before and after class, walking together and getting meals in the nearby dining hall. They also wish each other good luck before an exam, "especially if it's a harder class that we're struggling in." Robbie described how he has one friend who "would not wake up for class, so I call or text him" so that he will attend. They do not often talk about ideas from class unless they are helping each other understand the material or prepare for the exam. In other words, their academic discussions are more instrumental and goal-focused than intellectual. Through instrumental and emotional support for academics as well as social connections, Robbie's friends formed multiplex ties, which facilitates staying friends.

Throughout this chapter, I expand on the themes in Robbie's experience, demonstrating the work that students do to maintain friendships. Robbie maintains his friendships, for example, through the time they spend together watching TV and running. Propinquity made it easier for them to spend time together. When propinquity was no longer operating through classes, Robbie found himself intentionally reaching out to his friends to keep these ties. Because Robbie's friends are connected in multiple ways—providing social support, studying together, and motivating each other academically—his friendships are multiplex ties. In sum, this chapter goes deeper into the processes through which Robbie and other students maintain friendship ties as well as discussing why certain friendships are kept, while others are not. Later in the chapter, I highlight the different challenges to keeping friends that students face if they are tight-knitters, compartmentalizers, and samplers. I also discuss students' friendship networks when they engage in either "friendship funneling" or "friendship expansion" to maintain friendship ties.

## How To Keep Friends? Spending Time Together

Keeping a friend typically involves keeping in touch in some way. Although it may seem basic, this is an important insight for students' ability to maintain friendships. In Robbie's experience, as well as for other students I interviewed, three components emerged for maintaining friends:

1. Spending time together regularly,
2. Engaging in shared activities, and
3. Getting to know each other through conversation.

Spending time together in conversation and activities is the glue that holds friendships together. Lori told me how she formed her friends at UNH when "they started coming over more, and, yeah, then we just became really close." The ones that she was still close to in our second interview were the ones that "talk consistently" and that she "actually take[s] time to hang out with now." Whether it is hanging out in a dorm room, as Lori does, or getting meals together, or spending time in the same club or campus organization, time spent together is the foundation for friendship.

For most college students, it is both the total time and the frequency that maintain friendships. At UNH and Dartmouth, when I asked students to tell me about the last time they spent with a friend, often it was immediately before our interview. If not, it was typically the night before our interview. Tom's response to my question about the last time he spent with a friend was typical. He responded, "It's almost every day. For instance, this morning I woke up and my roommate, he's one of my closer friends, was sitting on the sofa, and he's, like, 'Where are you going?' I'm, like, 'Oh, I'm going to do this research thing to talk about my friendships.' A concrete example is two nights ago, we all played poker. And when I say *we all*, I mean, there's eight of us that live in the two apartments [right next door to each other on the Dartmouth campus], and we all sat down and played poker in our apartment." College students, particularly those at residential campuses, spend much time with friends.

Even at the community college, it was not unusual for students to describe spending weekly, if not daily, time with friends. David, a twenty-one-year-old second-year student in the HVAC program at MCC, told me: "Outside of college, I have a small group of friends. Eight to ten of them. We've hung out since elementary school, at least. Hang out almost every night. There's at least two of us hanging out every night at someone's house. We all live in the same town, pretty close to each other." Like most others at MCC, David regularly spent time with friends. As David's experience illustrates, MCC was different not because of the value students placed on friends, but because of the amount of time they spent outside of class with other students at their college.[2]

It is often reported that making a friend takes approximately forty hours spent together. Breaking this down more precisely, a recent study concluded that casual friendships form after spending somewhere between forty and sixty hours together in the first six weeks of knowing each other. To deepen this relationship and move beyond a casual friendship takes spending somewhere between 57 hours over 3 weeks and 164 hours together over 3 months.[3] My study was not set up in a way that enabled me to confirm these specific numbers, yet it is clear that keeping friends requires spending time together.

Related to spending time together is engaging in shared activities. Students on all three campuses reported engaging in a range of activities with friends, like David at MCC, whose friends hang out and talk, play video games, and watch TV together. Similarly, Robbie described spending time with friends watching TV shows, playing video games, going to the gym, going on six-mile runs, and studying together at UNH. Jane, another UNH student, explained that she prefers to study on her own rather than with friends but enjoys lots of other activities with friends. She described how they "sometimes go to the bars on Thursdays . . . relax, hang out, listen to music and play beer pong," as well as "going shopping, and getting food." Collectively these shared activities add up to a lot of time spent together and do the work of friendship maintenance.

The flip side of this is that friendships often became less close when my interviewee or their friends join a sorority or fraternity or a different one from their friends. Dartmouth student Tom, for example, explained about a friend, whom he listed in our second interview but not our first, "he rushed a different fraternity and so we weren't close for a while." They became close again when they decided to "make sure to grab dinner and hang out" together.

As Robbie's experiences show, spending time together is easier when propinquity is bringing you together than when you must intentionally go out of your way to do so. Will, a UNH student, noted that during college "you see your friends every single day, and you live with them, and you go to the dining hall with them." Propinquity enables keeping friendship ties.

As I was interviewing students, and they were telling me about the types of things they did with friends, I started to wonder if doing errands together makes students closer friends or if they do errands because they are close. Both things seem to be true. And more important is that the time they spend together solidifies their friendship. Dory, a student at MCC, told me about how she spends time with her friend Aubrey: they do "grocery shopping together, watching movies, going out for Chinese food, [and] we talk." Dory reflected, "She's a fun friend." Dustin, a Dartmouth student, told me about the last time he spent with a friend, which was with his friend Keagan. Dustin explained that he needed a mattress and Keagan needed sandals, so they went shopping together in a nearby town earlier that day: "We went mattress shopping, he helped me out, he laid on the mattresses with me, he seemed to enjoy himself, I purchased a mattress. We went to Walmart. I bought a bunch of towels and stuff for the apartment. We went to TJ Maxx and went shopping together. I ended up spending $60 on clothes I don't need, and Kevin bought sandals and clothes he didn't need. We got Dunkin' Donuts. Then I dropped him off at the house." Dustin wrapped this up by saying: "We enjoy each other's company, and we'll run errands with each other just 'cause it's more fun than doing it [by] yourself."

Students mentioned that they know that a friendship is close when they are willing to engage in any activity to spend time with that friend. Students' activities with friends range from mattress shopping to studying together to going to activities of a club they were not a member of. Tom and his best friend, Tucker, for example, worked on class projects together, even though they were for different classes. Tom liked that Tucker will "bounce ideas off" him and "he'll listen to me." Layla, another Dartmouth student, described a close friend, someone "that I know I can tell anything to" who is "an atheist," yet "she comes to my church on Easter, and she comes to all the Christian events because she wants to be with me. . . . at the end of the day she still retains what she believes in." Layla sums this up by saying that "relationships that are not nurtured will fail, right?" To ensure they do not fail, Layla and her friend nurture their relationship through engaging in activities together, even when those activities themselves are not of interest. Although friendships are often seen as fun rather than work, part of the work of friendships is spending time together.

Engaging in activities on a regular basis is a valuable way to maintain friendship ties. For example, Tyler's weekly poker night with five friends helps keep those connections. During her second year at UNH, Chandra mentioned that her "circle of friends started doing game night every Saturday." Chandra described game night as "a staple of all of my friendships," a place where they saw each other "consistently" and had time for "hanging out." Daily or weekly traditions, like studying, cooking dinner together, attending a club meeting, or going to a yoga class, helped students keep their friendships.

The third component of maintaining friends is continually getting to know each other through conversation. In my interviews, I asked students about the kinds of things they talked about with friends. Some noted that their friendships stayed at surface level, but most talked about more intimate topics, such as their backgrounds, struggles, and goals, at least with closer friends. These deeper discussions facilitate friendship ties remaining, particularly when propinquity no longer brings them together.

As long as propinquity is passively bringing people together physically, these friendships can also be sustained through surface-level conversations. Small talk can keep friendships going. Often, these conversations are about the topics that people have in common, such as classes when they are classmates and work when they are coworkers. David, who talked about how he hangs out daily with his friends from home, explained: "Through here [MCC], I haven't really made too many friends. I mean there's people I talk to and socialize with, no problem at all, but outside of school, there's like no contact unless it's about classes or homework. That's about it." Conversations about their classes can move people from acquaintances to friends but are likely not enough to keep the friendship alive when they no longer share the classroom connection.

Getting meals together also enables students to spend time together and engage in conversation. Campus dining halls increase the convenience of sharing meals, especially when both friends have a campus dining plan. Some students reported "grabbing a meal" regularly by walking to the dining hall after a class they shared or a class that met in a nearby building. This routine allows students to talk about a range of topics, including more meaningful ones. Melanie, for example, told me about grabbing lunch with someone right before our interview: "She was more of an acquaintance, but she seems really cool, so maybe we'll be closer friends. There was free soup in Collis Commonground [the Dartmouth student union], and I really like free food. So does she. So we went and got free soup. Then we ate it and found a spot in the sunshine in Collis and just like talked about how finals are stressful and home is not. It was nice." Campus dining halls and free food events increase the convenience of grabbing a meal together. These mundane activities, like eating free soup together in the sunshine, while engaging in conversation about their lives, are the building blocks of friendship.

Friends are the people whom students want to spend time with. Nancy, a UNH student, brought this up by saying that her friends "always find time for each other." When I was interviewing Dartmouth students right at graduation time, they often told me about the people they wanted to be sure to share a meal with before they graduated. Even if these were not close friends currently, this was a sign to them that it was a friendship that had been meaningful at some point in their time at Dartmouth. For example, in my interview with Tom, he described his reasoning for including two friends on his friend list: "the reason I put Sumedh and Surina down [on my friend list] is those are two people that I put on my list to make sure to grab dinner with and hang out with before graduating. And they're pretty much the only ones." Engaging in a common activity, in the form of sharing a meal, was not only something that maintained a friendship, it was also a marker of a relationship that matters.

## How to Keep Friends? Deepening Ties

Implicit in this earlier discussion is that deepening our friendship ties is a good way to keep them. When I asked for their advice for other students, my interviewees often highlighted developing meaningful friendships, not just collecting friends. How to keep "rewarding friendships" can feel mysterious. Students' experiences, however, reveal three specific components to this:

1. Having conversations about personal, not just surface-level topics,
2. Talking through disagreements, and
3. Being there for each other, even when it is not convenient.

The friends who stayed in students' lives over the two waves of interviews were more likely to be those with whom they had deeper conversations, as opposed to small talk. Researchers have found that it is not just talking that makes people friends or moves them from friends to close friends; instead, it is what is conveyed through those conversations. The amount of time involved in small talk ("talk about current events to pass the time") leads a relationship to be less close over time. In contrast, the amount of time spent talking about more meaningful things increases the closeness of the relationship.[4] Students mentioned a range of conversation topics they felt had deepened their relationships, including "family drama, relationship woes, mental health," fear of disappointing their parents, the culture shock at college and differences from their home community, and religion.

The process of deepening ties often involves making yourself "very vulnerable and honest," as UNH student May put it. May was describing a particular friendship, one that became closer once a friend shared that she has a "parent who's terminally ill." It can feel risky and, therefore, not always good or safe to share personal things with friends. Some of these conversations involve digging up difficult experiences from the past and sharing these with friends. For example, as Calvin was talking about his closest friend at Dartmouth, he explained how "that friendship came a lot from trauma sharing." He noted that they have "similar goals in dance and activism," and "we're both poor, we're both from working-class and from immigrant families." He described the feeling of understanding each other as "we're able to be real."

Vulnerability is such a key part of friendship that students often experienced a breach of trust when they discovered that someone they considered a close friend had not been sharing an important matter in their life with them. Students brought up times when they were surprised to find out that a friend had an ill family member, and wondered if the relationship was not as close as they had thought because this aspect of their friend's life was unknown to them. During our interview, Kylie excitedly told me about how she met her "two best friends" at UNH, noting that the three of them "really get along well." Later, she described her surprise in finding out: "Tragically, my friend almost committed suicide. And that was a freaking shock because she goes around with this big smile on her face. . . . I did not know this side of her. I didn't even know she had those thoughts in her head. And she had to leave and take the next semester off." Kylie was jolted by worry for her friend. However, she also felt jolted that her friend had not talked about this important topic with her. Kylie mentioned that this friend "taught me how to be really compassionate and genuine towards other people." They remained close friends, even after college. After the suicide attempt, Kylie's friend discussed her depression and challenges, bringing them closer together.

With one exception, students told me that the person or people they considered their best friend were among the closest relationships and those whom they talked with about the most meaningful topics. The exception is a UNH student, Heidi, who identified a best friend and explained that their relationship is "not close on an emotional level, we don't talk about a lot of things, it's just surface level," but they've been best friends for almost twenty years. In this case, the length of time they have known each other keeps the best friend tie in place, at least from Heidi's perspective.[5]

Talking through differences or disagreements is a second way friendships can deepen. When I asked Ella for her advice to a future Dartmouth student, I was surprised that she started out by saying, "It's okay to fight with friends and to get in a rocky patch with them." Ella gave an example of that experience with her friend Zane, noting, "We ended up yelling at each other and then going back to each other saying, I'm really sorry, and then having to work it out." Ella mentioned that after that, their friendship felt deeper and stronger.

Students remarked knowing someone was a close friend when they could talk about differences, such as about different ways they viewed the world. Dartmouth student Melvin told me about a friend who "expanded the way I look at things." Melvin said that his friend from Haiti had an impact on their friend group: he "forced us to look past Dartmouth" and make their worldview "more global." Melvin explained: "We don't all agree on everything, necessarily. But we're all approaching it from a similar-enough lens that we can see where each other are coming from, so that makes it kind of comfortable." As discussed in chapter 1, homophily often brings people together. However, that alone is not enough to maintain a friendship. Renata, a Latina woman, first-generation college student and second-year Dartmouth student, said it well: "We come together through common threads, but I feel like the differences made our friendship stronger." Talking and interacting across difference is something that deepens friendship ties.

The third way to grow meaningful friendships is to be reliably there for a friend and to feel that your friend is there for you as well. When I asked students what separated their closest friends from other friends, they often mentioned knowing that their closest friends would be there when they needed them. For example, MCC student Alexa talked about how her closest friends are there for each other "unconditionally," even when "it's not convenient at all, but you do it because you're invested in the friendship." May, a UNH student, described how she would "be there for" for her friend with a terminally ill parent; May would "listen to her," and "bring her food and cards." As another UNH student, Nancy, put it, "we always find time for each other."

Keeping friends by creating deep connections also fits with advice from a range of sources, including computer scientist Cal Newport's book, *Deep Work: Rules for Focused Success in a Distracted World*, where he advises to "quit social media" and instead have the goal "to maintain close and rewarding friendships with a group of people who are important to me."[6] It is discussed more extensively in the book *How College Works* by sociologists Daniel Chambliss and Christopher Takacs, who argue that students get more out of college when they have "two or three good friends" and connections with professors.[7] Having a few good friends increases persistence and makes students' college experiences more meaningful and impactful.

Having close friendships, where you can depend on someone, not only matters in college, but also contributes to happiness, physical health, and mental health throughout people's lives.[8]

## How To Keep Friends? Multiplex Ties

Friends who are connected to each other in multiple ways are more likely to be meaningful and lasting ties. The way Sasha described her closest relationships is a good example of multiplex ties: "my very close friends, we're not just academic friends, we're not just social friends, we're both." Sasha noted that some other friends faded because they were just academic friends or outgrew each other during their time at Dartmouth. Friends that are connected in multiple ways are known as multiplex ties.

In chapter 1, we met Safiya, a Black international student from Africa, who described her closest friends as important for the "support" and "loyalty" they provided her. When I asked her what "support" means, Safiya described it this way: "Support is anything from telling me I can do it on a test, to grabbing dinner with me, or checking up on me, [or] just hanging out and being able to talk to each other about anything and everything." She also described how they engage in intellectual conversations; as she explained it, "we spend a lot of time talking about our lives and we also have conversations about the world," including topics they do not agree on. One example is Pan-Africanism, about which Safiya noted, "I believe that it works in the economic sense," while some of her friends believe that it works not only economically but "also in a social aspect." Safiya described the multiple forms of support from her friends. At Dartmouth, they live together, which helps "mentally and emotionally too because even on a really stressful day, I would just go home and my friends would all be there." And she felt her friends "encouraged" her to do well academically. Based on her experience, she advised, "Just surround yourself with the people that will help you be successful." Having friends who provide emotional support, academic support, and a positive identity are multiplex ties. And they are meaningful ties to Safiya.

A recent book, *Connections Are Everything: A College Student's Guide to Relationship-Rich Education*, argues for the value of multiplex ties with friends as part of a "relationship-rich education." The authors' chapter "Connecting with Peers" encourages students to find and nurture a friendship that "supports you in a number of overlapping ways (academically, emotionally, practically)."[9] Similarly, *My Girls: The Power of Friendship in a Poor Neighborhood* shows how one source of this power is the "multifaceted" ways friends are involved in each other's lives, which the author also describes as "the versatility of their relationships."[10] Being "versatile" or connected in multiple ways is a strong force keeping friendships intact. These books echo the value of multiplex ties that I found for students at MCC, UNH, and Dartmouth College.

## How to Keep Friends? The Role of Technology

Technology has changed the way we live, communicate, and socialize. This has happened rapidly, with substantial change occurring in the lifetimes of the college students I spoke with. Technology, such as social media and smartphones, has made it much easier to stay in touch with people, including friends. Technology also makes it possible to make friends with people we have never met in real life. The impact of technology on our friendships is complex, neither fully good nor bad.[11]

The main downside of technology in students' friendships was the social comparison that led to students' feeling that they were not doing as well or having as much fun as their friends. Students spoke about how it is easy to feel lonely when looking at friends' social media posts, often through the shorthand expression "FOMO" (fear of missing out). Students recognized that other people's posts are curated to show the good parts of their lives. Yet, they still feel FOMO seeing how their friends "are having more fun than me," or look as if they are. These perceptions exist both for friends from home and for those down the hall. The social comparison was challenging for many students. Layla, for example, told how she "deleted my Facebook for eight months my freshman year because it was just overwhelming to be, like, I have so many friends, but then I felt really lonely." Negative feelings of loneliness because of social comparison were far more common than the stories students told me about friends and classmates using social media to bully them.

Every student I interviewed used technology to stay in touch with friends.[12] Technology, especially texts and social media, helped them keep up with friends, both those on campus and those far away. Students did this both one on one and in group chats or forums. For example, Dartmouth student Sasha told me about the group chat she has with Ian and Bryce. "We had a group text going since freshman fall, and I don't think there's been a day we haven't used it to check in with each other, which is really nice. When I was [studying] abroad, we definitely texted every day, FaceTimed a couple times a week. It never felt like—I don't know how to describe it. I'll miss them, but it's not like anything changes, we pick right back up where we left off when we're back together."

Some students use technology to keep in touch with groups of friends, some with individual friends, and some with both groups and individuals. UNH student Lori told me how she uses "this one group message" with her closest friends: "We just always keep in contact. If I texted any other, less close friends, they wouldn't really know what's going on in my life, like day-to-day everything. In that group message, we talk all the time, we tell each other everything." Lori elaborates that with her "less close friends," "I have no problems hanging out with them, it wouldn't be awkward at all." When I asked about the effort it takes to maintain her close friendships, she remarked that "it's easier because it's just one group message." Some students, however, note that their closest friends are those they keep in touch with both in a group message and one on one. For example, Heidi, another UNH student, explained that what separates her eight closest friends from the seven in her next level is that the closest eight engage in "talking more individually than just in a group message." Her closer friendships involve "hanging out" as a "group activity," and they also "hang out one on one." This happens both in person and through technology.

Students used social media to connect with friends in quick and regular ways. The examples given here contain many of the kinds of mundane details students share with friends, so they "really know what's going on in my life, like day-to-day everything." Technology companies have capitalized on this by showing students how often they interact or creating games or challenges, like Snapstreaks on Snapchat. Several students mentioned Snapstreaks as ways to stay connected, even with friends they see in person. Dartmouth students Dustin and his friend Moses have a 150-day streak on Snapchat. When I ask how this worked, Dustin explained how each day, you take a picture or video, "send it to him, and he writes one back." They see the number of days along with a fire emoji by their chat. Dustin believes "Moses will continue this Snapstreak for as long as is possible." As he thinks to the future, he told me, "That's like a way that we would continue to keep in touch for four years or until Snapchat goes out of business, I guess." Dustin and Moses live together currently, so they see each other in person every day along with communicating electronically to keep their Snapstreak going.

Students recognize that without propinquity working in their favor, it is necessary to be intentional about keeping connected, and technology provides the means to do so. Natalie recalls how her friendships were easier when she lived on UNH's campus: "when you're living so close to everyone, you didn't really have to do that in the first place, . . . planning things in my personal life." When she was not on campus, technology enabled her to keep in touch with her friends, and that required intention: "I really have to mindfully say, okay, I'm gonna text this person or call this person or make plans to plan a trip or something like that. I found myself really putting in more effort to make sure that those connections are still there because I recognize that I lost touch with a lot of people." Although technology has a lower barrier than face-to-face interaction, it still is not automatic. At least one person in the relationship must decide to connect. And the work of friendship necessitates that the connection be reactivated repeatedly.

Other students relied on technology in place of in-person interaction. Kari, for example, a forty-five-year-old MCC student, had never met her best friend in person, although they had been friends for almost twenty years and live only a few hours apart. They met in a chat room and stayed in touch mainly through texting. Pauline, a forty-nine-year-old MCC student, told me how she is able to maintain relationships with her eight closest friends, even after she moved more than a thousand miles away for a job after graduation. Pauline told me that these friendship ties, "those are the ones that I nurture . . . the friendships that I make sure that I work on and strengthen, and I keep in contact with," saying that sometimes that is through "a text message, 'Hi, how are you? I love you. Is there anything I can do for you today?'" And sometimes it is more in depth, like a phone call. Technology enables larger networks to be maintained across distance.

As Pauline's experience shows, technology can help students keep friendships when they are experiencing transitions. However, technology is not a magic bullet. It works to maintain friendships when there is effort behind it. For example, Ella told me how she easily continued to keep in touch with summer camp friends at Dartmouth using technology, but did not maintain any ties with her high school friends. Although her summer camp friends were separated by physical distance, they were very involved in each other's lives because of their efforts to keep in touch. Ella had maintained these sturdy, long-distance friendships for many years prior to Dartmouth, so the transition to college did not change the dynamic much. In comparison, Ella quickly fell out of touch with her high school friends once they no longer saw each other every day. Technology could have helped, but it did not, without intentionality to maintain these connections.

The COVID-19 pandemic also necessitated using technology to maintain at least some ties. I expected that the pandemic would disrupt and harm everyone's friendships. However, I found that was not the case. Some of the UNH and MCC students I interviewed had graduated shortly before the start of the pandemic, so they had just undergone that transition with their friendships when the pandemic brought about another transition. During my second interview, this is how Chris, a UNH student, described their friendships: "Honestly, I don't feel like things changed that much [because of COVID], because I had already graduated and my friendships with my college friends were already remote anyway. So that didn't really change. It was just that, if we were all gonna be in the same area, or, as the case may be, the same country, we wouldn't be able to get together like we had the previous year." The transition from in-person friendships during college to technology-based friendships after college that Chris had already accomplished made the transition to remote friendships during the pandemic mostly seamless.

An important part of keeping friends is doing the work of friendship. Spending time together is necessary but not sufficient to maintaining friendship ties. The work of choosing to invest in a friendship by keeping regularly in contact is easy when you regularly bump into each other on campus in clubs, classes, or dorms. It is takes intention when propinquity is not bringing you together. Most students recognize that their friendships are "worth the work," at least the meaningful and supportive ones.

## Why Keep Friends? Emotional and Social Support

Friends can provide social and emotional support for one another. Put simply, difficult things in our life feel easier when we have people supporting us. In an experiment that asks college students to report how steep a hill looks when they are alone, when they are with a friend, or when just thinking about a supportive friend, they reported that a hill looked less steep when they had friends by their side. In fact, even just imagining a supportive friend by their side made the hill appear easier to climb.[13]

Students on all three campuses report friendships that provide social and emotional support. In line with other studies of college students, the students I talked with reported leaning on each other for a range of emotional needs, including those related to their classes, romantic relationships, family, financial troubles, and other friendships.[14] Grace, a UNH student, described the support her friends provide: "It's just nice to, like, be able to fall back on them whenever I need them." Dartmouth student Layla described this emotional support as "someone who will be there for me."

What often distinguishes close friends from others is this support. Dartmouth student Layla highlighted this difference by saying, "I want to have friends that I can call at any point, and I know that they'll be there for me, versus people who just like my posts on social media." Paige, an

MCC student, told me that, in contrast to acquaintances, her close friends "are there for each other. We call each other. We text each other." Paige described these friends as someone "I can tell anything to . . . whatever is going on." Being able to count on this support is part of what makes these relationships meaningful and different from other people in her life who are not close friends.

Students rely on and appreciate indirect and direct forms of support from friends, including listening to one another's complaints and understanding what they were going through.[15] Dartmouth student Libby told me, "Your friends probably know when you're struggling, whether or not you admit it." She valued that sense that her friends understood her. UNH student Tyler noted how his friends "helped me a lot mentally and emotionally, too, because even on a really stressful day, I would just go home and my friends would all be there." MCC student Elyse especially valued the "emotional support" from her friends, noting, "You definitely need that." This support also echoes "shine theory," coined by the two best friends who co-wrote a memoir discussing ways they value and affirm each other's successes in their friendship. They sum this up by asserting that, among friends, "I don't shine if you don't shine."[16]

Friends also provide direct emotional support through offering verbal encouragement, congratulations, and providing help in busy or stressful times.[17] Libby described turning in a paper for a friend at Dartmouth or bringing them lunch even if they do not have time to eat it with you. Libby added: "Sharing an umbrella can make your day. I've stayed up late, even though I didn't have a lot of work, just to be with a friend who was really crunching. It sucks, but, looking back, I don't regret missing that sleep versus just supporting someone who I cared about." Layla shared a range of examples of this direct emotional support, including a friend who brought "a blanket and crackers and soup and Nyquil" when she was sick, and someone whom you can reach out to when you are worried, whether emotionally about a big test or "you can call at 3 a.m. in the morning when you find a spider in your room and you're like 'I'm scared.'"

One challenge with emotional support was when it was not reciprocal, and students would find themselves spending a lot of time and energy supporting others without receiving much in return. UNH student Cindy referred to "one-sided" friendships, where one person "needs a lot of support and they need to be with you all the time." She said that in retrospect this person is "not really a friend." While it is not necessary, or even possible, to be equal all the time in giving and receiving support, students note the importance over time in knowing that they will receive support from friends when they need it and will give it to a friend.[18]

Although students explained support in a lot of ways, a common one was referring to friendship support as "feeling like a family."[19] For example, when Layla described some friends, she phrased it as "they became like a family to me," Renata had two friend groups that she referred to as "familia," and Dawn described a group as "like family, so you'll always be there... We know that we're all gonna be there for each other at the end of the day... I'm really glad that I found that in college." Students' chosen family provides emotional and social support.

## Why Keep Friends? Academic Support and Motivation

Friends' support also applies directly to classes and academic success. In the previous section, we saw how Libby shared examples of emotional support as well as academic support, specifically, being present with a friend as she studied in the middle of the night. This type of academic support was experienced by students on all three campuses, and it echoes the findings of other research that documents both instrumental and emotional support that friends provide.[20]

Students described instrumental support for their academic work, including studying together, using flashcards to prepare for exams, sharing notes, and proofreading papers. At the beginning of this chapter, Robbie described how his friends provided academic support in a range of instrumental ways, such as teaching him material he did not understand and studying together. Robbie told me: "I don't think I would have been able to get through the whole mechanical engineering major on my own. So I feel like with their help, us studying together and us doing all the academic stuff together, I was able to finish the degree and get a job." At MCC, Monika explained: "Having friendships within nursing school is very important to me right now since this is a priority in my life and it's a huge focus, so having people who I can count on in school is very important." Monika noted that the people she can count on are those to whom she can ask questions about the material, who share notes, and who study together in the library or off campus.

Students also described emotional support for classes, particularly motivating and encouraging each other to keep studying and doing their academic work. Erin, a White woman and first-generation college student in her second year at MCC, told me, "I definitely feel like they have an enormous impact on my educational experience and on my ability to keep refocusing and keep going forward even when I'm starting to get tired."

The support of MCC friends also came up in a conversation I had with two friends, Emma and Hazel:

> EMMA: When you're down and out and you're stressed and you feel like giving up and you're at your wits end and then you turn to this person and they're like—
>
> HAZEL: You can do this. Yup.
>
> EMMA: When you're weak, I'm strong. We're going to get through this, we're going to get through this together. And it's almost like you create a better bond, a better understanding, a better love, and appreciation. Their goals are your goals, even. You succeed and I succeed by watching you. It's definitely different.
>
> HAZEL: Yup. I think so.

Emma and Hazel were not only talking about the academic motivation and support that friends provide for each other, they modeled it through their conversation. Friends implicitly support students' academic success by providing an environment where that focus is encouraged, or at least tolerated.[21]

This support from friends is especially important for students who feel marginalized on campus in some way. Jennifer, a Latina, low-income Dartmouth student, explained: "Friendship is the one thing that keeps people going. Especially minorities. Like people who are not used to this type of environment, and who are so closely connected to home where there's a lot of pressure. You're here because your family worked so hard for you to come here." Friends give each other academic support and model academic success. They sit with you while you are studying.[22] Friends' encouragement to keep going and to do better is also one of the ways they support each other's academic success.[23]

## Why Keep Friends? Fun and Enjoyment

Research and popular culture frequently highlight the social capital provided through connections, including friendship ties. While these benefits are real and important, as discussed in other sections, I also want to underscore the importance of friendships for pure enjoyment. To be sure, some popular culture sources draw on this as well: TV shows such as *Firefly Lane* and *The Sex Lives of College Girls* show the fun that friends have together, as do books such as *Big Friendship*.

The joy and fun of friendships came up in my interviews in a variety of ways. When discussing her best friend at Dartmouth, a big smile appeared on Uma's face as she told me, "One of the things that I love about our friendship is that we can do basically anything together and we know it will be fun." Talking about her friends at MCC, Erin added: "Seeing them makes the day better. And I hope they feel the same way about me." Capturing the enjoyment of friends, UNH student Grace declared, "All my friends are my favorite people."

Students discussed a variety of activities that were more fun with friends. Friends stave off boredom.[24] Melanie mentioned that her friend Ryley is "a really fun person to study with" because she "always brought such a bunch of energy to the table, which was awesome." Troy exclaimed, "Everything's always better with a friend."

Some "fun" friends, however, are actively distracting students from academic life. Violet, who transferred to MCC from a four-year institution, described lacking any academic connection with friends. "I've never had a friend ask me for academic advice." In another part of our conversation, she described her friends as "very distracting. All of them. Don't have a single friend I can sit down with and just work." Violet said that she had tried to study with them, but they were constantly interrupting her, and "don't see the urgency in trying to get actual work done, at least *my* friends don't." Thankfully, Violet's experience was not universal among my respondents. Violet, however, described keeping these friends because they were the people in her life whom she did not need to do something exciting with to have fun. As she put it, "We can just show up at each other's houses and not talk to each other and we had a great time." Fun friends can provide other forms of support—academic or emotional—but this is not always the case.

## Why Keep Friends? Identity: "You become a better version of yourself"

As students talk about their friends, they are also talking about themselves. Friendship is a chosen relationship, and students see themselves reflected in the people they associate themselves with.

Students often talk about knowing someone is their friend when they can be themselves around that person. Timothy told me about the friendships he made at UNH: "I really value friends I can confide in and be myself around, and people I feel like appreciate me for who I am." Another UNH student, Yusef, expanded on this point: "I'm just glad that I was able to make friends here, close friends, people I can be my true self with. 'Cause

I feel like the worst thing is to have friends and they think they know you, but they really don't. And it's because you aren't being your true self all the time." Students told me that when they can be comfortable with someone, that is when they know they are being their "true self." They feel accepted.

Friends contribute to students' identity development. Students talk about how friends reflect or bring out a particular side of them. As Ella described her path to making friends at Dartmouth, I was struck by how many clubs she had joined. Ella explained that although she had reservations about religion prior to college, she joined a Bible study group, and she noticed that she was her most "upbeat" and "cheery" self with these friends. Ella reflected on what this group meant to her: "It's not like it changes who I am, but it brings out a different side of me when I'm around them which I think is kind of a nice break from my other kind of trends that I have going on." Indeed, young adulthood is a particularly important time in the life course for identity development, and higher education is a relatively unique time and place to develop identities alongside friends.[25] Throughout college, students are developing their friendships and developing their identities and sense of self.

Some students also told me about how they intentionally try to form friendships with the type of people they would like to become. Terrence discussed this in relation to the balance between academic and social life he hopes to achieve at MCC: "I surround myself with people that highly prioritize academics over being social." UNH student Irina discussed this as well, attributing her approach to her mother's lesson to "look at the bigger picture. I mean it's not gonna matter that you got a 70 on this exam, it's not gonna matter that you got a C in that class, it's gonna matter who you wanna spend the rest of your life with, and who you, really, who you surround yourself with. So she [my mother] always says, 'What's within you surrounds you,' and I love that. My connection to people is definitely a big aspect of my success in school." As Irina and her mother discuss, friends both reflect and create our sense of self. Friends help us forge who we are.

Students talk about how identity development happens over time, so that the traits or qualities you seek in friends may also change. Tyler offers a clear description of this, advising UNH students to "make a lot of friends freshman year cause that's when people are coming out of their shell and meeting people. Then by sophomore year, try to find the people that make you feel like you want to be better or help you feel like you're being better and more successful. Then by junior and senior year . . . you know that you're compatible." He advised, "In general, surround yourself with the people that will help you be successful." Because friends reflect and create students' own identity, who you surround yourself with matters.

Friendship talk creates self-identity through constructions of friendship. Both the differences and similarities students note between their friends and themselves can be means of personal identity construction.[26] Tyler spoke about how his friends reflect both who he is and who he hopes to be: "very understanding and sympathetic." He goes on to discuss the importance of who he associates with: "You need to surround yourself with the people that you would like to become. If you hang out with people that put their academics to the side and decide that personal recreations are more beneficial, then you'll find yourself doing that, too. You congregate with the hive mind that's around you. And the people that I was with here [friends at UNH] cared about their academics.... Surrounding myself with those that are more knowledgeable in this field inspired me to do the same." Similarly, Nancy advises UNH students to "make good friends, not a lot of friends. Quality is better than quantity. And find people who motivate you to be a better version of yourself, but don't try to change you." Insights from students like Tyler and Nancy build the existing concept of "friendship talk as identity work," as students construct who they are and who they aspire to be by reflecting on similarities and differences with their friends.

## Why Keep Friends? Companionship

While not as common as the reasons discussed thus far, some students mentioned the importance of keeping friends so that they are not alone. These were not friendships based on intimacy or trust but based on "having someone." For example, UNH student Rachel told me how she valued having someone to spend time with. She felt like an important discovery for her was that "you can be friends with people, but not be best friends with them. They can just be someone to hang out with and talk to and stuff, but you don't have to, like, tell them everything." Rachel is making the point that friendships do not need to be meaningful or intimate to fulfill our basic needs for companionship.

Rachel's point also fits with research on social connection that shows that loneliness does not just feel bad, but also can negatively affect our health and longevity. The US surgeon general's report summarizes this research: "Lacking social connection can increase the risk for premature death as much as smoking up to 15 cigarettes a day," and it leads to an increased risk of heart disease, stroke, anxiety, depression, and dementia.[27] Social connection, including friendships, matters for our health and well-being.

In summary, there are many reasons why students keep friends: social and emotional support, academic support and motivation, fun and enjoyment, identity work, and companionship. Students' experiences also point to a few ways that they keep friends, including spending time together in person and through using technology, as well as getting to know each other more deeply. This all points to overarching issues in this chapter—friendship maintenance and friendship deepening.

## Challenges by Network Type

Because it takes work to maintain friendships, it is more efficient to maintain multiple friendships at once than to do so one at a time. This means that tight-knitters and compartmentalizers can maintain groups of friends collectively rather than just individually. For tight-knitters, this may be all their friends hanging out together in person for a game night, or it may be communicating with each in a fast-paced group chat. For compartmentalizers, this may be having two or three groups to alternate hanging out with or joining in their group chats.

Compartmentalizers are often doing different things with each of their groups, which also means that they get the efficiency of doing multiple activities or activating multiple identities through the different groups of friends they maintain. A Black man and third-year electrical engineering student at UNH, Otto, described how he alternated between groups: "something that I can't get from one friend, I just get it from another. I would say my friend group is pretty well balanced." Figure 2.2 shows Otto's multiple friend groups. Describing the different activities he does with different friends, Otto explained, "It's nice to have someone who is taking similar classes to study with. And then I have friends who I don't want to do anything class related with, so I'm just gonna go goof off with those friends and play video games or play some kind of sport." His largest group of friends were those he met as an RA in the dorms, and those are the friends he "goofs off with," playing video games or pool, or watching a movie together.

There are also downsides to maintaining compartmentalized networks. Each group takes work to maintain. And students find they must do so separately when the groups are different from one another. A Dartmouth student, Danica, described some of these challenges:

> I have a lot of friends and they're all in very different social circles. Lizzie's on the women's soccer team, Yolanda usually hangs out with the African American community. Chris [is in a different group] . . . They are all in very different social circles. . . . So it's really hard. I was talking to Lizzie about this last night, where it's just, like, we all crave to have this one

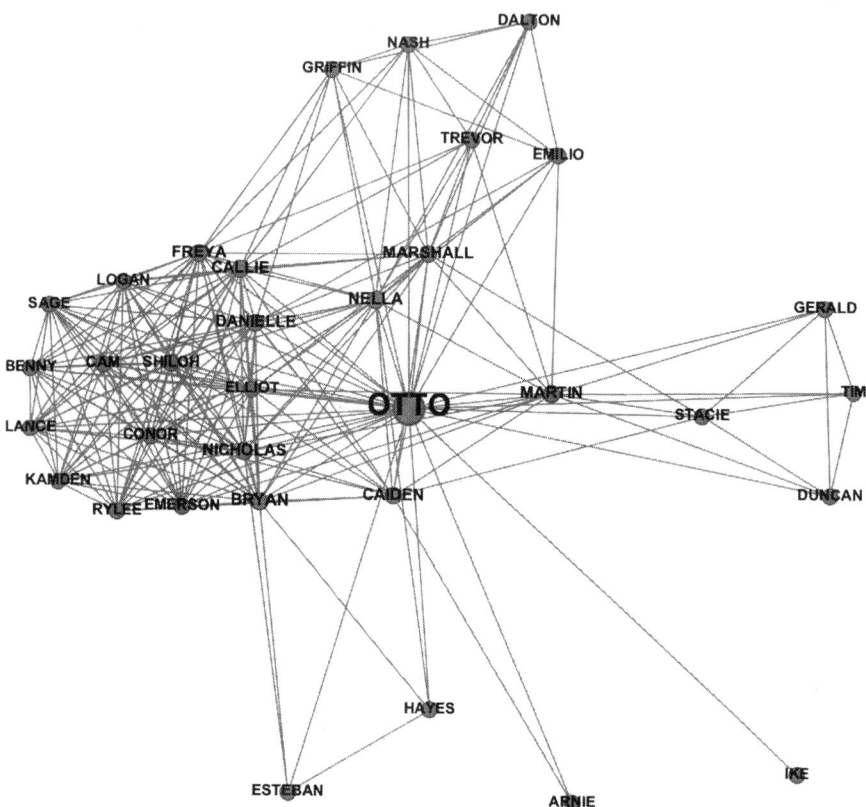

FIGURE 2.2. Otto's friendship networks, UNH year three.

group of friends that are always together. That can do things. That ask each other to go out. To go get dinner. To come and study. And she too has this problem where all of her friends are part of different groups. And it's really hard to find a way to string them all together.

Danica expressed the wish that she had a tight-knit network rather than a compartmentalized one; however, that also comes with challenges.

Students in compartmentalized or sampler networks often felt they did not have enough time to maintain all of their connections. As shown in figure 2.2, Otto described thirty-three friends and a compartmentalized network. When I asked him about his biggest social obstacle at UNH, he replied: "Even though it's not a bad thing, having too many friends, because everyone wants to hang out and you can't hang out with everybody because it's just impossible. So you have to pick and choose who to hang out with." If all of his friends knew each other, or even if he just had two groups to balance, it would likely not feel "impossible" for him to hang out with all of his friends. However, his multiple groups made this an impossible task, at least along with his classes, clubs, and on-campus job.

May, a UNH student who was a sampler, expressed similar sentiments. May explained that "the hardest part about it is, I have a bunch of different friend groups, and sometimes I wish they were a little bit more integrated... I definitely find that splitting my time between all my friend groups is really difficult." As with Otto, this likely would not be as big a challenge for May if she had a tight-knit group or fewer groups to balance.

Two primary challenges come up in tight-knit groups.[28] One is a social challenge. When the group starts to fracture, students may lose their whole network. Even without fractures, there is still an implicit pressure to remain in the group. In chapter 1, Melanie mentioned friends feeling "trapped" in their tight-knit groups. Similarly, Dawn told me, "It's so much easier to make friends at the beginning" of college, so that, once you have a group, you can feel "just stuck with that group."

The second is an academic challenge. Friends can create barriers to success by focusing on social life instead of academics. A range of scholarly work documents how social life can dominate students' time and energy at college. Friends may directly encourage each other to put off studying to go out or hang out; however, students more often described a more indirect, "subtle yet pervasive" peer pressure or a "nuanced... study-versus-socialize dilemma."[29] Although friends can implicitly encourage or explicitly pressure students to hang out or go out rather than study, students also had a range of coping techniques to achieve balance between their academic and social goals.

Pressure, however, was particularly strong in tight-knit networks, when the members of a student's friendship group were all focused on social life over academics. Pressure had less intensity in the less dense "compartmentalizer" or "sampler" networks, where students had other friends who might be more academically oriented. To achieve both academic and social goals, students "cultivated relationships with those who tolerated or encouraged academic involvement and used strategies of separation to protect their academic lives from friends who were academic distractions."[30] In other words, the potential of friends to distract students is real; however, students' responses to this indirect or direct pressure matters for their success.

While the majority of students' network types remained throughout college, there were also some that changed, as shown in Table 2.1. The largest group in my sample were compartmentalizers at both points in college: when I interviewed them near the end of their second year and at graduation. However, one-fifth of students who had compartmentalized networks

TABLE 2.1. Change during College for Dartmouth College Respondents, N=27 at graduation

|  | Sampler at Graduation | Compartmentaliz- er at Graduation | Tight-knitter at Graduation |
| --- | --- | --- | --- |
| Samplers | 2 | 0 | 1 |
| Compartmentalizers | 1 | 11 | 3 |
| Tight-knitters | 1 | 5 | 3 |

when I first interviewed them became tight-knitters by graduation. The next section discusses how the process of the "friendship funnel" led to this change. Also important is that two-thirds of samplers remained samplers and about one-third of tight-knitters remained tight-knitters.[31] This suggests there may be some personality or prior socialization at play that shapes the type of networks students have in college. Institutional factors, however, also come into play, as I proposed in *Connecting in College*. By examining these three additional campuses, I dig deeper into how institutional factors shape students' network types.

## Friendship Funnel

I heard about Troy before I met him. One of my earlier interviewees had suggested I talk with Troy because he was someone who had a lot of friends. Early in the interview, Troy noted that he had heard that perception about himself, but he did not agree. He saw himself as welcoming to new Dartmouth students, particularly other Black or first-generation college students. Yet, he believed he was selective, and becoming more selective over time, in who he considered to be a friend. The change in Troy's friendship network throughout college was an example of what I came to refer to as "friendship funneling."

Troy himself noticed that his friendships had funneled over time, although he did not use this term. When Troy described what he saw in his friendships over time, he called it "the natural progression . . . where you get involved in a bunch of things, you're a freshman and maybe sophomore. Then you start to narrow down on what really matters to you." This narrowing is the funneling of friendships, as they become more selective and more focused. Troy expands on this:

> The first two years of college you come in, and it's a lot of reaching out, and trying new things externally. . . . The latter two years, you start reflecting a

bit more, and then you start doing some internal work. [You're] focusing on your own growth, and examining your own growth, what you want, what you want to get out of this experience, and where you want to be, and all of that. At the same time, you start thinking about how you relate to your friends. As opposed to the first two years, a lot of everything on the outside affecting you.

Troy divided college into the first two years of "reaching out," and the last two years as focused on the "internal work," which narrows friendships to the meaningful ones.

Troy noted that he, like many Dartmouth students, aimed to make a lot of friends when he arrived on campus. As he got to know these friends better, he noted that he got past the "honeymoon phase" of his friendships and started realizing some of his friends' flaws. This ultimately helped Troy look inward, consider some of his own weaknesses, and make self-improvements. Troy exemplified this idea by discussing how he learned to see things from more people's perspectives, not only his own. As Troy continued and deepened his self-reflection and self-discovery, he felt he was left with a narrower pool but the most meaningful relationships.

As shown in figure 2.3, when I first interviewed him, Troy listed nineteen friends and had a tight-knit network. In the second interview, shown in the righthand panel, he became a compartmentalizer. Troy narrowed the previously tight-knit group, keeping six of those friends on the cluster on the righthand side, and adding two other clusters. The friends who appear in both networks are marked by an asterisk on the righthand panel. His friends from home, whom he grew closer to during college, are the two smaller groups separate from his core group at Dartmouth, which makes him a compartmentalizer.[32]

Like others who engage in friendship funneling, Troy started with more friends and funneled down to those that were most meaningful. Dustin had a similar path of friendship funneling, also moving from a tight-knitter to a compartmentalizer network.

However, this was not the only way that students engaged in friendship funneling. As shown in figure 2.4, Kira's network changed less in size, shrinking from eleven to nine friends, but changed from the compartmentalizer network shown on the lefthand side to the tight-knitter network shown on the righthand side. The friends who remained steady over time are marked by an asterisk. Kira kept some friends and replaced others, and her friends came to know each other over time.

A third pattern in friendship funneling is among students who all stayed compartmentalizers. Jenna, Libby, and Nicole all fit this pattern. Their

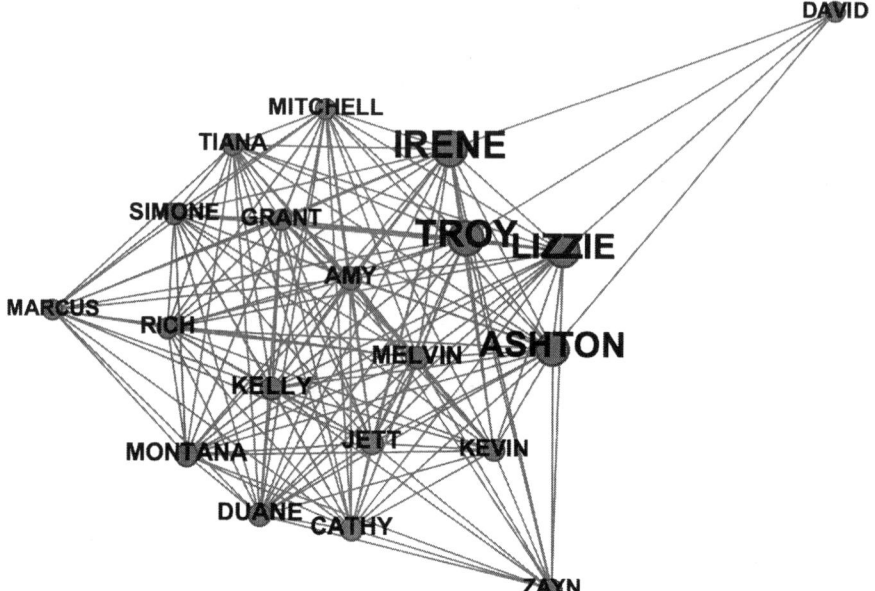

FIGURE 2.3. Troy's friendship networks, Dartmouth year two (above) and at graduation (on the next page). Note: asterisks indicate they remained friends.

networks, however, also shrank in size: Jenna's went from twelve to six friends, Libby's from twenty-five to seventeen, and Nicole's from twelve to eight. In other words, their networks maintained the compartmentalized structure, but shrank to one-half or two-thirds their original size.

Nicole described this process of network funneling: "I was friends with, like, absolutely everyone [at the start of college]. And then, over the course of four years . . . I [came to] value the depth of friendship more. So I think that that's changed over the years, because before I was just trying to have as many friends as possible." Throughout her time at Dartmouth, Nicole reevaluated what mattered to her in friendships. This led to changes in Nicole's close circle of friends, and in the quality of their relationships. Nicole went from being friends with "absolutely everyone" to a smaller, more meaningful group.

Rather than changing her "friendliness" toward others, Nicole changed her "investment" in others. It took a few years for Nicole to realize that she valued the "depth" of friendships more than the mere number of people she could call "friends." Nicole also mentioned that the six months away from campus that the D-Plan structured into her time[33] made her real friends more apparent. By senior year, Nicole was very comfortable with her six or

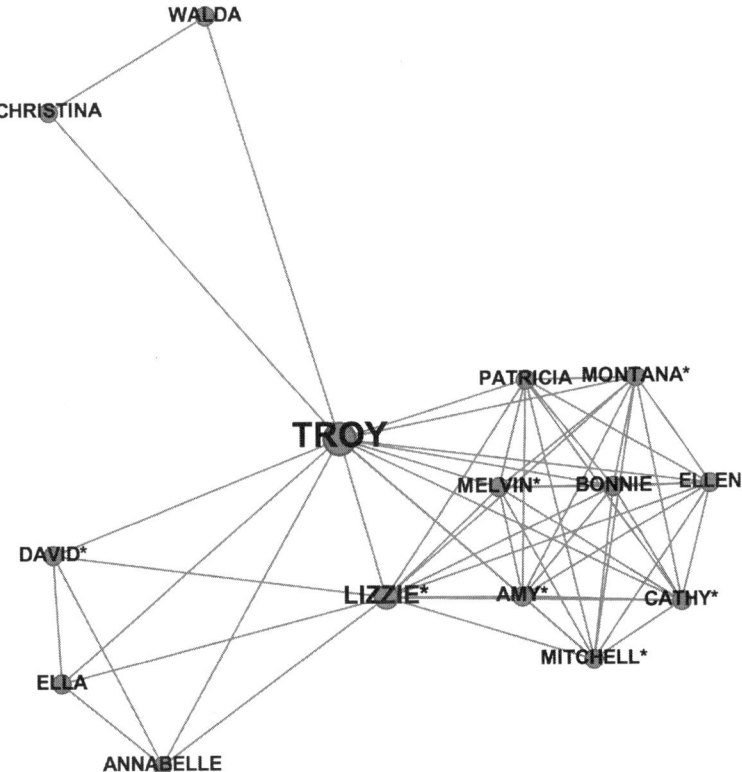

FIGURE 2.3. (continued)

seven close friends, who were different people than the friends she listed in the first interview. Nicole had four or five "second tier" friends whom she loved being around at Dartmouth, but whom she did not expect to stay close with after college. With graduation around the corner, she observed herself being generally more "careful" about friendships. Nicole explained: "I feel like I've built a small wall, or . . . more like, withdrawn from automatically thinking someone is a friend just because I realized people come and go."

All students face a trade-off between deepening existing friendships and branching out. Time is limited, and students who engage in friendship funneling seem to notice this more acutely. Dawn remarked: "I got less outgoing since orientation in terms of meeting new people. But within my friend group I've gotten a lot more open." While funneling can close students down to meeting as many new people, it can open them up within existing relationships.

Savannah's description of her friendships over time sums up the friendship funnel well. Savannah named ten friends during our first interview and

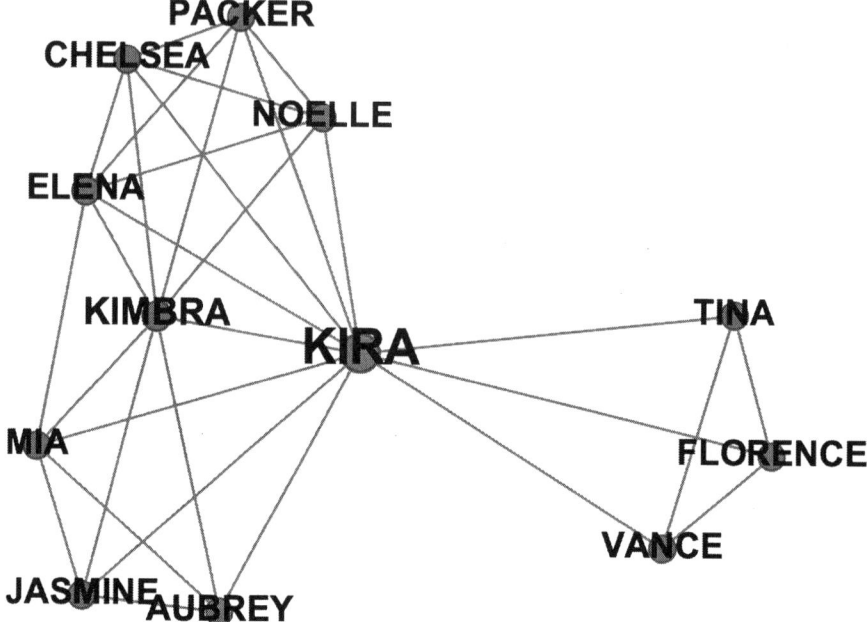

FIGURE 2.4. Kira's friendship networks, Dartmouth year two (above) and at graduation (on the next page). Note: asterisks indicate they remained friends.

five during our second. She explained this to me: "Freshman year I was, like, 'Yeah. Everyone's my friend.' And now I'm just kinda like, 'You know, I'm good with one or two people that I constantly see.' [Laughs]" She described this change as one that "definitely strengthened the ones that I like, the people who I enjoy hanging out with, people I don't find very taxing to be around." Savannah felt like the funneling served her well, removed those friends who extracted energy, and left her with meaningful friendships that enriched her life and supported her.

## Friendship Expansion

Many of the students who fit into the pattern of friendship expansion added a cluster or two of friends, as they expanded from a core of their tight-knit group to exhibit the compartmentalizer network structure. Layla is one example.

Layla's network is shown in figure 2.5. When I first interviewed her, she had a tight-knitter structure, with two friends who were less well integrated into her tight-knit group. At graduation, she had expanded from eleven to

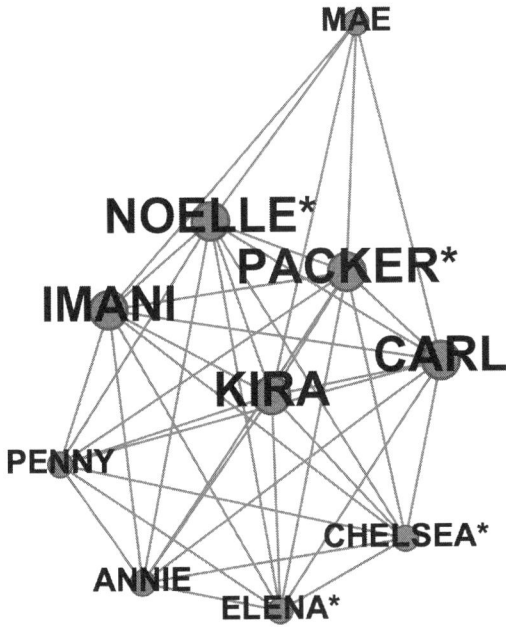

FIGURE 2.4. (continued)

fourteen friends, and notably had two clusters, the larger of which included two of the core members of her tight-knitter group from the first interview. The smaller group were three friends she made during a term studying abroad.

While some students expanded by adding a few new friends and keeping many over time, others expanded size by losing friends but gaining more than they lost. Layla was one example. As discussed in more detail in the next chapter on losing friends, Layla had friendship breakups with several friends, so she had a good deal of change in who was in her friendship network over time. She went from a compartmentalizer to a sampler. In her own words, Layla asserted, "I break up with people." At first, I expected this pattern to mean that Layla would show evidence of friendship funneling; however, she was constantly expanding her network. She described herself as someone who "came to college to get to know all different kinds of walks of life. And it was really easy for me to make friends. I feel like it's always been easy for me to make friends." She has shifted the groups that she affiliates with on campus throughout her college years, which has expanded her network over time. In our first interview, Layla was involved in the "Christian community on campus," as she describes it, specifically, the Christian Union student organization, as well as the first-generation student

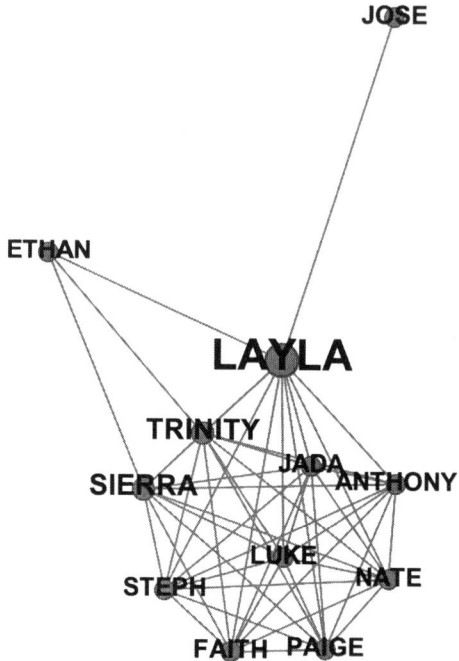

FIGURE 2.5. Layla's friendship networks, Dartmouth year two (above) and at graduation (on the next page). Note: asterisks indicate they remained friends.

community and several Latinx organizations. In the second interview, Layla remained involved with the Christian community, but not with the other identity-based groups. In the year before graduation, she described making friends through her sorority, study abroad program, and classes, particularly a public policy leadership program.

In the sampler network, on the next page in figure 2.5, Layla's three friends at the top were those she met during study abroad, who "all live in different parts of the world." Layla described them this way: "I really, genuinely, from the bottom of my heart believe these are individuals that I'll always stay in contact with." She noted, "All of us have already visited each other, in each other's respective homes, already." Teagan was a friend from her public policy leadership program, and Charlotte from her economics class. The students who were more connected in the cluster on the bottom right in figure 2.5 are mostly involved in the Christian Union. The two friends in Layla's network at both interviews—Ethan and Trinity—were also connected through the Christian Union.

Some students' networks changed in the opposite direction. This was the case for Renata, who went from a sampler to a compartmentalizer. As

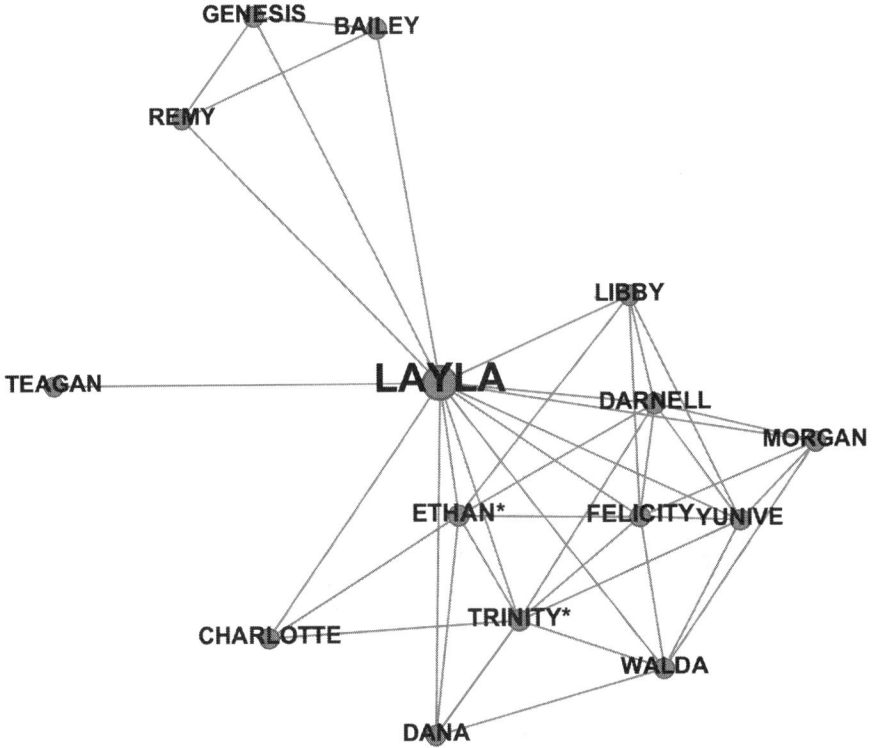

FIGURE 2.5. (continued)

described in chapter 1, Renata made friends through a range of campus programs and clubs, and intentionally connected them to each other by making sure they knew each other. In the second interview, she told me, "I still have the friend group that I started with, but that's kind of my side group" now. She also "formed a friend group with a lot of the people" she looked up to. She remembered thinking, "I wish I could talk to them, but they wouldn't like me." Renata got to know them, they did like her, and she still thinks they are "really cool." She expanded her network by adding a new cluster and becoming a compartmentalizer.

Other students expanded their networks without changing their network type. For example, Austin expanded the clusters slightly in his compartmentalizer network. This occurred after he and his girlfriend, Amanda, broke up. Amanda played a large role in his social and academic life, so he found himself with less support after their breakup. Austin reflected, "It actually forced me to reach out to other friends." Austin branched out, spending time doing homework with different people, "whoever I'd run into at the library." This also led to Austin developing deeper relationships with some of the friends he already had, because he was spending more time with them.

Similarly, Jennifer stayed a tight-knitter in both interviews, but expanded her network from nine friends to thirteen. During our second interview, Jennifer told me that her last year at Dartmouth turned out differently—and much better—than she had expected in terms of her social life. Jennifer's closest friends at Dartmouth had always been a year ahead of her, which meant that they graduated a year earlier, so she was "really worried about this year" because "all my friends are gone." She described how her friend group expanded to "a really big friend group, surprisingly, of people who I was not super close to before but became close to." As she told me about this, Jennifer got a big smile on her face. Propinquity brought them together through a political organization on campus. Rather than being a passive recipient of propinquity; however, Jennifer made a GroupMe group chat to reach out to them, hoping to "provide a space for people." Jennifer aspired to create a fun and comfortable space for students, much like what she felt older students had provided her. Jennifer described how this larger group would "hang out a lot" and "play pong," while the smaller circle of close friends would go out to eat and just talk. This smaller circle had "deeper conversations," and Jennifer felt that "I know more about their personal life outside of Dartmouth." As Jennifer's experience shows, expanding one's network does not mean sacrificing meaningful relationships for quantity.

## Takeaways

For students:

1. Take stock of your friendships, and make sure to invest in those you wish to keep. Where do you get emotional support, academic support, and enjoyment? Consciously put effort into maintaining those friendship ties.
2. For a friendship you want to keep, prioritize (1) staying in touch, whether in person or via technology—or both; (2) spending time in shared activities, whether it is watching TV, sharing meals, going together to a club meeting or class, playing tennis, running errands together, or studying alongside each other; and (3) talking with your friends to get to know them and help them get to know you. Share a couple of details at a time, including information about your background, struggles, and goals.

3. There are also three great ways to deepen a friendship: (1) having conversations about personal, not just surface-level, topics; (2) talking through disagreements; and (3) being there for each other, even when it is not convenient. Do not be afraid of showing that you are different from a friend or hold differing views; talking across difference can lead to deeper connections.
4. All three of the previous suggestions involve spending time with your friends and on your friendships. Rather than hanging out with whoever is around when you do not have other things to do or when they invite you to do something, schedule time with friends, just as you would schedule class or study time. Be intentional in spending time connecting with friends and with whom you invest that time.
5. We see ourselves reflected in our friends. Which of your friends do you feel like you can be yourself around? Which friends bring out a better version of you? These are the friendships to consciously put effort into.
6. Multiplex ties tend to be more meaningful and lasting ties than those only connected on one dimension. Reflect on which friends you are connected to in multiple ways, such as those who provide both social and academic support. If these seem lacking in your friendship network, you can craft them by trying new things with a friend, particularly one you have identified as meaningful through nos. 1 or 5 in this list.
7. Each network type—tight-knitters, compartmentalizers, and samplers—experiences challenges to keeping friends.

    a. If you are a tight-knitter, you have one dense group of friends, where nearly everyone knows each other. Socially, tight-knitters benefit from high levels of social support from friends, but find it difficult to exit the network. Along with spending time with the group, nurture a couple of friendships that are most meaningful. You can identify those ties using nos. 1, 5, and 6 above, and nurture those ties using the techniques in nos. 2, 3, and 4.
    b. If you are a compartmentalizer, you have two to four clusters of friends, who do not know each other. Compartmentalizers typically get social support from one cluster and academic support from another. The challenges of this network type come from the time and identity pressures in managing multiple friendship groups, which increases with more groups to manage. Focus on deepening ties with the group that is most meaningful for you, or a couple of friends who are most meaningful. Takeaways nos. 1, 5, and 6 above will help identify those times, and the techniques in nos. 2, 3, and 4 will help nurture those ties.

c. If you are a sampler, you have one-on-one friendships rather than groups of friends, with friends from different places remaining unconnected to each other. Samplers can find social support from one-on-one friendships, yet this network type can lead to loneliness and isolation. Maintaining meaningful ties is important, as with the other two types. Particularly important for samplers, however, is spending time in the activities mentioned in takeaways nos. 2 and 3 with multiple friends. Adding a community of support to the one-on-one support is an intervention against loneliness.

8. Friendship networks also change over time. Some students funnel, narrowing their friendships into the meaningful ones. Others fit into a pattern of friendship expansion, adding a cluster or two of friends. As you're expanding, make sure not to sacrifice meaningful friendships for more friendships.

For parents and other supporters:

1. Encourage your child to reflect on the amount of time they spend with friends and what they do together. Keeping friends takes time and effort.
2. Does your child spend time in shared activities with friends? Helping them think through what they enjoy and who they might do the activity with could be helpful. They can invite a friend along. If they do not have a friend who is interested, they can join a club and perhaps make a new friend who shares that interest (see chapter 1).
3. Having conversations about personal topics is a way to keep and deepen friends. Ask your child which friends they have that fit into this category. If they wish to expand or deepen, they can purposely share a few personal details at a time, including about their background, struggles, or goals.
4. Know that there are multiple types of friendship networks. Not everyone has one close-knit friendship group, some students have multiple groups, and others have mainly one-on-one friendships. Encourage your child to identify their network type and follow the advice above.
5. Know that friendships change over time. Some students funnel, narrowing their friendships into the meaningful ones, while others expand to broaden their networks.

For colleges:

1. Create and support programs, clubs, and organizations that provide students time together regularly, to interact and to deepen their connections with each other.
2. Working on projects together—in classes or clubs, for example—can help students keep friends and deepen these connections. Support professors and staff advisors to use such projects in their classes and programs, and to assign groups strategically rather than randomly or letting students choose.[34] There may also be times when it is useful to share directly with students that the time they spend on these projects is not just about accomplishing the project but also about building connections.
3. Know that when propinquity no longer keeps students connected (e.g., when they no longer live together or take the same class), they will need to put effort into staying connected. Providing common space where they can connect and resources for clubs can facilitate these connections remaining and deepening. Also, naming this phenomenon to students can help them see that it is the structure rather than the people that has resulted in the need for more work to maintain the friendship. When a friendship no longer feels easy, it is not always the friendship itself that is the problem.
4. If a student has difficulty keeping friends, share these three ways they can maintain a friendship: (1) staying in touch in whatever ways work; (2) spending time in shared activities; and (3) talking with friends to get to know them and help them get to know the student.
5. Because the students on your campus have a range of network types—tight-knitters, compartmentalizers, and samplers—offer activities and spaces that appeal to each type. For example, tight-knitters often want to attend activities, share meals, and hang out with a large group, whereas samplers more frequently attend activities and spend time by themselves or with one friend. Spaces and activities should accommodate and appeal not only to one type, but to all students.
6. If a student is comparing their friendship group to others they see or hear about, share with them that there are multiple types of friendship networks. Not everyone has one close-knit friendship group, some students have multiple groups, and others have mainly one-on-one friendships. Encourage students you work with to identify their network type and follow the advice above.

7. Help students reflect on whether they have meaningful friendships. If they want to deepen their friendships, they can reflect on how much time they are spending together and what they are doing together. Encourage them to be intentional about spending time with friends and whom they spend that time with rather than filling time with whoever is around. Share that three ways to deepen a friendship are to (1) have conversations about personal, not just surface-level topics; (2) talk through disagreements; and (3) be there for each other, even when it is not convenient. Perhaps it would be helpful to engage in shared activities that they enjoy, deepening their friendship along the way. Or perhaps they do not know each other that well, in which case they can purposely share a few personal details at a time, including about their background, struggles, or goals.

[ CHAPTER THREE ]

# Losing Friends: Breaking Up and Fading Away

When I first met Bill, he was beginning his third year at Dartmouth. He was a slim, quiet, and introspective Asian man, with dark thick stylish glasses and short-trimmed hair. Like most students I interviewed, Bill not only made many friends in college, he also lost many. Bill told me that he had "very different friendships" and "my friendships have changed a lot," yet the changes he described were not unusual among the students I interviewed.

Most students experienced much change in their friendship networks, yet they typically explained this change to me as unusual and unexpected. While students tended to expect the friendships they make in college to happen quickly and the friends to stay, it is not unusual for most friends—even close friends—to change. The average percentage of friends no longer in students' networks from the midpoint to the end of college was 61 percent. In other words, during that two-year span, students kept about less than half (about 40 percent) of their close friends. The paradox is that, although students perceived change in their friendship networks as unusual, it was not.

Bill made a lot of friends in college, and he also had a lot of friendships fade away. Bill's first friendships were from his orientation group, but these ties did not last. His first friends were other first-year students who attended the same multiple-day outdoor orientation program, called "Trips"; Dartmouth students refer to the small group of other first-year students in their same trip as "Tripees." Bill explained:

> In freshman fall, I was friends with my Tripees. After we came back from Trips, we'd . . . get dinner and hang out. Slowly, that kind of dissipated 'cause we're not that similar after all. We don't have much to talk about. And then as classes started, I met five other people from the dorm across from me. And they also happened to be Asian American, and also I was in

two classes with one of them. And that didn't really last because we also turned out to be very different from each other.

Each time he described friendships that did not last, Bill audibly sighed. He summed up these shifts by noting that his friendships have "changed a lot," conveying that this change feels unusual and unexpected. Data, however, show it is not unusual among college students.

Although Bill said he "was not really expecting" that he would make primarily same-race friends at Dartmouth, it was through meeting politically minded Asian students in an Asian activist club that he found more lasting friendships and his place on campus. Bill's network at the end of his second year of college is shown below in figure 3.1, and this group of campus friends is the tight-knit one on the bottom.[1] Bill talked about how they study in the same space because "it's nice to have other people

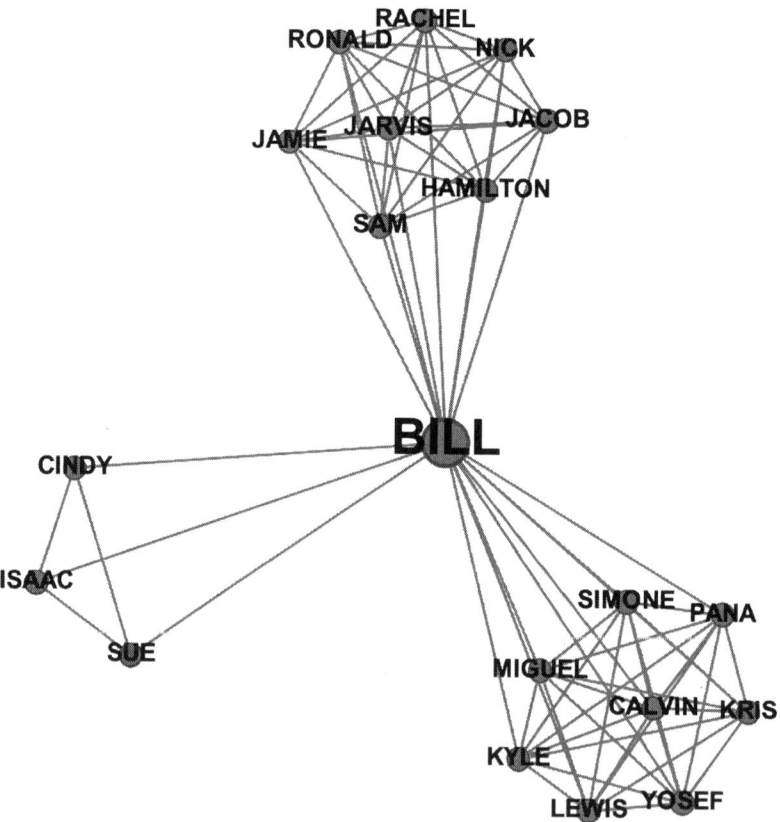

FIGURE 3.1. Bill's friendship networks, Dartmouth year two (above) and at graduation (on the next page). Note: asterisks indicate they remained friends.

working around you 'cause that kind of motivates you." They share with each other both the amazing experiences they have and the difficult ones. Bill remarked that "they're there for support," and it is "important" to him that the group "talk about our emotions." These friends sustained him for the middle part of college; however, they graduated before him, so then he was left alone on campus again. Bill's friendships faded because of changes in propinquity.

The changes in Bill's friendships also reflected changes in his salient identities on campus. In his follow-up interview, which took place about a week before he graduated, Bill described his closest friends as based on class solidarity rather than shared racial background. His racially diverse friendship group, shown below in figure 3.1, bonded on the basis of their working-class backgrounds and experience working at a café on campus.[2] Three friends remained in his network during that two-year period, and all three were ones he had met through the Asian activist club. They were part of one cluster in the sociogram on the previous page. Bill also listed seven new friends. With different friends in this group, Bill observed that they altered how they bond; for example, some friends help him when he feels "stressed about a paper," some "talk about our emotions to each other," and some "bond through making food." Even after losing friends at multiple points in his Dartmouth experience, Bill finds support and belonging on campus through his friendships.

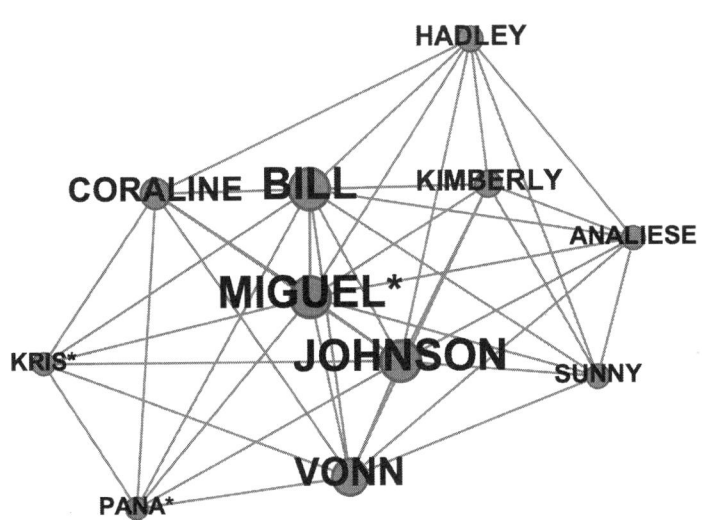

FIGURE 3.1. (continued)

Given the epidemic of loneliness declared by the US surgeon general,[3] losing friends might be expected to be a problem. As Bill's story illustrates, however, sometimes we make friends according to who is around, and they are not a great fit for us, so it is not surprising that those bonds fade. In fact, it can be better for us—our identity and our well-being—to lose those friends so that we have space and time for those who are more supportive and more reflective of who we are.

In the previous chapter, I wrote about how students keep friends. The other side of that issue concerns the friends they lose along the way, and that is the focus of this chapter. More friends are lost than are kept across the two interviews I did, and other research finds similarly high rates of turnover in friends. This means that the friendships students form early in college are not likely to stay until the end of college, and this is a normal process.[4] As May, a UNH student, put it, "the first person you meet isn't going to be your best friend all the way through senior year."

While we typically think of "breakups" in terms of romantic relationships, they are more common in our friendships—because we have more friends than we do romantic partners. During my interviews, students often mentioned someone they were no longer friends with. When I asked what happened, sometimes there were detailed stories, but more often it was simply that they stopped keeping in touch. Although these friendship breakups happen more frequently than we might think, even more widespread than dramatic falling-outs are those friendships that just fade away.

## Friendship Breakups

Some friendships end with these dramatic falling-outs or breakups. These breakups elicited a lot of emotions, including anger, sadness, disappointment, shame, and embarrassment. And they often erupted from a mismatch of expectations or needs in the relationship. Students told me, for example, about friends who stopped talking with them or turned their friend group against them, expressing embarrassment that this happened. Danica told me, "I've seen friendships crumble because of GroupMe," which is a messaging site used frequently at Dartmouth.

Friendship breakups can happen when students' expectations are not aligned. Dartmouth student Paige's former "number one best friend, we were like sisters," offers one example. Paige explained how their friendship had "recently fallen apart," mostly because of differences in how they prefer to stay in touch while apart. Paige's friend "sees the fact that we don't text every day or talk on the phone everyday as proof that I don't care about her anymore [and] I don't want to be her friend. And that's just not true. That's not how I see it." Paige concludes, "I still love her, but we've had too many fights over the fact that I'm not addicted to my phone with her. It's too much for me." She notes that "we're not friends anymore" because "what she's asking of me and what I'm interested in getting is just not going to work right now." The mismatch in their expectations and needs was too much, and their friendship dissolved.

Even when students seem certain that breaking up is the right thing, friendship breakups can still be difficult. This is true even for the person who initiates them, including Paige. For instance, in the example above, Paige was clear that "I still love her" but that the friendship was "too much for me." During this conversation, Paige paused, looked up at the ceiling, and said, "I hope it won't stay this way. I hope we can be friends again in the future." There is real pain in breaking up with a friend.

Breaking up with friends can also be a form of identity work, relating oneself as a moral, dramatic, or kind person through one's actions. For example, having friendship breakups was part of Dartmouth student Layla's identity. Both times that I interviewed her, Layla discussed many recent changes in her friendships, explaining that she preferred to terminate friendships and address the fact that they were ending, rather than letting them naturally fade. In her words: "I'm a very dramatic person. I like dramatic exits, so I break up with people." It was not that Layla was careless or cruel in how she broke up; in fact, I was struck by her willingness to engage in rather than avoid difficult conversations. Layla described how this unfolded in the three most recent friend breakups she had had. Once she recognized that the friendship was "not working," she "called or messaged them to tell them that 'our friendship is a little done. I just want to thank you for everything, and I wish you the best where you go next year [meaning after graduation].'" She also told each friend that although their relationship is not "gonna go any further from here, if my career can help you in any way, or your career can help me in any way, I hope we can have a professional relationship." She called this "the Dartmouth networking," so it was not that she wanted to cut off all ties with a friend, but that she wanted to make sure it was clear that the friendship was over, which is what she meant by a "dramatic exit." To Layla, breaking up with friends was a way she showed care about the quality of her friendships; having fewer friends gave her more time to "nurture" existing relationships.

Although Layla saw this method of breaking up as positive and leaving open the possibility that they might have a different sort of relationship in the future—not a friendship, but a "professional relationship"—it is not clear that her former friends saw it the same way. When I asked about her friends' reactions to the three friend breakups she initiated, she said that "no one responds" to her messages. However, she saw her ex-friend's reaction when she bumped into them on campus: "I saw one of my friends after I sent the email, and they looked very ashamed. And I thought it was interesting, because in this scenario, I addressed something that was unspoken these four years: one thing that happened our first year that we never spoke about. I wrote it out in our communication, and I feel like this person felt a little ashamed that maybe the conversation never happened, or maybe ashamed that they were called out." Shame was a common emotion that came up in friendships ending. Shame can hang over the person who was seen as failing in some way. At times, both parties can feel ashamed, although here Layla did not express shame.

Whereas the term "friend" can seem unclear at times, breakups remove that fuzziness. Layla said that she prefers the "dramatic exit" so that the relationship was clarified rather than left vague. In her words, "I like to close things. I don't like the fading away of things, because I'm a very kind person, so it makes me think, like, oh, it's gonna start again, and we're gonna be friends again. I like to be more serious with myself." While Layla phrased this as "more serious," I took it to mean that she wanted clarity. Feeling clear that the friendship was over felt better to Layla than the possibility that the friendship could be rekindled. Friendships typically have fuzzier boundaries than romantic relationships, where labels are more often—but certainly not always—applied to characterize something as a relationship or not. In contrast, labeling someone as "friend" does not clarify the level of closeness of the relationship. Yet, telling a friend that your friendship is "done" counters the fuzziness of the "friend" label.

As these examples illustrate, friendship breakups are typically intentional and the rupture clear to both parties. Another Dartmouth student, Danica, similarly noted, "I don't burn bridges, I obliterate them." She described a group of friends she was close to earlier in college, but recently fell out with. Danica told me: "To put it in my terms, I was salty. I was very, very salty." Danica characterized it as "I wrote them off," putting blame on herself for the break in their friendship. "That's part of the reason why that strain has continued for this long and why the gap between us has increased. It's definitely me perpetuating it, but for good reasons."

Students' friendship network also influenced how they experienced friendship breakups. Dartmouth student Ella, for example, described how she found herself spending a lot of time "complaining to my outside friends" about a friendship group that was "not good," and "not worth the energy." Ella explained that "it got to a point where I was like, I'm done." Having these "outside friends" was important. Ella told one, "You saved my life because you kind of filled in the little cracks and what I lost from a different social sphere." Being a compartmentalizer rather than a tight-knitter enabled this change: it made losing this group easier. Had Ella been a tight-knitter, she would risk losing all her friends, even by initiating a breakup with just one of them. Friends in tight-knit networks often "take sides." As a compartmentalizer, Ella received help during and after the friendship breakup from friends in a different part of her network.

## Friendship Fade-Aways

In contrast to friendship breakups, the fading away of friendships often happens unintentionally, and it is not always noticed by both parties. Friendships may fade away intentionally because one person in the relationship did not want it to continue, but they did not want to have the conversation that is necessary to pause or end a relationship. Particularly when it is a slow fade-away, one or even both people involved may not notice—at least for a while—that the friendship has faded. Unintentional drifting apart is often due to other changes in their lives, including in their class or work schedules, living locations, identities, or romantic relationships.

Austin, a White man and first-generation student at Dartmouth, was my first participant to draw a contrast between friends breaking up and fading away. In future interviews, when students told me that a friendship ended, I used Austin's language to ask them about this distinction. Austin told me that when his friendships ended, it was "never" a falling-out. Instead, he found that each time, "it just faded. It always would just kind of fade away. Which that's not fun to think about. [laughs] Like, oh, where'd they go? I haven't talked to that person in like three years." These friendships indeed faded from Austin's memory, not intentionally forgotten and the distance not consciously recognized for quite some time.

The most common way that students described their friendships ending was fading away because of lack of effort into keeping it going. Students described this as "we just kind of slowly stopped talking" (Nancy, a UNH student) and "they stopped reaching out" (Lindsay, also a UNH student). If the friends are not coming into contact on a regular basis, the friendship may fade without work by both people. Lindsay described how this happens: "I don't really go out of my way to see them, and they don't really try to hang out or anything," so their friendship has fizzled. Layla described the fading-away process as one where the relationship "could have meant a lot at that time, and then you just grew apart. And that's fine. You found new circles. You don't wish bad upon them. You're just, like, it would be nice if we were still friends, but we have a new life now." For Layla, Lindsay, Nancy, and many other students, their relationship did not intentionally end, but the friends "grew apart," each landing in a different place.

The fade-away might be felt more strongly or sooner for one friend. It may be that one person notices the fade or intentionally chooses to not put in the effort to keep the friendship going, while the other does not. In our second interview, Dartmouth student Savannah gave one example of a friend she had recently reconnected with. She told me how that friend texted her out of the blue, inviting her to dinner. At dinner, the friend told her, "I'm sorry I kinda ghosted you," and Savannah told her, "It's okay," while she was thinking, "I didn't notice" but "I didn't say that."

So as not to romanticize friendships fading away, I want to acknowledge that sometimes this experience can be painful. If the fade is only on one side, it can feel like ghosting to the other person. Jennifer, a Dartmouth student, explained how she was "really hurt" by a friendship that faded:

> I was really hurt that he stopped hanging out with me. I was like, "What did I do to him?" And then I ended up texting him in the spring. I was like, he's going to graduate, and it doesn't really matter if I offend him by asking him, "Did I do something to you?" And he was like, "I don't know what you're talking about." But I think he realized that he had shut me out and stopped talking to me, because a week later he came up to me and started trying to have a conversation with me. Then he asked me to hang out before he graduated because he knew I wouldn't see him for a while.

Jennifer expressed relief and delight that her friend wanted to hang out and saw their relationship as worthwhile. After graduation, he continued to reach out, and Jennifer excitedly told me that "when he came [back] to visit, he asked me to hang out."

Jennifer's experiences show the pain that can accompany a friendship fading away, and they also show that this rupture is not always permanent. When friendships fade, particularly because of changes in people's lives, it leaves open the possibility that the friendship can form again, particularly when lives change again to bring people together.

For friendships to be maintained, we must nurture these ties. Occasionally, we find friendships that continue even when they are ignored; however, more often friendships continue through time spent together in activities and conversation. When we are no longer spending that time connecting, the friendship might slip or fade away.

## Reasons for Losing Friends: Propinquity

On all three campuses, the main reason that friendships faded away was when propinquity no longer kept students in regular contact with each other. For example, students remain friends with their floormates until they move the next year, or they remain friends with classmates until the next term when they no longer share a class, or they remain friends with others on their athletic team or student club until one of them stops attending or quits.

When propinquity no longer brings friends together, they must be intentional about maintaining the friendship. A frequent explanation I heard for friendships fading away was that "distance and time has been the main deciding factor in hanging out with a lot of friends that I used to be closer with," as Austin put it. While students attributed this to distance, from a sociological perspective, it is not just about distance. Instead, it is that people now must be intentional about reaching out, whereas before their friendship was propelled by propinquity. Chris's explanation gets at the mechanism that matters for distance, which they refer to as "lack of proximity." Chris, a UNH student, explained: "It's a lot harder to maintain relationships when you don't see these people every day anymore." As the previous section on friendship breakups makes clear, it takes an intentional act to lose a friendship while people are regularly in touch with each other.

Some students lost many friendships that had been held together only by propinquity. Will is one example. At our first interview, when Will was a second-year student at UNH, he named fifteen friends, which dwindled to five at our second interview. Changes in where Will lived, his major, and his club involvement led to him losing a lot of friends as these shifts happened. He described how his first group of friends came together "because we lived on the same floor, and once we didn't live on the same floor, we don't have anything in common anymore, so we kinda lost touch." He lost other friends when he changed majors, which made it hard to keep in touch with friends once they no longer saw each other in chemistry classes, and he lost even more friends when a club he was involved in ended due to poor leadership, which made it hard to keep in touch without seeing each other weekly at meetings. Propinquity made these friendships feel effortless, but, without their paths crossing regularly, they were no longer compelled to reach out to each other, and their connection fizzled.

Students noted how these disruptions made them less open to future friendships, because they do not want to be hurt again. After losing friends at Dartmouth because of changes in propinquity, Nicole remarked: "I've built a small wall or withdrawn from automatically thinking someone is a friend just because I realized that people come and go. It hurts if you make such a strong friendship with people and then, they are off for a term, and then they come back and you are not really friends anymore. I had a really close friend while I was studying abroad. We came back, and we don't talk ever, which is weird. I felt hurt by that. And I think she did too." The "wall" that Nicole put up to protect her from feeling "hurt" also limited her investment into new friendships. She explained, "I'm just as friendly as I've always been, but it'll take me a minute before I'm texting you or really trying to get meals with you once a week." Friendships brought together by propinquity were easily disrupted when changes in propinquity occurred and both parties were not willing and able to invest.

Leaving a team or a club can disrupt students' networks by causing friendships to fade away. Propinquity is also the mechanism here. Nearly all varsity athletes described a friendship that faded away with a teammate who was injured or quit the team, thus they did not see them on a regular basis, and no one made an effort to stay in touch. As discussed in chapter 1, athletes spend an immense amount of time with their teammates, thus propinquity is a strong glue for friendships while it operates. Quitting student clubs or organizations or not regularly attending their meetings or events can also result in friendships fading. When Ella, a Dartmouth student, left crew (rowing) team because of some challenging dynamics with the coach, she noticed that her friendships with her former teammates became less close. Ella did not intentionally dissociate from her crew friends, but she saw them a lot less once she was on her own schedule, due to the lack of propinquity. Similarly, Bill talked about losing a friend after that friend realized their shared club "was not the space for him," explaining that they "just ended up hanging out less and less" once the friend "distanced himself from" the club.

The role of propinquity was highlighted for some students with the changes that the COVID-19 pandemic brought to their lives as well as changes after graduation. Although technology and social media certainly make it easier to stay in touch with friends across distance than in past generations, students still have to make the effort when propinquity is not in play.

Students struggled to maintain their ties during the early months of the COVID-19 pandemic when propinquity did not bring them together in classes or activities. Echoing these struggles, other research finds that college students' friendship networks got smaller during the COVID-19 pandemic.[5] Friendship drama also seemed heightened among friends who lived together during the pandemic, as they spent nearly all of their time together. Will, for example, referred to this as "weird COVID drama" among the friends in his apartment in spring 2020. He told me how one friend "wanted to move out, get out of her lease, then stuck us with a random person without telling us, in the middle of a pandemic. We called her out on that, and she dropped off the face of the earth, and we haven't heard from her since." With the friends who remained, Will lamented, "Living together was a mess. That was tough. A lot of politics got in the way." He described his friendship network shrinking because the friends had different ideas of what constituted safe socializing. During that period, Will said his roommates "spent time together just 'cause we were forced to 'cause we were living together and that was fun. . . . I saw my best friend maybe a small handful of times here and there. And the other friends I didn't see because they did not quarantine." While propinquity created closer friendships for Will with his roommates, not regularly crossing paths made it harder to maintain ties with his other friends, including his best friend.

Ties that propinquity kept together during college were also strained after graduation, sometimes fading away. For Natalie, a UNH student, the benefits of propinquity during college stood out to her only after she no longer had that regular contact that made keeping up with friends so easy. She described how, right before we started the interview, she had a conversation about this with her mother: "I was chatting with my mom, and I said, it's funny because when you're living so close to these people in school and you're around them all the time and you're always talking with them, it's hard to think that maybe you lose touch one day. After graduation, everyone kind of moves back home or they move to their own job opportunities. They go off and do their own thing." Natalie's comment highlights that it is not just the distance between them that matters ("living so close"), but the fact that they are no longer encountering each other on a regular basis because "they go off and do their own thing." Without propinquity, they must be intentional about reaching out. Often the result is that the friendship fades away because neither party is intentional about keeping it going.

At the end of each interview, I asked respondents how many of their current friends they expected to have in five or ten years, and I was surprised that many participants anticipated that the lack of propinquity after college would disrupt their friendships. For example, Shirley, an MCC student, answered, "I'm moving away next year and realistically I'm probably never going to talk to them," aside from her boyfriend. She matter-of-factly stated, "People fade away. . . . It's natural, I think." Moving will disrupt the power of propinquity to make connections seamless in the classrooms and office where Shirley currently sees those friends. However, other students' experiences also suggest that losing these friends may not always be forever.

If propinquity again brings them in each other's orbits, they may find their friendship renewed. College structures this through opportunities to connect in future terms in classes, clubs, or just the path that they take to or from activities on campus. It also can happen after college, for example, if people find themselves in the same city or industry. College, however, provides greater opportunities for propinquity.

The fading-away that happens with propinquity can influence people's sense of social support. Teddy, a UNH student, noted that he did not have a best friend and that his previous one was someone he was not currently friends with. It was not a falling-out; "we just haven't seen each other in such a long time. Do I feel like I could go to him if I had any problems? Not particularly. No." For Teddy, the lack of contact with his friend resulted in a lack of closeness. He no longer felt that friend was someone he could rely on. Without the regular contact that brought Teddy together with his best friend, they did not have opportunities to share and feel close, and their relationship faded. By our second interview, Teddy named someone as a best friend, with the caveat that "he probably considers one of them [another friend] his best friend. But I consider him one." The loss of a friend, particularly a best friend, can come with a long-lasting loss of social support.

## Reasons for Losing Friends: Identity Mismatch

College is a time of identity growth and change. Research on the life course identifies an "emerging adulthood" period that focuses on self-identity exploration.[6] As students' identities change, their friendships often change to reflect their changing identities. And sometimes students realize later in a friendship that they were mismatched from the start.

Because college is a time of identity growth, this itself puts strain on friendship duration. Some students recognize both the identity and friendship progression that happens. Lindsay, a UNH student, talked about how she saw people "change a lot throughout college, so it's hard to stay friends with people all four years." Libby, a Dartmouth student, told me about a "good friend" who "drifted apart after she joined a sorority," noting that "she changed a lot," becoming more focused on status and less on her art.

In describing how changes in her sense of self impacted her friendships, Sasha bluntly said, "You just outgrow some people." For Sasha, some of those times at Dartmouth she outgrew people were breakups and others were fade-aways: "the ones over [sorority] Rush ended definitively. The other ones faded, for sure." Many social psychologists who focus on identity discuss the role that other people play in our own identity construction.[7]

As coauthors, Amanda Koontz Anthony and I have previously discussed how people are often talking about themselves and doing what we refer to as "identity work" as they talk about their friendships. Using the term "friendship talk" as a subcategory of "identity talk," we describe the ways people manage their identities by talking about how they are similar to a friend now or aspirationally, and how they distance themselves from someone who is not like them. Referring to this as "betterment distancing," we identify how people engage in friendship talk to distance themselves from others—often former friends—whom they describe as possessing negative traits. In discussing this identity mismatch, they are constructing their own identity.[8]

Some students, like Savannah, engaged in betterment distancing, crafting her own identity as she talked about how she was different from her former friends. In an earlier chapter, I discussed how Savannah made friends in her second year at a study abroad program at Dartmouth. When she came back to campus in her third year, she returned with a changed outlook on life. The identity work she did while abroad not only brought her new friends, but also resulted in many friendships fading away. In Savannah's words, "I think a lot of my friendships have kind of died." Savannah felt she no longer had time for friends who were dramatic, negative, or overbearing. She faded away from these freshman-year friends. Similarly, Savannah quit a club [an identity-based one in her major] because it became a "high pressure, toxic environment" for some of her friendships. She also grew apart from her sorority because she felt that it also had too much drama and "weird friendship dynamics that are happening," and thus she felt it was not quite the right community for her.

The identity mismatch can become visible before, during, or after the friendship ends. Renata, for example, found refuge in her sorority at Dartmouth, but then after a term away, she came back and felt like her friends were being "really petty," so she distanced herself from that group of friends. Another Dartmouth student, Victoria, told me how fading away from several groups of friends helped her to recognize she was "a pretty relaxed person." She realized that she "felt overwhelmed having to spend time with them rather than wanting to spend time with them" because they were "very dramatic," so she began distancing herself from these groups of friends, embracing this more laid-back identity.

Students contrasted their own identity to those of friends in a variety of dimensions. Lafayette, an MCC student who later transferred to and graduated from a four-year university, discussed several of these dimensions as he was telling me about Blake, a friend he was close to in the first interview but did not list as a friend in our second interview. He explained: "Our lives simply just went in entirely different directions. I got a college degree, I work for a pharmaceutical company now, so very white-collar professional, living the American dream, whole thing. Blake still likes to party, still likes to smoke weed. Our lives just went in very different directions." When they became roommates—"very, very briefly roommates," according to Lafayette—these "diverging priorities" became too big. "We had a slight falling-out a few years ago, and we just have never spoken since." Lafayette used betterment distancing, explaining this friendship ending by drawing contrasts between the "very different directions" that their lives took.

Without the skills and desire to bond across difference, including understanding and respecting these differences rather than trying to change them, friendships often either break up or fade away. Earlier in this book, homophily came up as an important factor bringing friends together. Often, when students bond over a homophilic tie, this is a significant part of their identity, whether a dimension such as race or sexual preference, or an interest like a sport or hobby. This comes up in MCC student Dory's description of what she sees happening as her classmates try to make friends: "It's, like, you are working on becoming someone's friend, but you still call them friend because you are working to get out of the acquaintance stage. How I'd explain it [is] you're an acquaintance, but you're working to get out of the acquaintance fog so you can be that person's friend." Dory recounted how, as people get to know each other, they sometimes discover important differences in their beliefs. She noted that while some people can be friends despite these differences, other people have "really strong beliefs," such that when they notice that a potential friend "doesn't believe what they believe, they immediately start acting different or will completely stop talking to them." When there are "too many" important differences between them and "too much" judgment, Dory explained that one person feels, "'Oh, I can't talk to this person anymore.' Like, for instance, some people who believe in God and the people who don't believe in God. They could get along, and then once they find that out about each other, they start acting differently. Or one of them will try to convince the other one to believe in this and they just can't." Dory told me that when relationships unfold this way, the friendship ties lack "some sort of connection." In her words, "it ends up not working out."

When they detect these identity mismatches, students talk about "cutting" or ending these relationships. For example, MCC student Shirley told me about "weeding out" friends, particularly "short [term] friendships," with "people that make really bad life decisions or, not necessarily bad life decisions, but decisions that I would never do under any circumstances and I don't really want to be around that type of person. . . . I don't want to sound like a jerk, but I am not afraid to cut off relationships with people that I don't want to aspire to be like, [at least] to a degree." Similarly, Dartmouth student Bill talked about several "convenience friendships" that he had at the beginning of his first year that ended quickly once Bill realized, in his words, "you're not as compatible as you think you are."

The compatibility or mismatch of identities can change over time, including after graduation. Dartmouth student Dustin recognized this: "I would love to be friends with all these people in five years." However, he remarked, whether they are friends will be "a function with where we are in our lives." If they are going through similar things, they are more likely to still be friends. In contrast, if their identities are mismatched, they may well drift apart.

## Reasons for Losing Friends: Romantic Relationships

Romantic relationships tend to change students' connections with their friends. They can expand students' networks through, for example, attaching their partners' friends to their friendship group or strengthening ties with other couples when they are hanging out together with a significant other. It also leads to losing friends due to people having less time for existing friendships, through straining relationships with friends who get "too close" to romantic partners or when friends reveal romantic feelings, and through losing friends during or after the romance ends.

Many students mentioned friendships that faded away when those friends got into romantic relationships. Will, a UNH student, explained that his friends "have a tendency to lose themselves in relationships, kind of fall off the face of the earth when they start dating someone." This means that each time his friends enter a new relationship, "our friendship kind of changes and it is harder to get ahold of them." Will sounded sad as he described these changes. He sounded a bit resigned when he noted that he knows they will become closer again after the couple's breakup. These periods of fading in and out were not within Will's control, and they can test the strength of a friendship.

Students also mentioned friendships being strained when a friend dated or got "too close" to their own current or past romantic partners. Kylie, a UNH student who grew up about forty-five minutes' drive from campus, had several such experiences. She had a close friendship group in high school, and many of her high school friends attended another nearby college. Kylie recalled: "A lot of them changed, branched out. Especially my friend Amie. I noticed her changing a little bit through high school. But then when she went to college, I guess she just wanted to do the big partying and drinking scene. And I was hurt by an action of hers where she dated my boyfriend a few weeks after we broke up. So, that was not very good." Kylie concluded that they "haven't really talked" since then. The trust required for friendship was broken by this action, from Kylie's perspective. She also told me about a "falling-out" with, as she put it, "my best friend from childhood. . . . He was a really good friend to me until I dated one of his friends. His friend ghosted me, and I didn't take it well. And I especially didn't take it well when my best friend started hanging out with my ex-boyfriend more often." Kylie remarked, "I stopped talking to him. . . . We haven't really talked that much ever since."

Students also felt strains in existing relationships after their friends broke up with a romantic partner, with whom they themselves had become friends. With an exasperated tone, UNH student Heidi remarked that in their friend group: "When no one was dating these people anymore, people got mad if you were hanging out with them. So, like, Arianna dated Clint, and I became really good friend with him, but they broke up. Leah's dating someone else now. So, now, it's just one of those things, where we can't really hang out like we used to." Although Heidi does not hang out with Clint anymore, she explained, "We'll text and stuff. But I don't really tell Leah, like, 'oh yeah, Clint texted me,' because I don't want to start anything."

Revealing romantic feelings to a friend could cause the relationship to end, either quickly or after a while. Even if the romantic feelings are mutual, if it does not work out romantically, it may also break up the friendship. UNH student Otto explained: "We start as friends, and then you think you could have a potential partner, and then it doesn't work. Then, all of the sudden, it's like you can't go back to being friends. It gets messy. So you push away from that person, even though, once upon a time, you were really close, but as just friends." While students discuss the "benefit" of a romantic partner who is also a friend, they also describe the downside of losing a close friend if it does not work out.

When romantic partners also consider themselves friends, breaking up can also lead to losses in their broader friendship networks. In my initial interviews with both Austin and Amanda, they each considered the other to be one of their best friends. As romantic partners, they broke up the year before our second interview, and both described the breakup as "sad." It also disrupted both of their friendship networks. In chapter 2, I discussed how Austin went through friendship expansion after the breakup, adding friends to his network that he regularly encountered through propinquity. Amanda's network size changed little, but she lost the two most central friends in her network—Austin and her best friend, Sasha. Amanda explained that Sasha had ghosted her last year. Before winter break, their friendship seemed "totally normal" to Amanda, "and then I get back, and Sasha just didn't want anything friend-wise." Sasha did not respond to texts, so Amanda decided, "If that's how it's gonna be, that's okay, I can accept that. Then I tried meeting her in the fall, 'cause it was senior year, and I was, like, I don't actually know what happened." When they had lunch, Amanda asked, "What even happened?" and Sasha told her, "All you would ever talk about was your boyfriend." Amanda continued, "And I was like, 'Well, no, you had just asked me about him.' And I didn't know what to say. And then that just kind of fizzled out. [nervous laughing] Weird." Amanda said several times during this story that "I'm okay with it," but she seemed hurt and confused by how the friendship ended.

Sasha's version of their breakup also indicated that it was related to Amanda's romantic relationship, but the details differed. Sasha noted that the "falling-out," as she called it, was because:

> Amanda only ever talked to me about her boyfriend and her boyfriend problems. It got to the point where I was like, "You literally haven't asked me how I'm doing in six months, and all we ever talk about is 'Austin this, Austin that.'" I confronted her about it. I was like, "Look, I'm not your therapist. Sorry, I can't do this anymore." Then it was the whole, [Amanda said,] "You're not supporting me" thing. Rah. [laughs] I was just, like, "I just don't have the emotional bandwidth to deal with this right now." I was really stressed out junior year. I was dealing with health stuff, and I was like, "I just can't."

Sasha noted that Amanda is "now dating this guy that, he and I had a pretty bad history, so, yep, I don't mind that friendship fading." Even if she did not "mind" that friendship ending, this changed Sasha's friendship network.

As this example shows, romantic relationships can lead to friendships ending during the relationship as well as in the breakup. Amanda's romantic relationship contributed to losing her best friend Sasha, and, with the breakup, Amanda also lost her friendship with Austin as well as with Austin's friends. While the romantic relationship disrupted Sasha's and Austin's networks, it had the most dramatic effect on Amanda's network. With breakups with her two closest friends, Amanda described it as "my friend group totally flipped." Amanda explained how she had previously hung out in Austin's fraternity house, so her "social spaces changed because of that [their breakup], too, just where I would hang out." Changes in romantic relationships can disrupt students' broader friendship networks.

## Reasons for Losing Friends: Reevaluating the Friendship

Friendships also faded away or broke up because one person realized that the relationship was not that valuable to them. During the interviews, students talked about realizing that a friend was not really that close, was not someone they really wanted to spend time with, or was not that good a friend. When this type of friendship loss happened, it was usually intentional, as a result of one party deciding to put less into the relationship or more into other relationships, which left little for the one that consequently faded away.

Sometimes the reevaluation was realizing they had never truly been close or had much in common. Dartmouth student Ella named the biggest social obstacle she faced in the first two years as realizing that the first group of friends she met were "not forever friends." Rather than a breakup, they drifted away as Ella instead worked to strengthen bonds and spend more time with friends in other groups, specifically, friends she knew from summer camp and those on her varsity crew team.

I also heard about moments when participants felt hurt by a friend, and they ended up reevaluating the relationship as not as close or meaningful. Jennifer told me about a close friendship that ended: "I stopped being friends with her because there was this guy that I liked, and she started talking to him, and I was, like, 'Oh, no. This is not someone I want to be friends with.'" Jennifer took her friend's action as a reflection on her character, reevaluating the relationships as not meaningful to her, and the friendship faded away.

Students told me how "drama" becomes a negative in a friendship when it is not balanced by a meaningful connection, and this reevaluation is a step toward the friendship ending. Sydney, a Dartmouth student, described her friendship group this way: "I just got tired of all the drama. Some of my friends had drama with other people, and I didn't [want to] get dragged in to be, like, 'Oh, I don't want to go to this place, I don't want to hang out with them, and that's because so-and-so is there.' I didn't have a problem with so-and-so, but I'm friends with them [the friend that does have a problem with so-and-so], so it was just very weird and lots of tension. . . . By the end I was like, 'I've got to go.'" After reevaluating these friendships, Sydney stopped investing in them. Another Dartmouth student, Melanie, provides more detail about how these friendships can end. Lamenting that "people sometimes suck," Melanie explained, "I just have developed a relatively low threshold for that. For the most part I just don't get involved with things like that. But, yeah, I don't think it's that hard to lean out of those situations.

I think that my roommate's friends freshman year are a good example of that." Melanie eventually came to see them as "a toxic little group" and in response she "just leaned away." She remembered, "They'd invite me to things, and I'd be like, 'I'm busy.' I would not invite them to things. By not spending very much time together, we became very clearly not close. Yeah, that has been a pretty fair way for me to escape things." Related to the identity changes and "betterment distancing" identity work discussed earlier, students reevaluated their friendships as negative, dramatic, or toxic.

Because of this reevaluation, students decided to invest less in the friendships that were "negative" or "taxing." Savannah talked about how she "gradually stopped hanging out with" some friends, keeping the ones whom "I enjoy hanging out with." When I asked her, "What do you think made for that change?" Savannah replied, "I just realized that being at Dartmouth was so emotionally and mentally taxing that I don't need other people to be that for me as well." Elaborating on the "taxing" behaviors that led to friendships ending, MCC student Dory described noticing that a friend was not treating her well. When they had plans to "just hang out," her friend would "trick me to do something else," such as "Can you stop at the store? Can you pick this up for me?" Dory explained, "After a while, even if you're as naive as me, you're gonna start thinking . . . I can't take it anymore. I just can't. And I keep biting my tongue in when I want to say something." Looking back, Dory realized that this has been a pattern for a while, where the friendship was not reciprocal: "I just couldn't [any] longer stay [friends with her]. If I did stay in it, it would be this vicious cycle of so-called abuse to me as a friend. It shouldn't be so much pressure to be all you can be for that person. It should be like, 'Hey what are you doing? Are you doing all right?' Like, 'What's going on?' Not like, 'Oh, can you do this for me? Can you do that for me?' You know, 'Can you get this done for me?'" After Dory complied and did the favor, her friend would say "all right, bye," no longer willing to hang out together. Eventually, Dory reevaluated this friendship, recognizing it as too one-sided. The lack of reciprocity led Dory to end the friendship by no longer responding to her friend's texts and requests. It is certainly true that friendships may not be reciprocal constantly. However, nearly all respondents expressed a belief that friendships should be reciprocal over the long haul. When one party realizes the friendship is not reciprocal or is draining, they may (and should!) end it or at least have a conversation about it.[9]

Often, realizing that a friendship is unhealthy does not feel good. Sometimes, it leaves students feeling "used," "abused" or "pressured," as Dory described it. Other times, it leaves them feeling "hurt" or "sad." MCC student Alexa described this painful evaluation of realizing that your friends are using you. Alexa discussed how "I've lost a lot of people that I considered friends before. Because I realize it wasn't really me but what I could do for them that was the reason that they were hanging out with me." Calvin, a Dartmouth student, described reciprocity and being "genuine" and "authentic" as important values in friendship. Calvin let friendships fade when there was "no longer a joy of giving" or when he found himself wondering why he was putting in the effort. Calvin described how this process unfolded: "realizing that my effort has no return. And slowly, slowly [I] catch on to, like, this is actually not a friendship. It's not mutual. It's not reciprocal . . . that's when the falling-out happened. It's slow [and] a lot of sadness." Calvin described his one-sided friendships as having small "cracks" or "leaks" that gradually turned into a break. He was looking for "more thoughtful and considered friendships."

Like Dory and Alexa, Calvin felt "extracted" by his friends and groups. Echoing the "mom" role in Blake Silver's research on cookie-cutter selves,[10] Calvin named that "my role usually in a friend group is that I provide emotional support or logistical support. And usually in the background." He ended friendships after feeling like someone was using him for the transaction, for the "social capital" rather than for "personal interaction." For example, Calvin described realizing his time in his fraternity was "not fun. I want to have fun with my friends here." Instead, he said, "I was bringing all my female friends to the frat," which he saw as like "feeding lambs to these people," which "was very obvious to observe after two or three events." Once Calvin realized this, he said, it "was really easy to depart."

Living together as roommates often intensified incompatibilities between friends. Sasha described how this happened with her friend Blake. Sasha, Blake, Ian, and Bryce all got an apartment on the Dartmouth campus together the previous year, their junior year. It brought Bryce, Ian, and Sasha closer together, but led to the end of their friendship with Blake.

> Blake was the worst roommate I've ever had in my life. So disrespectful of boundaries and items. If anyone went grocery shopping, he would just help himself to your food. He was just dirty. And he was in [an a cappella group], he would have all these [a cappella] events in our apartment and then wouldn't clean up afterwards. There'd be drinks everywhere and our apartment would smell weird. Once, one of his friends threw up in our bathroom, all over our toilet, and he just didn't clean it and was like, "Not my job," and I was like, "Yeah, it is." Just really egregious.

Sasha described how her roommates were relieved to find out that Blake would not be taking classes in the spring, which meant he was not able to stay in their on-campus apartment, so they found another roommate. "We pulled in the other roommate, and then Blake decided he was gonna live in our living room, unilaterally made that call . . . to literally live in our living space and hadn't consulted us about it. And we were like, 'no,' so there was a very intense falling-out." Blake "just basically refused" to move out of the apartment, so they ended up contacting the campus housing office, which told Blake, "You can't live in their living room. You need to leave."

Along with living together, other transitions facilitated reevaluations of students' friendships. There were two big such events that happened during my data collection. The first was graduation from college, which particularly came up the second time I interviewed the Dartmouth participants, since I scheduled these interviews within weeks of their graduation. Students were typically very introspective about their friendships and intentional about how they would spend their last bits of time on campus with their classmates and friends. For example, when I asked Calvin to talk about his college friendships, he responded, "I've been thinking about this. As a graduating senior, I was thinking about this. And my good friend and I were talking about a friendship that fell apart." Calvin explained that they were talking through, "Do we want to have a meal with them and sit down so, as we exit this place, we're both in a peaceful place?" They had not decided because they realized that although "in our head, that was the intention," it is not one they can "mandate." They talked through how their ex-friend might "not want that" and might have their own agenda.

Students used transitions, such as parting ways at the end of college, as a time to reevaluate their friendships. When I asked Kira how many of her current friends she thought she would have in ten years, she replied: "I wouldn't be surprised if I'm not friends with any of them in ten years [laughs]." Kira clarified, "You go through cycles of your life and, realistically, the people you're friends with in college might come back to each other every now and then at reunions or whatever, but I don't expect to really stay in close contact with any of them." Initially, I found this response surprising because she had just told me that she liked having a smaller intimate group of friends and felt particularly close to two friends, noting that "I wish I had more friends that were like Elena and Chelsea." When I interviewed her two years later, Kira was not friends with Chelsea, instead listing Elena and a new friend, Carl, as her two closest ties. She reflected that even with these closest ties, "I wish they knew more about me," noting that "they tell me more about themselves than I tell them about myself. That's just where I'm comfortable. I don't know if that's a bad thing." With Kira and others who told me they did not expect to remain friends with people they were close to, it seemed that having someone to feel connected to was more meaningful than the specific person.

Dartmouth student Layla spoke about the transition at the end of college in a particularly captivating way. She noted that in the past year, she had been thinking that "when you're gonna move on to another step in your life, you start packing up things and it's not just your clothes that you pack up. So ending relationships, here. Or, I guess, it's interesting to say like *cutting* friendships here and there. Because I feel like if it was a real friendship, you wouldn't need to necessarily cut it. So cutting relationships here and there." In contrast to the friendships that are cut, Layla mentioned the importance of "taking this moment to look at what I've picked up in my bag, the stones that I wanted to really interact with, or the diamonds in my bag." The meaningful friendships are the diamonds.

The second transition that facilitated friendship reevaluations was the COVID-19 pandemic, which disrupted normal patterns of propinquity and, consequently, interaction patterns as well. Lafayette, a charismatic MCC student, was the leader of a couple of campus clubs. Through these clubs, Lafayette met a lot of people on campus, acquiring many friends. Between the two interviews, Lafayette experienced much change in his friendship networks. When asked why this change might have happened, he replied: "COVID-19 has been one of those events in our lives where it really, when it comes to friends, it separates the wheat from the chaff. You really know who your friends really are in crises like this." Lafayette noted that "I very rarely ask for help" and "I've always been the type of person that if anybody needs help, I'm always willing to give it." Like others, he found the pandemic to be "a very stressful time," and he distanced himself from friends "who required or wanted all that attention, I just wasn't able to give that to them." Lafayette found the pandemic to be a moment that forced him to reevaluate his friendships. While he noted that he lost some friends, he defended these changes by saying that it was not "good" or meaningful friends who fell away.

Patrice, an MCC student, encourages her peers to reevaluate their friendships by thinking of their future self and imagining how they may look back on their college years. Although she was just in her first year at MCC, Patrice advised: "Be very careful in how you pick your friends, because no matter how old you get, you're gonna still think about college. You're gonna look back at it. It's part of life, and you don't wanna look back at it and think, hmm, I never should've been with that person, I never should've had them in my life." Although Patrice phrases this as who you "pick" as a friend, it also relates to who you lose as a friend, or which friendships you allow to fade away. If students might look back and think, "I never should've had them in my life," then Patrice argues that it is wise to end the relationship.

## Network Type

The way that friendship loss—both friendship breakups and fade-aways—unfolds differs by students' network type. That is, friendship loss is experienced in different ways by samplers, compartmentalizers, and tight-knitters.

For samplers, friendships seemed to end often, and they posed little disruption to students' friendship networks overall. Samplers were especially likely to have multiple friendship breakups happening at different times, not all at once. They were more able to have multiple, sequential losses because a rupture in one relationship is less consequential for their network as a whole. They can lose one friend without it leading to problems with their other friendships since these friends are one-on-one relationships.

Samplers lost friendships without much impact on their network as a whole. Ciara, an MCC student in the liberal arts program who had a sampler network, told me: "I've been in a lot of rough roads with friends. I've had a lot of best friends. We were friends for about six months, and it just crashed and burned. That's been a pattern for a couple of years now . . . It is a lot of fair-weather friends. A lot of, they'll drop me, a lot of drama, continues on and on and on." The frequency of departures from Ciara's network was not unusual for samplers. Losing friends, moreover, posed little disruption to her network because most of her friends did not know each other. Therefore, the connections among her network were not disrupted. Sasha, another student with a sampler network, told me about quite a few friendships that ended, first in her sorority, then in her study abroad program, then with her best friend Amanda. Although losing friends could be emotionally taxing, it did not disrupt her broader network much. Similarly, Danica, who had a sampler network, told me that she was frustrated with quite a few friends in her network, in her words, "so tired of the toxic environment" and "so tired of having people thrown under the bus and having people be shamed." She was able to leave these relationships by leaving the GroupMe group chat without worrying that she would lose all of her friends.

In contrast, when compartmentalizers have friendships that end, they may lose a cluster of friends. Because their friends are typically embedded in one of the two to four clusters of friends in their network, losing a friend would change that cluster in some way. The loss has an impact beyond the one-on-one relationship. Losing the friend or the cluster can certainly feel hard in the moment; however, compartmentalizers have another group to fall back on.

Victoria was a Dartmouth student who had a compartmentalized network both times I interviewed her. She told me about friendships that faded away in her varsity sports team after four of the five women in her graduating class quit. She also lost friendships in her first-year floor and her sorority over her time at Dartmouth. Although the specific clusters in her friendship group changed, she only lost one cluster at a time, and she was able to build another cluster around the same time. For example, when she joined a sorority, her friends in her first-year floor faded away. Reflecting on these changes, Victoria told me that these shifts in whom she considered friends helped her to realize she was a pretty "relaxed" person, so she began distancing herself from people who were a "burden." This shaped the "scattered" nature of Victoria's friendship networks.

Losing friends typically causes the largest disruption to tight-knitters' friendship networks. When tight-knitters had breakups, they interfered with relationships throughout the group, not only in that one friendship or cluster. For example, UNH student Lindsay explained how this unfolded in her tight-knit friendship group: "Lizzie and Willow started not liking each other, and then me and Hillary started not liking each other. So the friendship group just kind of disbanded. Willow, for some reason, doesn't really talk to me that much anymore. And now I just talk to Carter and then no one else from that friend group, even though Lizzie and I were close, which is sad.... It's just awkward.... We just had a falling-out." Because Lindsay's network was tightly connected, changing one relationship reverberated into other parts of her network.

When students lose a friend in a tight-knit network, it can lead to more self-reflection. Another tight-knitter at UNH, Chandra, told me: "Some of the stuff that I went through with my friends, particularly the people I'm not friends with anymore, I would say helped me to figure out what my boundaries were and what my priorities were, and my interests, I guess. Because being friends with those people and then realizing that I didn't want to be friends with those people was a pretty big shift. They were so important to me for a few years." Students with tight-knit networks described the most drama and difficulty with losing friendships. This disruption to their network leads to them reevaluating their friendships and then sometimes reevaluating who they are, in line with the discussion in chapter 2 about the identity work that occurs in friendships.

Technology makes it clear who is part of the group and who is not by inclusion in the group text or message. Students talked about carefully navigating what to do when their friend group had an issue with a particular friend. Do they remove that person without telling them, do they have "the friend talk" first and then remove them, do they all leave that group, or do they remain there but no longer communicate on it, instead starting a new group where they continue to talk without that friend included? This is not a concern if someone is a sampler, but it is a topic that comes up for both compartmentalizers and tight-knitters, both of whom navigate dynamics among friends.

Another dynamic that was intensified in tight-knit networks is the difficulty of letting a friendship fade away or break up, even when students recognize that it is not working for them. Students rightly recognize that the change to this one friendship will lead to a change in their other relationships. As discussed earlier, Dartmouth student Melanie described how she sees people sometimes who feel "trapped in [their] friendships." She explained: "I know from talking to people who I'm acquainted with, but not close with, that many of their close friends are people that they really don't like. And that they just felt like they had to stay friends with because it is such a tightly packed, small community." Tight-knitters are more easily "trapped" with friends they "really don't like" because the tight-knit bonds that provide social support also make it challenging to exit.

Losing friends may feel bad or make a person feel they have failed in some way, but it is a normal part of relationship cycles. Part of the pain of friendship breakups and fade-aways, when students do not initiate these actions, is the power of feeling chosen. Research on sexual desire and hooking up focuses on how "it feels good to be wanted,"[11] and I find that these feelings also apply to friendship. In turn, it does not feel good to be rejected. Not only is it normal to lose friends, but this change in our networks also leaves space to make or strengthen friendships that fit or support us better. Melvin, who experienced much change in his friendships over the four years, put it well when he told me his advice for Dartmouth students: "I would say find a close group of friends but be open to friends coming and going. Don't force friendships with people."

## Takeaways

For students:

1. As you find a close group of meaningful friends, some friendships will end. It is not unusual, although it can hurt and feel confusing.
2. If the friendship is meaningful to you, it is worth putting in work to help it last (see chapter 2), but, if it is not, do not be afraid to let it go.
3. Some friendships end with dramatic falling-outs or breakups, but more often friendships fade away when propinquity no longer keeps you in regular contact with each other, when you notice an incompatibility or mismatch of identities, or when romantic relationships change.

4. College is a time of identity growth, and this can put strain on friendships. Either you may change or your friend may change in a way that makes it hard to maintain the friendship.
5. Even when you know the friendship is not meaningful or supportive, it can hurt to feel rejected or not chosen.
6. Friendship loss poses less disruption to sampler networks than to compartmentalizers, who may lose a cluster, or tight-knitters, who often find their whole network disrupted. Tight-knitters often feel the biggest disruption. Tight-knitters also are more likely to feel "trapped" in their friendships or that they "don't like" their friends, and find it lonely to think of ending these friendships.
7. If you are worried about disruptions to your network, focus on making new friends (see chapter 1) or strengthening the ties with existing friends (see chapter 2).

For parents and other supporters:

1. Your child likely will lose friends during college. This is normal.
2. Although it may feel bad and be challenging emotionally and socially to lose friends, they can rebuild their network. As friends leave the network, there is more time and energy for other connections.
3. To rebuild, they can focus on making new friends (see chapter 1) or strengthening ties with existing friends (see chapter 2).
4. Losing friends may also be helpful to them, particularly when that friend is no longer meaningful or supportive, as it may aid in their identity development or open up time for new, more meaningful friendships to form.

For colleges:

1. Colleges can support students by normalizing that they will not keep all the friends they make in college. Although it may feel bad and be challenging emotionally and socially to lose friends, losing friends is not all negative. It leaves more time and energy for other connections. Losing a friend may also be helpful when that friend is no longer meaningful or supportive or through recognizing that they are no longer well matched because their identity or goals have changed.
2. To support students in rebuilding their friendship network after losing a friend, they can focus on making new friends (see chapter 1) or strengthening ties with existing friends (see chapter 2).

3. Losing friends can disrupt student organizations, roommate groups, and so on. It may require emotional support for the individuals involved and support for the organization through this transition.
4. The impact of losing friends will not be the same on each group, and it is not just about individual resiliency, but also about network dynamics.
5. Students in sampler networks may experience less disruption than compartmentalizers or tight-knitters.
6. Compartmentalizers have a group to fall back on, even if they lose a cluster.
7. Tight-knitters often find their whole network disrupted; to avoid this, they may remain in these groups. Despite feeling "trapped" in their friendships or that they "don't like" their friends, tight-knitters often find it harder to end these friendships than do compartmentalizers and samplers. Colleges can support students by recognizing this as a network dynamic rather than just a failing of an individual student. Colleges can also normalize change in friendship networks and support students who wish to shift their networks.

Part Two

# HOW INSTITUTIONS AND IDENTITIES SHAPE THESE PROCESSES

[ CHAPTER FOUR ]

# College Characteristics: How Networks Differ by Institution Type

As a cheerleader who was active in her sorority and in leadership roles in two other campus clubs, Amanda struck me as a very involved student at Dartmouth with a bubbly personality. She came to my office for our interview during the summer after her second year, a time referred to as "sophomore summer" or "Camp Dartmouth" by many students. Amanda described herself as enjoying multiple interests: "I like being part of different clubs." She also made many "good friends" that are "not necessarily close. Like, I wouldn't go to them for anything like love advice." With meeting so many people in many different places around campus, Amanda also experienced many friendships that "just kind of faded."

When I asked her why so many friendships faded, Amanda tugged on the dark curls that had escaped her high ponytail and responded: "That's a good question because, for example, my freshman floor, we were super close. We would all go to meals together, and we would do a lot of activities. But once sophomore year came, actually freshman summer to sophomore year, everybody left. D-Plans changed. We just didn't make an effort to really seek each other out as much because everything was just so different." Amanda's reference to D-Plans is shorthand for a schedule where each student chooses which terms to be on-campus and off-campus during their second and third years at Dartmouth.[1]

Although she did not use the term "propinquity," Amanda described how not regularly crossing paths with friends made her second year feel "so different" from the first:

> We didn't have that close-proximity thing where we would have to see each other. Because we live[d] together [freshman year], we'd always be, like, "Oh, do you want to go get food?" 'Cause you were there. We all moved to different places because of the D-Plan. A lot of people went

away for freshman summer or were gone for sophomore fall or winter. Inherently, the D-Plan takes a big role in that. A lot of people just went away, and unless you already had very close relations you don't really maintain that. [My best friend] Sasha went away for the spring [of their second year], and we spoke a couple of times because we put the effort in. But I didn't really get to talk to her that much until she came back [this term]. For me, if I don't feel super close to you in the first place, I'm not going to probably maintain that.

Amanda had a quite sociological understanding of how propinquity made her friendships easy. She also noted this structural force (the D-Plan) that disrupted her friendships, making it so that a friendship had to be actively maintained in order to be kept. Amanda explained: "Partly, it's just the nature of college [that] we all just do different things. A lot of my floor actually had gone to the same sorority, but I didn't [join that sorority]. So, I didn't see them as much for those reasons as well. So, we all just kind of went our separate ways in the way of the Dartmouth schedule. That played a big role in it for sure." As discussed in earlier chapters, friendships shape and shift for all students, so Amanda is correct when she asserts this is "partly . . . just the nature of college," and she is also correct in noting that the extent of these disruptions to propinquity are starker at Dartmouth than at many other colleges.

As discussed in the previous chapter, when I interviewed Amanda again at graduation, she was no longer friends with the two people who had been closest to her in the first interview: Sasha, her best friend, and Austin, her boyfriend. Toward the end of her third year, Sasha started to withdraw from their friendship. Amanda described that she kept texting her and trying to initiate a meeting. When they did meet, Sasha told her that all Amanda did was talk about her boyfriend, so she did not want to be friends anymore. Shortly after that, Austin broke up with Amanda. As a result, Amanda explained: "My friend group totally flipped. And [my] social spaces changed because of that, too, just where I would hang out. Things like that were all different." Amanda said that these changes in her friend group made her feel "super nervous going into senior year. Things that I've had constant for three years at that point, totally just fell apart. And I was rattled because I was, like, oh my gosh, I don't have any constant friends. I had Megan and Chloe, but they were gonna be off in there 'cause they were juniors." Not only did the D-Plan disrupt Amanda's friendships during her second and third years, as her friends were on campus at different times than she was, it also disrupted the new friendships that she made across class years as those friends were away during Amanda's last year, when she was on campus all three terms.

Another big change to Amanda's network was that she was no longer active in her sorority. When I asked about this, Amanda explained that she backed off from her involvement partly because Sasha was an officer in the chapter, so "the tension with Sasha" made things feel "uncomfortable." More generally, Amanda concluded, "It just wasn't my place. I didn't depledge or anything. I'm still a member. I'm just not really involved at all."

Amanda's friendship network and how these relationships unfolded would be less likely to happen at the University of New Hampshire or Manchester Community College than at Dartmouth College. Specifically, her path was shaped by Dartmouth students' tendency to dabble in lots of activities on campus, including sports that would often be students' only activity on Division I campuses, such as UNH. Her path was also shaped by the movement of her schedule and that of her peers and friends off campus and on campus, not always in sync. They would come together, then part ways, then some of them would come together again, and so on. In other words, the D-Plan shaped Amanda's friendship network, facilitating its compartmentalized structure, which is the most common network type for the Dartmouth students I interviewed.

Although the D-Plan, which requires students to take terms away from campus in their second and third year (fall, winter, and spring), is unique to Dartmouth, it highlights many of the features of campus structure and organization that impact the formation of friends on all campuses. Amanda's story highlights the role of friendships made in dorms and in clubs, and it explains the advantage of propinquity in propelling people together and the disadvantage to relationships when those regular patterns are no longer there. Amanda lost two important friendships, which did not have much impact on the structure of her friendship network, but had a big impact on the content and experience. She remained a compartmentalizer, yet the rhythms of her friendships changed substantially.

Campuses shape students' networks, including encouraging (and discouraging) network types through their organization. As shown in Table 4.1, my sample at Dartmouth has more compartmentalizers than the other two campuses: 63 percent of my Dartmouth sample are compartmentalizers, compared to 44 percent at UNH and 46 percent at MCC. The largest network type on any campus is compartmentalizers at Dartmouth, which make up nearly two-thirds of my sample at Dartmouth. As Amanda's story suggests, compartmentalized networks often reflect students' moving between groups, and the D-Plan facilitates such movement. Therefore, the structure of how students move around (and off and on) campus is reflected in their friendship networks. Tight-knitters are more common in my UNH sample than the other two (35 percent compared to 19–23 percent), and

TABLE 4.1. Friendship Network Type by Campus (percent)

|  | DC (N=35) | UNH (N=34) | MCC (N=26) | Overall (N=95) |
| --- | --- | --- | --- | --- |
| Samplers | 14 | 21 | 35 | 22 |
| Compart-mentalizers | 63 | 44 | 46 | 52 |
| Tight-knitters | 23 | 35 | 19 | 26 |

Note: This table shows the percentage of my sample on each campus with each network type.

samplers more common in my MCC sample (35 percent compared to 14–21 percent).

UNH has more tight-knitters and more samplers than does Dartmouth. As tight-knitters, at UNH, students tended to find one place or one group of friends to stick with, often a group they formed in the initial friendship market. Dartmouth students tended to balance multiple groups, therefore, more often fitting with the compartmentalizer structure. As shown in Table 4.2, my samples at Dartmouth and UNH are similar in terms of network size; students listed twelve friends, on average. So, it is not so much the number of "closer friends" that differentiates the two residential campuses as the connections (or lack of connections) among those friends.

Friendship networks at the community college differ from those at the two residential campuses. At MCC, networks are smaller (eight compared to twelve friends) and less dense (average density of 43 percent compared to 53–58 percent), fitting with students' stories about spending less time with friends and making fewer new friends on campus, especially friendships that last. It also reflects the role of residential campuses in encouraging students to develop more tight-knit ties between their friends, through spending time with friends on campus and in campus activities. These happen more often at Dartmouth and UNH than at MCC. At MCC, more students are samplers, with more disconnected networks and one-on-one friendships.

In this chapter, I spotlight key features of each campus that facilitate different friendship processes and network types, using examples of students' experiences on all three campuses. Sometimes students themselves noticed those differences, as did Amanda, but more often these differences exist unnoticed as just part of a college experience. To be sure, there are differences in precollege friendship networks and precollege characteristics that also shape students' friendship networks in college. I discuss these throughout but focus on what happens during college.

While I highlight differences across campuses, I also want to note the many similarities in friendship network characteristics across the three

TABLE 4.2. Friendship Network Characteristics by Campus

|  | DC (N=35) | UNH (N=34) | MCC (N=26) | Overall (N=95) |
|---|---|---|---|---|
| Size (mean) | 11.9 | 12.3 | 8.2 | 11.0 |
| Range of size | 2–25 | 4–39 | 3–16 | 2–39 |
| Density (mean) | 0.53 | 0.58 | 0.43 | 0.52 |
| Modularity (mean) | 0.20 | 0.18 | 0.24 | 0.21 |
| Betweenness centrality (mean) | 0.33 | 0.27 | 0.47 | 0.35 |

campuses. The range of network size overlaps, as do the other network characteristics—density, modularity, and betweenness centrality. Also, at each of the three campuses, I found all three network types—samplers, compartmentalizers, and tight-knitters. I also found more compartmentalizers than the other two types on each campus.[2]

## Manchester Community College (MCC): "Making friends is a little bit more difficult on a commuter campus"

At MCC, students would often bring up how they find it hard to make friends in a community college environment. For example, Lafayette, a Latino man and a second-year student at MCC, told me: "Making friends is a bit more difficult on a commuter campus than it is at a campus where everyone stays on campus ... [Even when] people want to stay on campus a little bit longer, at the end of the day, [other] people leave. And you won't see them until the next day, until you come back here."

Propinquity is less likely to bring the same people together often, which is the main reason friendships are "more difficult on a commuter campus," as Lafayette put it. Opportunities to connect regularly with the same peers are less frequent at MCC because students spend less time on campus, they participate in fewer club meetings and events, and they have fewer opportunities to connect without planning it. Students might strike up a friendship, then their schedules change, and they no longer cross paths.

Before turning to look at the campus structures in more detail, let's look at some differences in the students. As I was first getting to know students in each interview, I asked them about how they ended up at college and at that institution. The answers to these questions told me a good deal about students' goals, interests, and background. MCC students' answers to these questions differed from those of students on the other two campuses. When I asked Lev about his decision to attend MCC, he told me: "To be honest with you, it was just really affordable. Especially with having a lot of these 'sister schools' that a lot of my credits will get transferred over [to][3] . . . I'm paying half [the cost] here, then all that will be transferred over. So it will be the easiest route for me and most affordable." Other students described some turns in their journey to MCC, such as Violet, who ended up at MCC after losing scholarship money in her first year at an out-of-state private institution, or Anjali, who planned to start at a four-year institution until it was time to make concrete financial decisions. As Anjali described it, she "applied to out-of-state schools because my friends were going." She was accepted to several, but then her brother told her that "out of state would be more expensive, so I was like, 'Okay. I'll just start from community college.'" Anjali ended up at MCC because it was the closest to her home and her family's convenience store, where she continued to work.

Almost all MCC students brought up affordability and the convenient location of the campus to their home or work. Very few students mentioned a particular program's strengths; the exceptions to that were nursing and HVAC, where students would sometimes note these program's reputations for placing students into jobs after graduation. Students' advice for their MCC peers often focused on classes rather than social life. In our second interview, after Kari graduated from MCC in interior design, she advised, "To be honest, I would tell them to concentrate on their academics. They can be social after they graduate, but school ain't cheap and you need to get the most value out of it that you possibly can." Lev similarly offered advice to take as many classes as you can at MCC. He felt it was important that students know they could save money in this way by transferring up to ninety credits.

The advantages associated with the cost and location, however, also entail a different and more challenging structure for making friends. Ruben lamented: "I do wish I went to a university, but I just do not wish for that debt. Just living in a dorm, to not worry about anything, having all that social [life and] also having the ability to study." While Ruben believed it would be easier to be more academic ("to study") and to be more social if he lived in a dorm, he did not see the gains as great enough to outweigh the financial benefits.

### MAKING FRIENDS AT COMMUNITY COLLEGE

Not all MCC students noted that it was hard to make friends at MCC, but most did. Although many reported these challenges, all but three of the twenty-six MCC students I spoke with made at least one friend at the college.

On average, MCC students made fewer friends on their campus than did students on the residential campuses. At MCC, students' networks contained 44 percent friends who attended MCC and 67 percent friends from home, with 9 percent friends from home who also attended MCC. This is nearly half the number of friends from campus as found for the residential campuses and more than twice the number of friends from home. The small proportion of college friends they reported encouraged sampler networks.

Another difference in how students described their friends at MCC compared to the residential campuses was how deep and lasting friendships from campus become. Paige, an MCC student, explained: "You become acquaintances, you're friendly with each other, but I haven't really made any lasting friendships at community college. Maybe it's different at a different school, but that's been the main thing for me." At Dartmouth and UNH, students often described spending a lot of time with college friends and noted the multi-layered and meaningful impact their friends had on them. In contrast, MCC students tended to describe their friendships in a more shallow or one-dimensional way. For example, when I asked Mira, "Do you feel like you've changed as a result of the friendships you've made in college?" She asked me, "Changed, as in—?" and I clarified, "Any way, good or bad?" Mira replied, "I would say good. I mean, I haven't become a drug addict or anything like that. So I would say that's good." Friendships were "good," but there was not much texture to them, maybe because propinquity did not bond students together through repetitive interactions that transcended one setting. This fits with other research on community college experiences showing that "many students did not have relationships that extended beyond the classroom."[4] These more one-dimensional connections also encouraged the sampler network structure common among the MCC students.

Spending time on campus helped students to form friendships with MCC peers. Ruben, who was in his fourth year in the nursing program, offered the following advice to his peers: "Study on campus, and use your breaks to see what's going on on campus. Because otherwise clinicals take us away from campus." The campus had several places where students could go between classes. Students most often went to the library, the cafeteria, or "the pit." In the library, they would most often study. There were multiple spaces in the library, including those with wooden chairs and tables, and those with upholstered furniture where they could sit on couches or chairs. In both spaces, I saw some students sit by themselves and others in groups. The cafeteria also had an open seating arrangement, food at a range of prices, and pool tables. I saw students sit by themselves and in groups throughout the tables in the cafeteria area. They were eating, studying, and occasionally engaging in games of pool. Attached to the open area of the cafeteria was "the pit," where students could sit on comfy couches to study as well as for club meetings later in the day. Some of the hallways also contained groups of chairs, where students could spend time outside of class. Therefore, it was not that spaces to hang out or encounter MCC peers were lacking, but rather the culture and organization of time that served as barriers.

The amount of time students spent with friends was less on average and varied more at MCC than at the residential campuses. Some MCC students, like David, reported that his friends "hang out almost every night." At the other end of the range was Ciara, who noted that the last time she had spent with a group of friends was "a couple of years ago," and it is about "every other week" that she spends time with any one friend. Similarly, Tania told me that she could not remember the last time she spent with a friend, but she thought it might have been "a couple weeks ago" when they had lunch together. At the residential campuses, no student told me it had been more than two days since they had spent time with a friend, and almost always it was within the past day.

Because community college students had fewer deep and lasting friendships, the weak ties that they made may be all the more important. As mentioned in chapter 1, most MCC students had modest if not small numbers of "weak ties" in the form of "less close friends." For example, MCC students reported on average fifteen "less close" friends, compared to twenty-six at Dartmouth. Only Violet and Ruben had high numbers of weak ties among the MCC students.[5] These weak ties—also called "bridging social capital"— can be important for introducing students to new people and information, such as those that can bring about job opportunities.[6] Weak ties can also become close friendships, as discussed in chapter 2.

Students at the community college also differ in whom they report talking with about school-related topics. Many MCC students first name an advisor or a professor. Students at UNH and Dartmouth almost always first name friends. Often, they mention parents second, and some also name advisors or professors, but only in a couple of cases without naming friends first. Students like Pauline noted that MCC professors "go out of their way to help . . . as long as you're willing to do your part." She clarifies that they also will not "bend over backwards for a student that's not going to give the effort." Pauline also noted staff members who go "above and beyond" to advise clubs, start a food pantry, and give advice. She mentioned specific staff members and even the president of MCC who "came on Saturday, on her day off" to attend the Christmas party for the single parents' club Pauline had helped organize. Similarly, Erin mentioned that the staff "care. They know your name, they know what you're doing here, and where you're from, and they know a little about you. They do. They remember. Even the president. She will remember your name and what you do and who you are." Tania mentioned that the staff are "really nice people" who "really care about you," and Patrice said that "everyone here is really caring." Lev also told me how "they're really caring" and "always there to help." When I asked for an example, Lev told me how his advisor visited him in the hospital, which was about an hour's drive, after Lev was in a car accident, and "they even did a card for me in class." Students recognized caring staff as resources at MCC.

## ACADEMIC PROGRAMS

The highest density networks I found at the community college were among students in two academic programs: nursing and HVAC (heating, ventilation, and air conditioning). Even students not in these programs noticed that the students in them tend to be tightly connected to each other. For example, pointing at the nursing students, all wearing scrubs and sitting together in the cafeteria, Lafayette, a political science major, described, "They are very tight-knit, and they kind of have to be. Their schedule is very different, and they have to rely on each other." Like athletes who wear uniforms on game day, the nursing students are visible and identifiable not only in terms of their academic program, but as a peer group that spends time together outside of class.

The friends that students made in classes at MCC were more narrowly academic friends than those at the residential campuses. When I asked Terrence, a twenty-four-year-old White working-class man, about his decision to come to college, he described how six years ago, "I started college right out of high school. I was also working seventy to eighty hours a week, so I didn't do very well." He described how he went from being an "honor student" in high school to getting "a 0.8 GPA my first semester" of college. Terrence smiled slyly as he continued, "I made a lot of poor decisions and ended up dropping out of school after my second year," after not getting into a nursing program. He then "got a full-time job in construction" as a "laborer and heavy machine operator for three different construction companies." He described how "finally I got a really nice construction job with a cushy salary, and I had pretty much everything worked out to where I was pretty comfortable in life, and I wasn't happy, and [when I] looked around, my supervisors weren't happy." Once Terrence realized that, he described "the next step" as "I went back to school, got into the nursing program right away." He described how in the nursing program, "we started with sixty-four [students in the program]. We're down to thirty-eight of the original class." He explained, "A lot of my friends were the ones that ended up dropping out, so that was interesting as well. But I have a new clique. I guess you could say that we're all really close, and we all do really well." In response to my question about why the others left, he offered one word: "priorities." When I asked for more detail, he said they "were just not doing enough studying or had a lot of family stuff going on." Terrence described himself as a "social butterfly," and he has made friends at MCC.

The friends he made at MCC, however, were friends who mainly studied together. Terrence told me that among his group of MCC friends, he was closest to Bryce and Amber. These two friends have remained close with him, while "everybody else kind goes in and out as they find the need to." When I asked more about Terrence's friendship with Bryce and Amber, he noted that they mainly just see each other to study, "I wouldn't call us, like, buddy buddies." He explained: "I think we've hung out not in school maybe three times in the course of the last year and a half." The day before our interview, they had studied together: "We all got together at Bryce's house, and we went over NCLEX [State Board Exam for Nurses] questions and reviewed our notes and all that good stuff. And then I couldn't concentrate, so I shotgunned a beer. Then we kept studying. And that was that. [laughs] But it wasn't exactly a hangout. It was more just studying. The beer was just an extra. We all had a beer, and then we just kept studying." When I asked more about their study sessions, Terrence explained how they get to know each other while they are studying, blending the academic and the social. Terrence told me, "It's probably like 70 percent studying, 30 percent distracted nonsense, which is often personal stuff that we all share with each other. We spend more time with each other than with our significant others or family. I work a lot . . . so I'm either at work or with them for the most part." When I asked whether he found it more helpful to study with friends or by himself, he replied: "I tried the whole solo studying first semester, where I tried to work full time and go to school, which I barely passed. That's when I got a 75. Wasn't working out too well. And then I really started focusing my studies with them and I've been [higher] . . . The last test, I was the highest score." His MCC friends supported each other academically.

Although most students found it hard to keep friends they made in class, the classroom was an important way that students made friends at MCC. Patrice provided one example:

> I have a friend, Allen, that I just made. He's in my major. I actually sat next to him the first day of class because nobody was sitting with him,

and I was, like, come on, honestly? So I sat with him, and I started talking to him. And you find out, when you do that, people are the funniest, and you don't even know. [laughs] Like, he's so funny. He makes me laugh so hard, and we have a great time. And I'm really excited because I do have one class with him next semester. I'm really pumped about it.

Patrice's story makes clear that she is open to making friends. Since they met recently, it is unclear if their friendship will be a lasting one, and Patrice does not consider Allen close enough to include in her friend list.[7] Nonetheless, propinquity bringing them together in a class next semester in the elementary education program at MCC makes it more likely that this bond will continue. Also striking is how unusual it seems that students have a sequence of classes together, since Patrice mentioned that she is "really excited" and "really pumped" to be able to see Allen again next semester in a class.

Sharing multiple classes, especially over multiple terms, helps students make and keep friends. Mira met her friend Ciara through a class project, and they've now had multiple classes together. Ciara is the main person Mira studies with, and they often both struggle to understand the material. They struggle together, though, and Mira believes that the relationship grows stronger as they spend time together studying. They both work part-time (about twenty hours per week) along with taking classes, so they find it hard to find time to see each other outside of work and school. This past term, they scheduled classes together so they would be physically present on campus at the same time. While Mira's friendship network is low in academic resources and density, she values her connection with Ciara and feels that it keeps both of them motivated to attend class and continue with their education.

The students going through MCC as a cohort, like Terrence, included more MCC students in their friendship network. Specifically, the students who are in nursing and HVAC bond together more because they are not just in one class with a particular student, but they end up taking a series of classes together. It helps form lasting and meaningful friendships when students take more than one class at a time with a friend or end up sharing both a class and a clinical experience or being in a club together. It also helps when they share a class for more than one semester.[8] Both happen frequently in nursing and HVAC. There are two cohorts in HVAC—an evening cohort, which includes more older students and those with full-time day jobs, where students are often taking only one class at a time, and the other a daytime cohort.

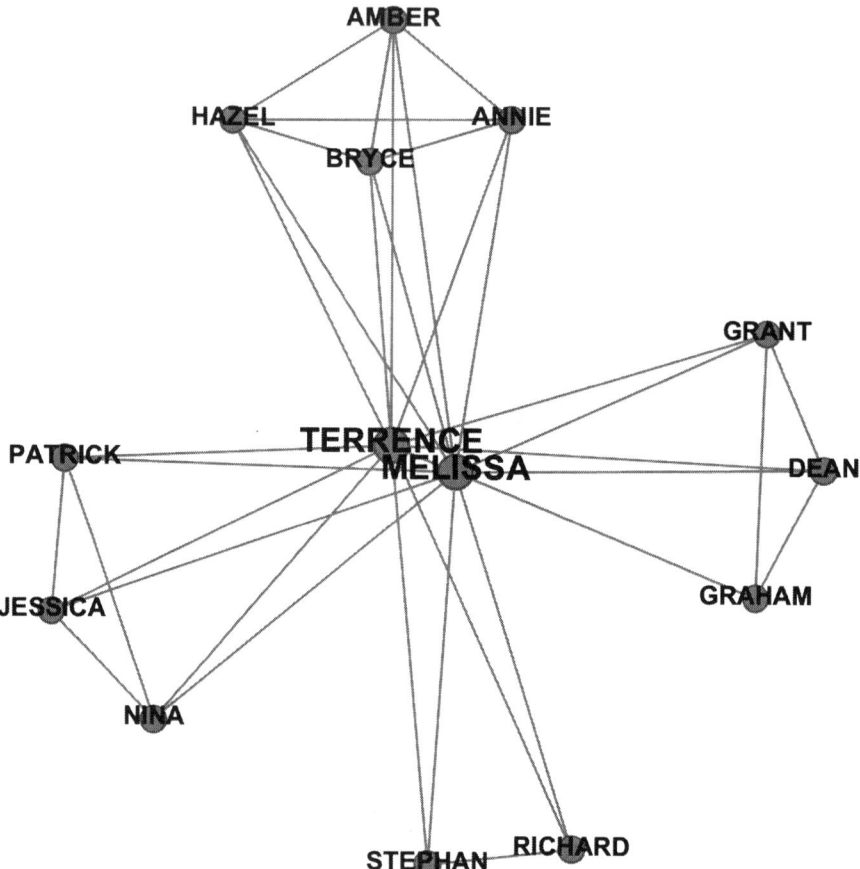

FIGURE 4.1. Terrence's friendship network, MCC year two.

The friendship network of a nursing student, Terrence, shown in figure 4.1, is typical of students in these more tight-knit programs. He has several groups of friends, including a group from high school, a small group from the community college he attended before MCC, and a group from his job as an EMT (emergency medical technician). His fiancée, Melissa, is well connected to all his friends. The group at the top of his network are his nursing friends: Bryce, Amber, Hazel, and Annie. He told me how they met in class, study together, and have friendly competition over their scores on the exams. Terrence was getting to know Annie better as they were both preparing for a medical mission trip to Ecuador on winter break. Often, HVAC and nursing students formed a cluster of friends in the student's network, as Hazel, Bryce, Annie, and Amber did for Terrence. Terrence had a compartmentalized network.

Outside of these two programs, students did not often make lasting friendships in class. In chapter 1, I shared several stories from MCC students, including Violet who compared the "acquaintances" she meets in classes to the friendships she makes in clubs due to the deeper interactions. Friendships do occasionally form in class, such as Mira and Ciara, who met through working on a group project and continue their friendship through intentionally scheduling classes together each term.

## CLUBS AND ORGANIZATIONS

One reason that I chose MCC as a research site is that more than thirty clubs and organizations were listed on its website—substantially more than for other community colleges in the area. Because I recruited through campus clubs and organizations, my interviews overrepresent these views among students; therefore, MCC students are likely less involved in clubs and less connected to campus on average than what I present here. As I was walking around campus, I noticed flyers for club meetings and events. I used these same bulletin boards to post flyers to encourage students to participate in my study. Students found out about clubs in the same ways I did—looking at the list on the school website, stopping by tables at the club fair, noticing flyers posted around the school, and hearing about clubs from other students and staff.

Another institutional difference is how clubs are less effective in helping facilitate friendships at MCC than at the residential campuses. Propinquity and time on campus work against forming and keeping friends at MCC. Part of this is that students in clubs at MCC spend less time together than those in clubs on the residential campuses (that is, they meet less frequently), which is related to the fact that most students are only on campus for their classes, and they are working more hours at jobs off campus. Another part is that they do not "hang out" on campus as much, if at all, so they are not readily available in the evenings or weekends for club meetings and activities.

The process to start a club seems easy—fill out some paperwork and collect signatures—but there were several structural barriers to clubs being successful. Skip described his experience: "They had a club fair, and I went and learned that you could start your own club. You just needed a certain amount of signatures." So, Skip collected signatures from students who said they were interested in a darts club, and he submitted the correct paperwork to the Student Senate. He even found a local darts store to sponsor the club, allowing them to borrow equipment, convincing the owner that "this seemed promising." However, it did not happen quickly enough for Skip to capture his peers' excitement.

Skip went on to explain that it "took so long" to get the club approved by student government. He told me: "That took almost another six months. Because the next student [government] meeting wasn't for another month. And so by the time we got our equipment there were only three people left. Everybody [else] had either left the school or lost interest." He sent an email to ask what day worked for them, and "most of the people said Friday was open for them." So, Skip scheduled it for the last Friday of the month at 2:00 p.m., emailing everyone: "You don't have to stay late. It's only going to be about a twenty-minute session" and "If you're running late, I will be there until at least 5:00." Skip was "disappointed" and "shocked" that despite sending the reminder and being flexible with time, "only one person showed up." Skip exclaimed, "He got a private dart lesson, and he loved it. He really did. And we played a game of darts." This happened the week prior to our interview, so Skip was still trying to make sense of what happened. Wondering if maybe Friday was free in people's schedules but not a good day because of the effort to come to campus just for the club meeting, Skip contemplated, "Maybe if that's their day where they don't have any school, why would they want to come?"

Although MCC listed more than thirty clubs and organizations on its website, most were inactive at any given time. For example, Skip noted that MCC "used to have a basketball team here. They used to have a softball team." But it's hard to keep teams organized because people's schedules change from term to term, and they are not on campus when they do not have classes. Alexa told me they were thinking about joining clubs, but they noted, "It's just hard with my work schedule and class schedule. Most of the clubs that I want to get involved in, they just don't have meeting times that I can get to. Even before, when I was doing night classes, they still didn't have good meeting times for me."

Even when they wanted to join, students found it hard to make the time to attend meetings and participate. Alexa explained what's "hard" about club meetings: "it's either like two hours after my class gets out and I'm not going to wait around here for two hours. But I'm also not going to go home and then come back for it." Alexa noted that it is also challenging when "I'm going to have to leave to go to work right after the meeting's over." Alexa explained their decision-making process: "Well, I could get there, but I would have to come and then stay for the shortest amount of time where it's acceptable and then leave. But that's not what I want to do at the clubs. I want to be able to sit there and enjoy them and have it as an actual activity rather than just something I need to go do [quickly] and then go take care of my responsibilities. I don't know if I'm actually going to be able to do any clubs here at all." Dory similarly described that at the club fair "I signed up for a bunch and they emailed me. It's just, there's no time. Time is not my friend this semester." Given everyone's different schedules, it is seemingly impossible to find a "good time" for clubs to meet on a commuter campus.

Students noted problems not only with joining clubs but with staying involved. David explained that he did not continue in a club because "they meet after class when I have to go to work, so it just doesn't work out time wise." Ruben told me how he tried guitar club and the anime group, "just dipped my toes into it," and then "nursing school came crashing hard as I was dipping, so I had to dip out." As Shirley put it, "Everyone is a commuter. The culture here is different than a university because nobody lives here." Students' competing demands with work and classes make it harder not only to join but to stay involved in clubs, when they also have to come back to campus just for a club meeting, because it is not already in a place where they live.

Kari talked about the challenges competing demands pose, even when she is a member of a group and can attend meetings. An additional barrier is the (little) time she feels she has to get to know the group members. She noted that the other members are acquaintances, not friends. Kari clarified: "People that I would wave hi to in the hall but not people that I would go have lunch with or sit down and talk to for anything other than being in the group, meaning I'm sure they're perfectly nice people, I just haven't had the chance to get to know them. There aren't that many clubs here at MCC. It's just, there really aren't many because this isn't a typical college campus. We don't live on campus. Most people are part-time. Most people are very part-time, one or two classes at a time."

Keeping a club going takes good scheduling and an engaging student leader. Clubs have adapted to these schedule challenges. Violet, one of these engaging student leaders, explained how they adapted a large campus-wide event so that more students can participate in some way:

> Judging will be happening October nineteenth, during our Harvest Day event. That way, we'll have jack-o'-lanterns and scarecrows all over the student center, which is really exciting. And this is a nice project because it means that you don't necessarily need to be there for the judging, which is always one of our big problems with events—that people need to be at the event. But this time, you can just drop it off and you have about two weeks to work on your scarecrow. So you can get together at random times . . . [and] it can still be a class-wide project, or an office-wide project, club-wide, whatever you want it to be.

I was on campus during Harvest Day as well as the week leading up to it, and it did feel like a special time on campus. They had many jack-o'-lantern and scarecrow submissions, and they had a sizable crowd for the ceremony where they announced the winner.

## AGE DIVERSITY ON CAMPUS

Although community colleges seem more welcoming to and diverse across age groups than do traditional residential campuses, students older than their twenties often experienced age as a barrier to making friends and more generally fitting in on campus. When forty-five-year-old Kari attempted to get to know the students in her classes, "asking them questions, trying to engage," she noted: "They're more focused on each other." She said, "They'll ask each other questions more often than asking me questions, unless they want an older person's perspective, like if they would ask their parents something, then they'll ask me, which gets awkward." Similarly, in response to my question about the biggest obstacle to her socially at MCC, Erin replied: "I'm a lot older than most of the people here. . . . The biggest obstacle is that I'm thirty-four and they are eighteen. So we're in very different places in our lives and we have very different priorities and very different thought processes. And they like anime with weird people and knives and strange colors, and I like a lot of different things than that. . . . There's a few people that are my age, and I do definitely relate better with them." In her midthirties in our first interview, Erin was majoring in liberal arts but thinking about changing to data analytics and wondered if she "might find more older students there."

Erin discussed how she felt distance from the other members in a club, even when it seemed like they should have much in common, given the club's focus: "You plan events together and activities together, and so you're planning themes and decoration. And some of the stuff they come up with, I'm, like, 'What?!? [laughs] You want to do what?!?' We had a table for the library club this year at the club fair, and the girl put up the computer and was playing these gruesome anime videos, gruesome." The age difference comes up in both classes and clubs. Both these settings also have the possibility to transcend the age difference by bringing students together based on common interests. For example, Skip, who was fifty-one years old, noted age as a barrier to relate to other students in class and study together, but was excited about how common interests in the darts club could help the age difference feel diminished.

## BENEFITS OF COMMUNITY COLLEGE RELATIONSHIPS

Despite having fewer friends on campus and often feeling like it is harder to make friends at MCC than on other campuses, students also described the positive impact their college friends had on them. As noted in the introduction, Erin described her college friends as having "an enormous impact on my educational experience and on my ability to keep refocusing and keep going forward even when I'm starting to get tired." She considered having friends at school "a constant reminder of why you're here and what you're doing." Even though community college friendships are often fleeting, they can be meaningful. The seeds planted in friendships can bring large rewards for students, even more when they invest more in these relationships.

Although dense and resource-rich networks were not the norm at the community college, some students formed them through clubs or majors. For example, Pauline, a White woman in her fifties who is attending MCC to learn marketing so as to help her boyfriend with his new business, told me about the friends she formed through a club for single parents. She described their interactions: "We can call each other, doesn't matter what time, and talk about things. If someone's missing from the group for a week, we always text them and make sure that they're okay. That kind of stuff, that doesn't happen with a regular group."

Along with friendships, students named other relationships formed on campus that were important. On all three campuses, including MCC, students named specific staff, faculty, and administrators who helped them navigate campus and craft friendships there. Many students described MCC to me as a caring place, where you are more than a number. For example, Erin noted that people at MCC "know each other and care about each other and care about us, with the same capacity, which is great." Erin explained that students and staff belong to the same clubs, and the set-up of the campus is such that clubs often meet in the open atrium area, which means that the topic and members are noticed by the people walking by. For example, the music club meets there, and Eric noted that "some of the staff in that club are not people that you would ever look at and be like, 'Oh, yeah, he's going to play guitar right in the middle of the student center,'" but he does. Erin explained: "You learn about them, they learn about you. They do. It's true. Even for someone like me, who's not a super socially oriented person." Erin summarized: "It's very community-based, very family-ish here." Even after recounting some challenging experiences she had on campus, which I discuss in the next chapter, Patrice made a similar comment to me, concluding, "I feel like everyone here is really caring." Researchers have noted the importance of connections and a resource-rich education beyond friendships on residential campuses,[9] and I find that MCC students also experienced and benefited from these relationships with staff, faculty, and administrators.

## The University of New Hampshire (UNH): "Just find a niche"

The public flagship campus of the state, the University of New Hampshire is the type of college attended by most students who attend four-year colleges. Smaller than many main campuses, at 11,000 undergraduates, UNH is located in a college town and offers a wide range of majors, schools, and academic programs as well as student clubs and organizations. Its website lists more than 250 clubs and organizations on UNH's campus, and a little over half of students live on campus.[10]

In contrast to the MCC students who typically described making friends as challenging, few students at UNH described it that way, even when they had difficult moments. For example, Yusef, a middle-class Black student and bioengineering major at UNH, told me: "Making friends wasn't really hard. I was a social person before UNH, and I remain to be a social person during UNH." His friendship network, shown in figure 4.2, reflects this social orientation as it includes friends he has had "since birth" and from high school, college orientation, the varsity football team, and a group study session.

Building on the parts of Yusef's story presented in the introduction, I highlight features of UNH's campus that shaped his feelings of loneliness and the friendships he formed. Even though Yusef considered himself "a social person" who meets people well and gets along with a range of types of people, he described some bumps in his friendship path at UNH. Before Yusef moved to UNH, he knew some people on campus because they had gone to high school together. Yusef described how he asked one of them and then a second to "room with me," explaining that both said, "'No, I just wanna meet new people.' I was like, 'That's cool.' But I was hurt by it." He ended up with a roommate who was a second-year student. Yusef described how he had moved in and unpacked. Surprised that his roommate had not arrived, Yusef texted him, "Are you coming? And he's like, 'Yeah, man, I'm a sophomore, I move in later.'" Yusef took a breath, looked directly at me, and said, "I didn't know that." Yusef went on to tell me about his roommate who, as a second-year student, "already had his own friends, so me and him didn't really click or talk. I understand we have different personalities, but

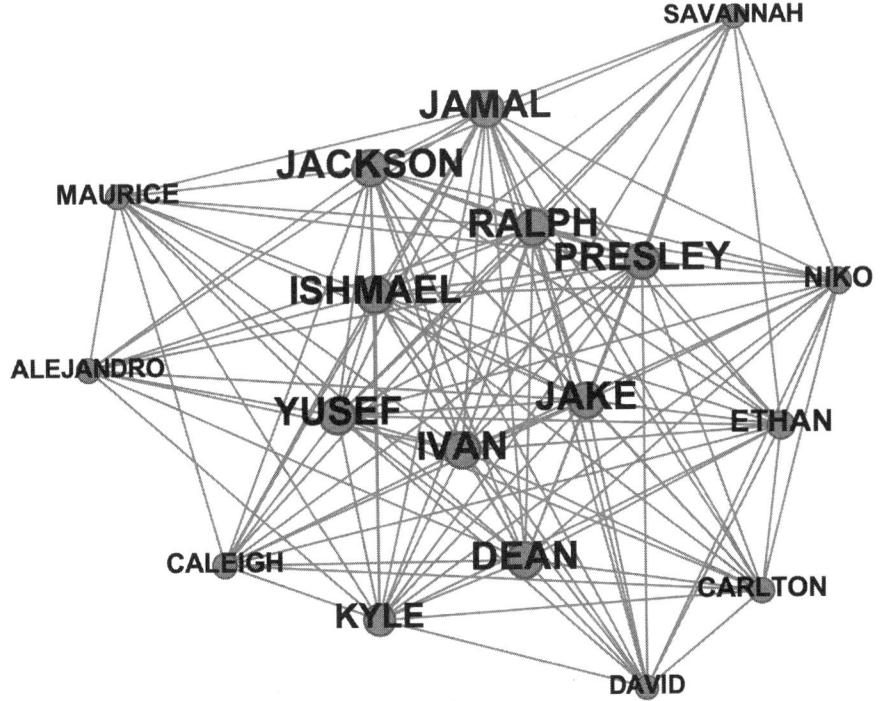

FIGURE 4.2. Yusef's friendship network, UNH year three.

it just seemed like he wasn't really engageful or trying to be friends. So I just let it be." Later that semester, in November, his roommate moved in with a friend "upstairs." Yusef then asked one of his friends from the football team to move in with him.

Yusef relied on his tight-knit group socially but not academically. He rarely studied with friends or talked about his classes with his friends. His friendship group was particularly meaningful for him in terms of his identity as a Black man and as someone who enjoys connecting with others and learning about them. In response to my question about whether he has changed because of friendships that he's made in college, he quickly replied, "Of course." Expanding on this point: "With every friendship you make, it's like another part of you gets exposed that you didn't know was there before. So, I feel like with every friendship I ever have, I always took a little bit from them." By this Yusef means that he learns, grows, and changes as a result of each new friend. Yusef is talking about himself and his identity as he talks about his friends, in line with the earlier discussion about friendship talk as identity work in chapter 2.[11] Each friend impacts his identity.

## ACADEMIC-SOCIAL BALANCE

Students at UNH, like those at Dartmouth, told me about a range of strategies they used to intentionally balance academic and social life. None of the MCC students discussing balancing academic and social life before I brought it up. Students at the residential campuses experienced more of a blending of academic and social life, and they typically felt they needed to be intentional about balancing these two spheres. Without being intentional, students were worried that they would become either "too social" or "too academic." Will, who entered UNH as a devoted computer science major, was worried about the latter. Will noted that he "too quickly" focuses on academics. He explained how he values both, and he makes sure to not tip too far toward academics. Will remarked: "I count being social and seeing my friends as really important in my life," noting that "if I'm not social, I'd probably go insane."

I asked each student to fill out a series of scales to compare themselves to other students, and these were markedly similar across the three campuses on the one that ranged from academic to social. With 0 as "academic" and "9" as social, UNH students rated themselves as 5.1, Dartmouth students as 5.0, and MCC students 4.7, on average. This was the only identity scale to come out squarely in the middle.[12] Given the differences I saw in students' academic and social experiences on the three campuses, I was struck by how, on average, students on each of these three campuses saw themselves similarly situated between academic and social. On all three campuses, students saw themselves as halfway between academic and social, on average. This resembles students' responses at the four-year "Midwestern University" in *Connecting in College*, suggesting that this may be a widespread, if not universal, goal of students.

At residential campuses students discuss spending time with friends as necessary to achieve balance in college. This came up at UNH as well as at Dartmouth. Abigail, a pre-vet student at UNH, was like Will in tipping to the academic side. She not only explained how seeing friends is important, but also noted that her friends push her to be more social: "They like having me around when it comes time to be serious about school. And I like having them around when it's time, especially on the weekends, to be social. 'Cause they know if I don't hang out with them, I'm probably gonna be in my room doing homework on a Saturday night." Rather than considering it unwanted pressure—at least most of the time—Abigail welcomes her friends' push to the social side. To Abigail, her friends complement her in their greater interest in the social aspects of the campus, and they help her achieve better academic-social balance.

## MAKING FRIENDS AT A LARGE PUBLIC UNIVERSITY

Students at UNH expressed seemingly opposite sentiments about making friends at a large public university: some said that finding where you fit can be easier with more people, and some said that the sheer size of the campus can be daunting. Sometimes both sentiments came up in the same interview. I am also struck that while students experienced this at UNH, a campus with 11,000 undergraduates, other campuses in the United States dwarf UNH in size. For example, there are almost six times as many undergraduates at Arizona State University as at UNH.[13]

May, who is studying business at UNH, is one of the students who felt intimidated by its size. When I asked her about her biggest social obstacle in college, she quickly responded:

> The amount of people that are here. There are so, so, so many people. So it's really hard at the beginning to find a group or your group. Whereas in smaller schools, where it's more like a high school, you see who people are, you see what they like and what they do, so it's easy to identify, these are people I connect to most in this way. So I'll go just introduce myself or something like that. But with a school like this, there's just so, so many different people that it's really hard to find those people.

Given the thousands of people on campus, students can find it hard to locate the ones who share their interests or values, the ones they want to "connect to most," as May put it.

Other students saw the size as having advantages, often related to homophily. The size provides more opportunities to find people with similar interests or identities because there are likely more people on campus who have those interests or identities. Daisy, for example, gave the following advice to a new UNH student:

> Join some organization [or] group or just find a niche. I know a lot of people push clubs, but, for me, work could be a sense of community as well. So finding where you fit in and finding people who like what you like. Whether it's going to series about racism on campus, and there's just a group of people who are all really committed about making campus inclusive, finding those people ... who like and are passionate about what you are. Since it's such a big school, you will find whoever you need to if you look in the right places.

Students also discussed that the larger student body meant that there were more activities to do and more "stuff going on" around campus. Daisy pointed this out: "Because we're a big school and we always have stuff going on, it really helps create friendships among people. Opposed to if I was at a little school, and I just wanted to sit in my room 24/7 'cause there was nothing to do, or everybody left on the weekends. A lot of people stay here. Just the campus-wide feel keeps people here and wanting to stay here and make friends." The activities happening around UNH's campus made it feel like a vibrant place to me, and one that would be welcoming to many students. In the next chapter, I delve into the experiences of students, especially those from marginalized backgrounds, who did not feel as welcome.

Being a residential campus, where students live, go to class, eat, attend meetings of clubs, study, and often work, means that students encounter other students all the time. The patterned ways that they do so on campus means that they often see the same people over and over again. Chris, a sociology major who lived with their parents, explained: "If I weren't in school, I definitely wouldn't have had the same avenues to meet people. And I'm not really the type of person to just go out and socialize with people. If I hadn't gone to school and just went straight to working, I'd probably just work and then go home and be by myself and isolate. I might have a couple close friends and online friends, but I would have had less of a social life. The campus climate has given me more of an avenue to meet people." Even though Chris does not live on campus, the campus is a residential one where students spend more time than they do at the community college. Natalie, an event-planning major who is in a sorority, expands on the "campus climate" that Chris referred to: "Being at school and kind of being on top of everybody, it was so much easier to connect with people because there's the different layers. So, you had the class friends, you have people you met at the parties, you had the people that you had clubs with or the different sororities. There was a lot of different opportunities to connect with people right in front of you." As a residential campus, UNH encourages—and expects—students to form friendships on campus. Propinquity gives students the opportunity to make and keep these connections as they see the same people around campus, particularly in spaces they regularly inhabit.

As discussed in chapter 1, clubs, pre-orientation programs, and dorms help students make friends on residential campuses, particularly during the initial friendship market that exists in the first few weeks of students' first year. Pre-orientation programs, like the outdoors- and volunteer-focused ones at UNH, help students make friends early on. These programs also help students get in the mode of being friendly and meeting people. Even if they do not make friends there, they are practiced for doing so in orientation and in their floor early on. Pre-orientation programs, however, are short-lived compared to the time that students are living on their first-year floor.

Propinquity makes students' first-year floor an important place to make friends at a residential campus. Often, I heard from students, "we became a big group of friends." However, this also makes it feel alienating to students when they do not click with their first-year floor. This experience is subject to some randomness in personalities. However, there are two things at UNH that decrease the tendency of students to click with their first-year floor.

The first is living in a single. Without a roommate, students are less likely to connect with others on their floor. Initially I found this surprising since I expected that people in singles would be more in need of connections on their floor, without a built-in potential friend in their room. However, being in a single also meant that you did not have a built-in friend who could go with you to floor events or ease the way into other friendships. It seems to make the barrier harder. Irina is one example of a student who lived by herself the first year and did not make friends on her floor. She noted that other students on her floor "have their own big groups, but I do get along with them," also noting they are "on good terms" but not friends. Students were often used to having their own room at home, so thought it would be useful to have their own space. However, it seemed to exclude them from some of the benefits of propinquity. Even when they kept their room doors open, students in singles were less often around when others were bumping into each other and making plans.

The second is that it is harder to make friends in a mixed-year dorm. As discussed in chapter 1, students at UNH had the option to live in first-year-only dorms or mixed-year dorms. Choosing a mixed-year dorm might seem like a useful way to make friends across class years, and occasionally that worked out or the small number of first-year students there bonded together. However, more often students reported feeling lonely, as they were expecting to make friends in the dorms and the non–first-year students were not because they already had friend groups. The friendship market was not widely open in these spaces.

A final way that propinquity shapes students' networks on residential campuses is through Greek life. Students not only join activities with their sorority sisters or fraternity brothers, but often live together in the house. Students bond together through the time they spend in formal activities as well as in informal time hanging out and studying in the house. Friendships formed through sororities and fraternities are an important part of many residential campus experiences. They also are sites of problematic and discriminatory behavior, often reinforced and hidden by friendship groups.[14] Several students I spoke with at UNH excitedly told me about helping to found a new sorority on campus. Even though they were not yet able to live there, the amount of time they spent together planning for the organization and engaging in activities together led to a number of new friendships.

These features also shape the network types that UNH students tend to form. The most common type at each campus, including UNH, was a compartmentalized network. Students tended to have two or three groups of friends, friends who know each other within the groups but not across them. For example, Rachel's friendship network, shown in figure 4.3, is divided into friends from home and friends from her sorority. Her friends from home stay in touch mainly through a group text. Grace (see figure 1.2), Morgan (see figure 1.4) and Otto (see figure 2.2) are also compartmentalizers, with networks discussed in earlier chapters.

About one-third of UNH students are tight-knitters, which means they form a dense cluster, often around a group on campus, such as their sorority or first-year floor. Their close friendships may be only within that group, or they might have close friends from other places that they introduce to that group, such as friends from home or work. Yusef's network, discussed earlier and shown in figure 4.2, provides one example of a tight-knit network mostly based on Yusef's campus friendships within the football team, along with friends from home whom he has integrated into that group. Robbie's tight-knit network (see figure 2.1) is discussed at the beginning of chapter 2. For tight-knitters like Yusef and Robbie, almost all of their friends end up knowing each other, which provides social support.

About one-fifth of my UNH sample are samplers, who have made a friend or two in a range of places across campus but have not connected these friends with each other. The students who are samplers at UNH often felt a lack of belonging with the campus and with peers,[15] and they lacked social support. While they had friends, the lack of connections between their friends meant that these ties each took effort to maintain, and often samplers focused on work or academic life at the expense of their friendship ties and social support. The students who had sampler networks did not find a supportive group during the initial friendship market, and the weak secondary markets at UNH made it hard for these students to make friendships later. While the more expansive networks of the samplers meant that they had bridging ties that could bring new information and other resources more easily than dense ties, the lack of a sense of a belonging and social support were significant challenges.

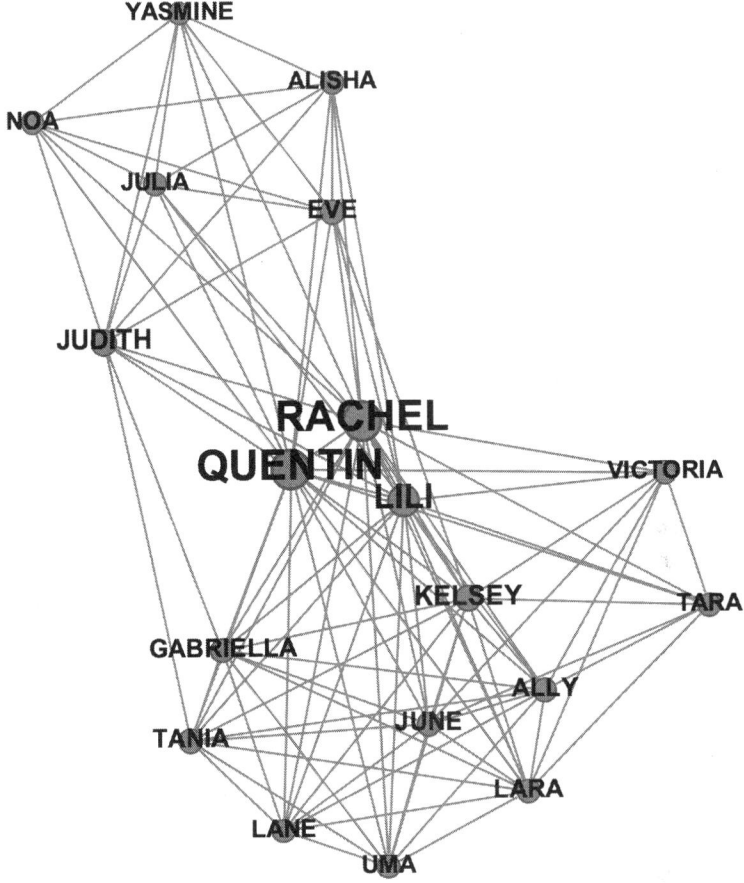

FIGURE 4.3. Rachel's friendship network, UNH year three.

## Dartmouth College: "The academics [are] impossible to survive without having close friends"

As an Ivy League school that is rated among the best colleges in the United States,[16] it may not be surprising that being a student at Dartmouth is an intense experience. When I started my research, I had been at Dartmouth for four years, and I had become accustomed to the fast rhythm of campus life there. It was the following year, when I was spending time at UNH and MCC, that I was struck by the difference.

Dartmouth is an intense place for students; intense both academically and socially. The students who attend are high achieving and are often used to being at the top of their class.[17] While a few of the students I spoke with described Dartmouth as not as challenging academically as they expected, most commented about the academic demands and intensity. Often in doing so, they brought in aspects of the importance—and the difficulty—of balancing this with equally intense social demands. For example, Danica exclaimed: "Everything moves so fast that I feel like we have to sacrifice interactions with others to do work."

Paradoxically, the things that intensify the social pressure at Dartmouth are the same things that students found appealing when choosing it. While students' decision-making process in choosing Dartmouth varied, often it included an escape from the city or, as Amanda put it, "I like the outdoors. It's really beautiful." Uma described her first visit: "I just fell in love with the campus and just felt like this was what a college should look like and what a college should feel like." Another student, Jodi, explained her decision: "After looking at other colleges in the Ivy League, I just fell in love with this place, just the whole atmosphere, what they stand for, and the quarter system. I just love being in the middle of nowhere." In fact, Dartmouth's motto since its founding in 1769 captures this well: "A voice crying out in the wilderness."[18]

This wilderness means that students' pool of friends is rather limited to the Dartmouth campus. When a college is in a city or near another college, students find themselves with opportunities to make friends more widely.[19] At Dartmouth, however, students' sense of belonging on campus was magnified because there were few alternatives. This can create deep and meaningful bonds among students. It also can lead to students feeling even more isolated and alone. These feelings of what Durkheim refers to as anomie were intensified even more during the pandemic when there was a suicide cluster on campus, as noted in an excellent sociology honors thesis at Dartmouth.[20] Students also refer to the insular campus culture here as "the Dartmouth bubble."

PROPINQUITY AND THE D-PLAN

The D-Plan, part of what Jodi referred to as "the quarter system," certainly shapes students' friendships. As discussed in earlier chapters on making, keeping, and losing friends, it shapes each of these processes. It makes it easier to form new friends after the friendship market as more students at Dartmouth than at a typical residential campus, like UNH, are looking for friends in their second and third years when their existing friends might be off campus. It makes it more challenging to keep friends because propinquity does not keep friends together as well throughout the four years. And it makes it easier to lose friends, which can be good if the friendship is not working well, but can be bad if the friendship is one that is meaningful but takes more work than the participants are willing or able to put into it.

Libby gave an insightful explanation of the difficulties that the D-Plan poses for friendship: "The test of a friendship can really be seen with a D-Plan, because (a), you're required to make new friends, if your friends are off or people who you [just] kind of thought of as friends are going to be close friends now, vice versa, or just people who maybe you're kind of close with, but you don't feel the need to stay in touch with them while you're not going to see them for two terms." Libby concludes that such people are "probably not going to be your lifelong friend" but may be someone that you end up being friends with because of convenience.

As mentioned in Amanda's experience that opens this chapter, according to the D-Plan, students are on campus together their first year, but they choose when to be on campus during their second and third years. This disrupts existing friendship networks. It also drives students to join Greek houses as a way not only to make friends, as happened at UNH, but also to have a network to return to on campus. In other words, joining Greek life gave students continuity on campus. Even if their closest friends remained off campus, they would have a place they belonged and a group of students to do things with each time they came back to campus.[21] Students joined Greek houses in their second year, and they typically lived in those houses for the first time in sophomore summer, which was the time period when I was speaking to them.

This meant that during sophomore summer, students were often getting closer to that group of friends. While joining a Greek organization can lead to new friends, it can also strain students' other friendships. Students talked about feeling "dumped" by their previous friends, not only when they first joined a Greek house, but especially when they lived there for the first time during sophomore summer. In the lore, "Camp Dartmouth" (another term for sophomore summer) is a time that students get really close with their friends. Because of this reputation, students were often surprised when their existing friends who were living in Greek houses for the first time were not getting closer to them, but were in fact distancing themselves. Sophomore summer is a time when it could feel particularly lonely to be unaffiliated, as discussed in more detail in chapter 5. It also can be isolating if you are not able to live in your sorority or fraternity because of the limited spots, so you are not able to build those deeper bonds because of limited propinquity compared to your sisters or brothers who live in the house together. There are several ways that Greek life can both isolate students and increase social belonging.

Going abroad can also shape students' networks. In the previous section, on UNH, I detailed how students make new friends abroad. That also happens at Dartmouth; however, since more students go abroad and they do so at different times, students are often in the position of needing new friends on campus.

Even if students themselves did not go abroad, their friends' schedules abroad and in internships and otherwise off campus change their own networks. I did not hear this from any students at UNH, but it came up multiple times at Dartmouth. Dartmouth students explained how this forces them to either expand their networks or be lonely. This expansion is not just to peripheral friends, but also to close friendships. Dani talked about how she had to "fill a void" when her "support system was gone" with her close friends not being on campus the prior winter term, so "I found a lot of other people who I grew closer with." Similarly, Melanie told me:

> I've developed a set of several best friends because of the D-Plan. At the end of my sophomore fall, I was very close with [Ryley and Connie] and a few other people, and they all left while I was on campus. I was like, "Uh, what's this void? I don't understand." And so I made close friends with a girl who's now one of my roommates [Susan]. She's definitely one of my best friends to this day. Then, when I was off campus, during my off terms, I lived with [Mikayla]. And she's absolutely one of my best friends at this point. All four of those people, I would say, are inner circle best friends. But definitely during different phases of Dartmouth.

Propinquity influenced who Melanie spent time with as well as who were her closest ties. She explained: "The people that I spent time with dramatically changed every term."

The disruption to friendship networks that the D-Plan structures forces students to be intentional regarding whom they connect with and not to rely on propinquity to fill the "void." That's the "test of a friendship" that Libby refers to above. It also can expand or deepen students' bonds with those they see regularly because of propinquity. In other words, students may expand their networks when they find themselves on campus without a friend group, as Amanda explained at the opening of this chapter. They also may deepen their relationship with the few friends who remain with them on campus when most of their friends are away. Tom, for example, described how he became closer to his best friend, Tucker, because he "was one of the few people here junior fall. I feel like we got very close as a result of that." As Dani put it, "the D-Plan is very interesting in both facilitating and impeding" friendships. It facilitates the formation of new friends and impedes students' ability to maintain existing friendships, requiring more intentionality than when propinquity brings them together seamlessly.

### DARTMOUTH ACADEMIC LIFE

Dartmouth students are high achievers, working to balance social life with the academic demands of an Ivy League school on ten-week quarters. Students balanced these competing demands by integrating academics into their friendships more than on the other two campuses and by relying on friends for academic support. As Jennifer told me, "The academics here make it impossible for people to survive without having close friends."

Danica noted that "the way that Dartmouth is, it really tears people apart. Everything moves so fast that I feel like we have to sacrifice interactions with others to do work." She describes these sacrifices as the daily decisions she makes about how to spend her time. For example, the night before our interview, she "had dinner with my best friend who was my freshman roommate." Danica described how they were "talking and having a good time. I really needed that so I can be happy, and I could recenter myself after all this stuff has been happening with all of these other communities." However, "I turned in my assignment late because I did it. I felt like it was worth it [laughs], of course, but it sucks that we have to decide between those two things." Having only ten weeks per term gives an intensity to academic life that a fifteen-week semester does not have. In the short quarter, Danica's decision to have dinner and a conversation with a friend "on a Monday night when that's when the week's starting" was a trade-off for Danica's grade.

The positive part of that is the greater number of multiplex ties at Dartmouth compared to UNH or MCC. More often than on the other campuses, Dartmouth students were engaging academically in some way with the friends they spent time with socially.

Most Dartmouth students' time is full with classes, clubs, and perhaps a job or two, so students end up studying together quite a bit, or at least being in the same space while doing classwork. For example, Tom told me how the night before our interview, he and his friends were working on a computer science assignment together, "just sitting down with our laptops," occasionally talking about the assignment, but mostly in the same space for company, for motivation, and because "it's more fun." As Dawn puts it, "everything's always better with a friend," including doing your homework.

## DARTMOUTH SOCIAL LIFE

While the rural setting, fast pace, and academic intensity of Dartmouth can help students bond with each other, it also can make students feel profoundly left out. Danica described Dartmouth as "this very, very hectic place where Greek life is important [and] athletes are gods." Students' lack of belonging was often related to their marginalized identities, and I delve deeper into this in the next chapter. Here, I focus more on other structural and cultural aspects of Dartmouth as an institution.

Students on all three campuses imagined that other students were having more fun than they were, yet feelings of loneliness are magnified in the wilderness. Layla explained, "Dartmouth gives an illusion within the social scene for students that the more friends you have, or the more people think you have friends, the cooler you are, or the more FaceTimey . . . That's a word, the more 'FaceTimey' you are." Such feelings are amplified by social media, with the curated life students can present on places like Instagram. Comparison has become never-ending with social media. Students, however, note that it is particularly hard at Dartmouth, especially when roommates or classmates are saying what a great time they are having at Dartmouth, and you are feeling lonely. Strikingly, a national survey finds Dartmouth students three times more likely than those on other campuses to say they would not talk to anyone if they "were experiencing serious emotional distress."[22]

The pressure to be social at Dartmouth and to engage in high-status activities, particularly Greek life, impacts many students. Chapter 1 includes a discussion of how Uma "joined [a sorority] mainly because everybody else was going through rush. And it seemed like a very Dartmouth thing. And it seemed like a very central part of the Dartmouth social scene to be in a Greek house. So, that's why I went through rush even though I absolutely hated rush." The picture Uma painted of getting swept up in rush sounds like the peer pressure created by the campus culture in the "party dorm" at a large public university.[23] It also sounds similar to the implicit pressure from the campus culture pushing students into finance and tech careers at Stanford and Harvard.[24] Despite the pressure to join what "were supposed to be fun things," Uma found herself "wish[ing] that I was spending the time with Ellie and Isabel," her two best friends who did not join. She de-pledged after realizing, "It never really felt like a comfortable place for me."

While joining a high-status Greek organization might appear as a solution to students' friendship troubles, students often found that it created new difficulties. In Dartmouth's student newspaper, a fourth-year student reflecting on her friendships over her college career wrote: "In my sophomore year, the twin forces of the rush process for Greek life and the D-Plan came along, changing my perception of my so-thought-to-be stable friendships. While some freshman year friend groups make it through these changes, there is the all too common occurrence of a friend group ending with a bang (my group ended with more of a whimper)."[25] Like the author in the student newspaper, students often found that, despite joining to have a "solid base" of friends, Greek life destabilized their existing friendships. Given the instability created by the D-Plan, many students' friendships changed, whether with a "bang" or a "whimper," because of structural aspects of the campus.

Sports teams pose both advantages and disadvantages for making friends, and the high proportion of varsity athletes at Dartmouth makes this a significant division in the social scene. Like Greek life, the proportion of students involved in varsity sports is significantly higher at Dartmouth than at UNH. This can intensify the pressure to join, as can be seen with Uma, and can also create strong division between who is affiliated and who is not. Dartmouth students often used the term "NARP" to label themselves and others as a "Non-Athlete Regular Person."[26] Organizations also differ in terms of status, which can leave nonmembers feeling marginalized, often those who are already from historically marginalized groups.[27] For those who enter college on a varsity sports team, they begin the friendship market with a group of friends, as discussed in chapter 1. That helps them feel like they belong from the beginning. But if those relationships do not work well later on, they may not have many friends to fall back on. The D-Plan seems to counter this a bit by making it easier at Dartmouth than at UNH to make new friends midway through college through joining a new club, for example.

Students at Dartmouth reported more "close friends," in the next level out from their "closer friends," than did those on the other two campuses. Students' descriptions suggest that the intensity of social life and the D-Plan expanded their number of these weaker ties. Some of these were due to sports teams; for example, Austin told me he had fifty friends in this next level, most of whom were on the varsity football team with him, while Jenna's fifty friends were also mostly from her varsity swim team. These are examples of bonding social capital, given their focus on similarities and inward-looking characteristics. In contrast, Dani said she had thirty to fifty friends in this next level, which included her "camp friends" from the summer camps she attended growing up, her older sister's friends, and some from her sorority and from high school. Dani's network was more outward looking, with more possibilities of bringing in different resources. Both types of social capital can be valuable; bonding social capital in helping students feel supported, and bridging social capital in accessing a range of resources.[28]

Dorms are another structural feature of Dartmouth's social life that impacts friendships. While dorms encourage friendships through propinquity and homophily, they also facilitate diverse friendships for some students. At Dartmouth, first-year students were assigned a roommate based on students' answers to a pre-matriculation survey about sleeping and study habits. Students told me how they likely would not have crossed paths with their roommate because they often appeared to be quite different, yet they became friends through living together. Propinquity brought them together regularly, and they discovered things they had in common that were not surface-level. Thus a "random roommate" assignment was not completely random because it was based on commonalities in their survey responses to questions like whether they study in their room, wake up early, and are tidy. In this Dartmouth differs from UNH and many other schools that allow students to pick their own roommates. In picking roommates before they arrive on campus, students are relying on existing networks (social capital) and, particularly when they meet on a Facebook group, surface-level homophily. Thus, Dartmouth is encouraging more diverse networks through this institutional feature of the housing policy. In a study of Bowdoin College, researchers similarly concluded that first-year housing policies, specifically assigning roommates, stand out in how they constructed "diverse" floors and "seeded some lasting friendships."[29]

## CAMPUS ORGANIZATIONS AND NETWORK TYPE

While compartmentalizers are the most common type at each institution, I find the most compartmentalizers at Dartmouth. The D-Plan, the academic and social intensity, and the tendency of students to be intensely involved in organizations all encourage compartmentalized networks. Some of my faculty colleagues refer to Dartmouth students as "dabblers," and while that fits the data in some respects, it does not capture the intensity with which they throw themselves into activities. They do each of these different activities with serious intention. The duration, however, is uncertain and often not long-lasting.

Danica, who had a sampler network both times I interviewed her, explained how her friendships took shape over college:

> The community that I have found have been all the people that I've kind of just cherry picked along the way that are friends with each

other. It's been really weird mixing those groups. So, I have my athlete friends still, I have my friends on the field hockey team, and the soccer team, and the swim team that are very much like A-side [in a top sorority], wealthy, White, wonderful individuals. . . . Then I have my very-within-themselves, semi-insular Latinx folks who are all friends with each other.

Both groups (that is, the "A-side, wealthy, White" friends and the "semi-insular Latinx folks") are small (three people each). These small groups, along with an additional unconnected friend, result in a low-density network that provides weak social support for Danica, as is characteristic of sampler networks.

Students' involvement in clubs and organizations is another factor shaping their friendship network, with heavy involvement in a couple of organizations encouraging compartmentalized networks. At UNH, students tended to pick a couple of clubs and stick with them more, fitting more with tight-knit networks.[30] In contrast, Dartmouth students seemed to jump around more, which fits more closely with sampler or compartmentalized networks. In chapter 2, which focuses on making friends, there are several good examples of compartmentalized networks at Dartmouth since it is the most common network type. These include the networks of Kira (figure 2.4) and Bill (figure 3.1) during college.

Many students end up as compartmentalizers or tight-knitters because of their experiences in orientation and pre-orientation programs. For example, Dawn noted that she made friends quickly in international student orientation, and "I kept most of my friends through orientation." Dawn observed that at the start of her first year, "everybody is trying to make friends, but that settles down in a few weeks," yet "I just stuck with that group and we're still the same core group now, two years later." Jorge's compartmentalized network included two groups: one from Trips and the other from international student orientation. About the latter, he noted, "We had a week before everybody else got to campus where we just did events all day, so we got to know each other pretty well then."

Students' experiences show that campus structures shape their friendship networks. As relational sociology suggests, students' agency also shapes the networks they form. Pairing quantitative measures and mapping of network structure with qualitative measures of students' experiences and meanings across three postsecondary institutions sheds new light on the value of friendship. It also reveals much about how friends can matter on the path to academic and social success, and how this path is shaped by the structure of each postsecondary institution.

## Takeaways

For students:

1. If you have not yet made the friends you are looking for, there are opportunities to do so, drawing on the structure of the campus you attend. How campuses are organized can make aspects of friendships harder or easier. In other words, it may not be a personal failing in your friendship skills or likability.
2. If you find yourself at a school where there is a change in which students are present term to term, there are likely strong secondary friendship markets. These secondary markets provide opportunities to make new friends, either when you find yourself on campus without friends or wanting to make new or different friends for any reason. However, these disruptions also make propinquity less powerful with existing friendships, which means that keeping friends requires more intentionality (see chapter 2).
3. If you find yourself at a school that has weak secondary markets, where the initial friendship market is the main opportunity to make friends, seek out the secondary markets. You must be more intentional in finding these opportunities to make friends through clubs and activities, particularly those that meet regularly (see chapter 1).

For parents and other supporters:

1. Students have opportunities to make friends throughout their time in school. Yet, how campuses are organized can make aspects of friendships harder or easier.
2. Help your child identify whether their campus is one where there are strong secondary friendship markets. If so, making new friends is easier, but maintaining existing friendships may be more challenging on this campus.
3. To capitalize on the existing secondary markets, encourage your child to attend activities or events that they are interested in and that meet regularly. Encourage them to be open to meeting people and intentional about following up with the people they meet, inviting them to an activity or meal (see chapter 1).

For colleges:

1. Knowing that propinquity helps friendships to form and ties to remain means that investing resources to support continuity in residential life, clubs, and class schedules will help make these processes easier.
2. When propinquity brings people together, relationships can feel effortless. This means that students may stay in unhealthy relationships when propinquity makes it easy. Help them understand that structural changes may mean that friendships that were once easy now require work, and help them reflect on whether those friendships warrant that work.
3. Support and encourage the development of secondary friendship markets, which facilitate students more easily making new friends past the first few weeks of their first term on campus. High-status activities were troublesome secondary markets as students frequently felt social pressure to join and even greater loneliness and rejection after they experienced rejection from members. Effective secondary friendship markets include clubs and organizations that meet regularly and involve a project or collaborative work.
4. Assign roommates rather than allowing students to choose their own. This will encourage deeper relationships between people from different backgrounds. It disrupts surface-based homophily and draws on propinquity to help students craft meaningful friendship across difference. Also provide resources to staff and students for how to interact across difference, so that the burden does not lie with the minoritized student to make this relationship work.
5. While mixed-year dorms may seem like good opportunities for first-year students to make friends with students who have been on campus longer, unless there is an open friendship market, these relationships will not happen. Supporting activities and spaces that encourage students to get to know each other and spend time together regularly will encourage these connections.

[ CHAPTER FIVE ]

# Student Identities: How Race, Class, and Gender Shape Networks

Sitting in a private study room in Dartmouth's library, Danica described moving from an urban area in the South to a small college in rural New Hampshire as a "culture shock." [1] Identifying as a "light-skinned, Latina[2] woman" who attended a high school that was "half Latino, half Black," Danica noted that this was "the first time" she felt like a minority, a feeling that "became very real very quickly" at the predominantly White college.

Used to feeling comfortable in these minority spaces, Danica attended the first Latinx event that she heard about, a club meeting. Danica was surprised to feel "shunned" and "rejected" in this space. She recalled the moment she experienced how she was used to "being Latino" as not fitting the accepted way at Dartmouth:[3] "I can't talk in Spanish with everyone" and "I can't blast music in Spanish like I would anywhere else because I would get looks." She summed up her experience as "made to feel uncomfortable in spaces that are supposed to be safe and accepting."

Feeling "shunned" rather than accepted among other Latinos, Danica felt she "had to pack that part of my identity away," and she turned to her varsity sport teammates for friendship. However, she felt they "automatically rejected" her, explaining that "the team is very clique-y." Despite spending "two hours each day" with them at practice, Danica did not feel included. She described the disappointment of "seeing them on Snapchat or their Instagram where they go get ice cream or go out to [dinner together], and I'd never get an invite. I asked some of them, the ones I really like, to get lunch with me, and they do. Even then, I'm not invited to the social events or anything like that." She summed up her experiences with her teammates: "my social dynamics with them have always been terrible."

Danica tried other clubs as well, capitalizing on the secondary friendship markets at Dartmouth.[4] In her words, she would "dabble" in different communities on campus. For example, she joined parliamentary debate, "but didn't like the format. I wasn't crazy about the people either." With these other clubs not working out, Danica kept interacting with and hoping to make friends with those in the Latinx community and on her varsity sports team.[5]

In addition, Danica saw joining a sorority as a path to feel a greater sense of belonging and make friends on campus. In the fall of their second year, Dartmouth students can join Greek organizations, and Danica signed up for sorority rush. Danica described herself as "very, very excited. I was so excited about this process."

She was looking forward to rush, even though she "had also gotten a lot of heat for it from the Latino community, for rushing, because it's a White thing to do." When I asked what she meant by "heat," Danica explained how her Latinx peers criticized her: "'Why are you assimilating? Why are you fitting into the Dartmouth culture?'" As she continued in sorority rush, she responded to her Latinx peers in her head, repeating: "You don't let me fit into the one that I am part of already, so don't get mean for me wanting to try to find something else."

Despite feeling hopeful that joining a sorority would be how she could fit in, Danica ended up feeling more left out. She described rush: "It was very overwhelming. It's speed dating. I kid you not. I talked to at least twenty-five girls. And I was exhausted by the end of the day." Danica found it disappointing, because her hard work did not result in her finding a community. She told me, "I didn't get any of the houses that I wanted. I did get one [house invite] . . . but decided to drop because of the social status of the house." She said, "It's all a social hierarchy and I refuse for Dartmouth to label me a loser." Danica went on, "I felt that the house that did give me a bid would've labeled me a loser, and I'd rather have no social capital than a bad rep." She let out a big sigh and told me this outcome was "very disappointing." In particular, she feared what her social life would look like in "sophomore summer," when there were fewer students on campus and many of those lived in their Greek houses, noting that "being not affiliated makes [summer] a very, very lonely and a terrible thing."[6] Danica explained the divide that she felt this would create between her and the friends she was working to build as "all of them" would be invited to weekly sorority events "every Wednesday, Friday and Saturday nights," but she would not, noting that this "really bummed me out."

Danica did not get a clear answer for why she did not end up "matching" at any of the houses she wanted to join, yet class seems to be one issue. Danica told me that class influences her interactions on campus, sometimes in ways people can easily see and other times in more subtle ways. One way "you can definitely see" class divisions is through "the Canada Goose thing," as she described it. She exclaimed, "You don't need an $800-plus jacket up here. It's just a symbol of status. It's a symbol of wealth. You can see who has it and who doesn't. And that's the divide."[7] Other markers of class inequality include how students spend their time during breaks between terms, working versus vacationing, and how often and how easily they can go out to dinner in town rather than in the dining hall.[8]

As Danica put it, "race, ethnicity, and income are very real barriers. Very, very real. I know that there's some groups of people here that I will never talk to just because their Dartmouth bubble and their Dartmouth experience is defined by class and by race." Danica explained the cost of friendship across these divides in more detail than did most participants. Often, students told me that friendships within their racial and class groups felt "easier." Danica elaborated on this point, describing friendships with White upper-class students as "pretty exhausting. I'm not against teaching them. I'm not against letting them know about my narrative. I'm not against any of that. It's just exhausting having to do it. It's exhausting having to explain myself. It's exhausting hearing them say something that is slightly problematic. In fact, having to explain to them why it's problematic and then even having them maybe not understand." In our first interview, she referred to some friends as "wealthy, White, wonderful individuals"; however, by the second interview, Danica had grown to feel more distant from these ties. She told me, "I don't have a White friend because they don't understand me and it's very exhausting." She explained, "Of course, I haven't given up on it, but there's multiple barriers for me to even get to that level" where she would interact with someone from that group. Although Dartmouth is statistically diverse in terms of race and students may sit in the same classrooms and dining halls, that does not mean that they interact with each other.[9] As a light-skinned Latina who does "not have the big thick black coarse hair," she is better able to fit in, "to move in White spaces a lot easier than a lot of my [Latinx] peers." She describes her parents coming into wealth for a few years but being "poor" both before and after those years. These experiences allowed Danica to know what it was like, for example, "to be in a submarine off the coast of Hawaii" and to "not have food on the table and not be able to afford internet." She noted, "I find myself in this very weird position where I feel like I'm a part of both worlds, yet I'm rejected from both of them." She felt like she did not fit in among the White, wealthy students on campus, including those in the sororities she sought to join, or with the Latinx community at Dartmouth.

After her first year on campus, Danica went home for the summer, and "I realized just how much I missed being myself." Through going home, she noticed that she "just had to pack that part of my identity away" at Dartmouth. So, when she came back to campus, "I was in the Latino fashion show this past Friday, and that's probably the happiest I have been here since I got here, and it was because I was able to be me. I was able to express being Latina, and speaking Spanish, and dancing, and being part of who I was again. To be Tex-Mex and just be myself for the first time." Danica again attempted to make friends with Latinx students and participate in Latinx events.

Danica ended our first interview by telling me, "I'm trying to manage these three social circles that aren't necessarily the best. Trying to develop healthy and genuine relationships is very hard." She lamented, "I know that I'm not a terrible person. I know that I can make friends. But I'm just, like, why don't I have more?" Danica wanted more close friendships at college. The three circles she referred to are the Latinx community, her varsity sports team, and the sororities she tried to join. Her friendship network in this first interview is shown on the first panel of figure 5.1, and it includes three friends in the Latinx community (Lizzie, Chris, and Yolanda), as well as four friends she did not make at Dartmouth.

When I interviewed Danica again as she was getting ready to graduate, she described the ups and downs of the past two years: "My junior fall and winter were really bad because I was dealing with the [romantic] breakup and she had become my best friend . . . It was a very dark time. I would say it's probably the darkest time I had at Dartmouth." She also "re-rushed" and "put in the work," explaining that she "became really good friends with the rush chair" and got to know numerous other women. Yet, she still did not get in. Danica explained: "I don't know who, I'm not allowed to know" who voted against her bid at that house. She wondered if she did not get in because she did not "have the clout, the label, the social capital." She believed if she had gotten into a "good house," then "I would have had everything I wanted." Danica felt like the second rejection was harder, she was "more angry," and "I lost it. Oh, I was livid forever. I was very angry the entire term." The rejection felt harder a second time when "I actually put in the emotional and social work to get this, only for it to be taken away."

Her friendships continued to change, yet it seemed that in her fourth year at Dartmouth Danica finally felt like she belonged. "Will I say I found community? No. But I made it. I think that's just as good. I'm content in it." After being away from campus on off-terms spring and summer of her third year,[10] she quit her varsity team, primarily because of the strained connections with her teammates. She explained, "I was finding fulfillment in every single way aside from socially. . . . They were not my friends. I didn't feel comfortable with them. I just felt like I couldn't be myself." Danica said that

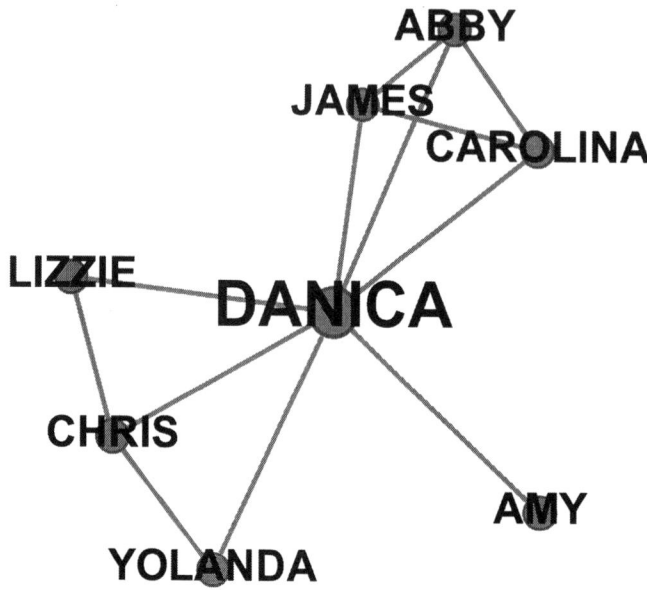

FIGURE 5.1. Danica's friendship networks, Dartmouth year two (above) and at graduation (on the next page). Note: asterisks indicate they remained friends.

they "are not friends. We're all cordial, and I mean that in, like, if I'm walking on the sidewalk, we say hello. But getting lunch, texts, phone calls, going out, nothing. And I am more than okay with that. There was a lot of hurt in that entire experience." She also reflected on the differences between how she expected to be involved in Greek life and how her experiences unfolded: "I like the competitive aspect of pong, and that's how I enjoy Greek spaces. I've realized and accepted that's all they offer me. The friendships I've found [and] the communities that I've found have all been outside of those houses."

Sampler networks are particularly lonely when students seek a different type of network. For example, Danica's sampler network felt lonely, even when individuals within it were supportive. Danica told me: "senior year has been probably the best year I've ever had at Dartmouth. My communities and my friendships are not what I thought they would be and not what I wanted them to be, but they're exactly what I need them to be. Everyone in my life fulfills a different role in a different aspect of my personality." Her description of her friendships was full of these different personalities. She described introducing some of her friends who did not know each other and "who would have never met otherwise if it wasn't for me. It felt like a crossover episode. I'm, like, 'What's happening?' You two are touching

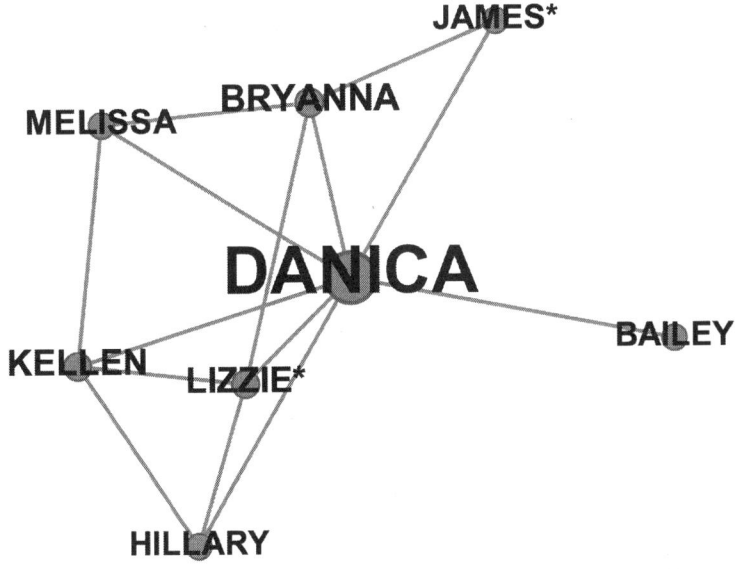

FIGURE 5.1. (continued)

lives when I'm the bridge. It's very weird." Danica's friendship network at graduation is above in figure 5.1.

The loose connection of her network reflects the race-based marginalization she experienced on campus and feelings of not belonging in several groups on campus, including her varsity sports team, sororities, and the Latino community. Danica's sampler network left her feeling lonely. Because her friends were not well connected to each other, she did not feel the strong sense of social support characteristic of tight-knit networks, yet the close friendships that Danica developed over her four years provided some buffer against this loneliness. Danica's first-year roommate, Lizzie, "is my best friend, my sister, like I will tear a building down brick by brick for her." Danica described her jealousy and then pride in seeing Lizzie "come into her herself more, I saw her grow." Lizzie and Danica's brother, James, were her two consistent friends across the two interviews. At graduation, Danica also felt emotionally close with Melissa. She described the emotional give and take in their friendship: "I went and held Melissa's hand when she got an IUD," and "if I'm emotionally needy, she knows that I just need company, so she opens up her room to me. I've slept on her floor." They see each other nearly every day, watching TV (*Game of Thrones* was their current choice) and meeting up on campus together, especially for meals. They stay in touch in between on social media: "We send tweets to each other all the time." Compared to the deep loneliness Danica expressed in her first interview, when I spoke to her the second time, it was mixed with gratitude for some deep connections: "I really, really like and appreciate our friendship."[11]

Danica told me how she was often comparing her sampler network to the tight-knitter network that she yearned for, one that our culture often idealizes. As mentioned above, she "realized and accepted" that she did not find her friendship group in Greek spaces or in her varsity sports team or squarely in the Latinx community on campus. Yet, she still compared herself. Even though Danica was conscious that she was comparing herself to others whom she saw as having an easier time or better friendships, she still found these comparisons challenging: "I thought that my friendships had to look like the friendships that everyone else had. A lot of people have their herd, their little crowd, and it's very hard to break into those crowds. I tried for a very long time. But I just kind of realized that I thrive off of being with people that aren't like me. I don't get bored, I learn something new, and they fulfill different aspects of me that, like, Dartmouth doesn't give me a space to do." Instead of the "herd" or tight-knit network of one group of friends, Danica found social support through patching together friendships from a range of places on campus. She described how she crafted a sampler network, plus other "weak tie" friends, after finding that the space she wanted on campus "doesn't exist": "So, I've learned to take up space and be in spaces that aren't necessarily physical, but I can still create. I can move in more White spaces with my more elitist White, wealthy, well-off friends, but I can also still satisfy my ethnic identity with my Latinx friends, and, like, we go to the Latino House, or we go to their room, or we go to OPAL [multicultural center], and we find a space, a physical space, even if it's just our own room, to be ourselves and really express that part of me." While sampler networks can feel lonely, they also can enable students to connect with multiple aspects of their identities, one relationship at a time.

As Danica's experiences demonstrate, making friends at college involves navigating race, class, and other identities. Her experience also shows that it can be difficult to disentangle how a single identity matters, thus necessitating an intersectional approach. Students are not defined by just one of their identities, but they are individuals composed of multiple identities that vary in their salience over time and in different contexts. Danica did not experience a smooth time in the initial friendship market, and she was intentional about reaching out during several secondary friendship markets. Yet, it was not until much later in college that she was able to craft friendships that she felt supported her, which she described as "genuine and healthy relationships."

Danica's story shows the isolation students can experience because of a marginalized identity on a predominantly White and elite campus. Danica's sampler network provided her with some important one-on-one friendships, but not the widespread support of the tight-knit networks that she often compared herself to. Danica's story also shows how bonding with peers based on this marginalized identity can be a source of belonging, yet it also is not a panacea. Indeed, it can bring its own challenges. The role of homophily in shaping friendships and bonding social capital is the focus of the next section. The following section discusses some of the identity-related challenges within friendship networks, including hostile ignorance from friends. I end the chapter by describing some additional characteristics of students' networks, particularly how gender shapes network structures.

## Homophily and Bonding Social Capital

While many students whom I interviewed mentioned expecting or wanting to connect with people unlike themselves, diverse friendship networks were not as common or as easy as students expected.[12] When finding themselves at a new place, students often expressed wanting a sense of the familiar or home. In response, students formed homophilous friendship bonds. Such bonds are often noticed among students of color, but happen among other groups as well, including White students, as noted in a bestselling book.[13] They develop bonding social capital, which refers to the social and psychological support from people through these homophilous ties.[14] When UNH student Yusef explains how his friends who are minorities "stick together" and "give each other support," he is describing this bonding social capital.

Jennifer's experience highlights how a tight-knit and homophilous friendship group can offer multiple benefits of bonding social capital, including social support and support for academics. As discussed in chapter 2, the term "multiplex ties" refers to the multiple ways friends are connected to each other, such as sharing academic advice, intellectual discussions, and social support. Jennifer is a Latinx student at Dartmouth with multiplex ties within her tight-knitter network. Although most tight-knitters build their friendships around identity-based groups, Jennifer was the only one in my sample who did this the year before she arrived on campus. Jennifer's first experience at Dartmouth was at the admitted students weekend, where she clicked with her host, Lucia. She said, "I really liked my host, who is now my best friend here. She was also from LA, so she knew what the transition would be like." Jennifer said, "I was really lucky. It was super easy for me

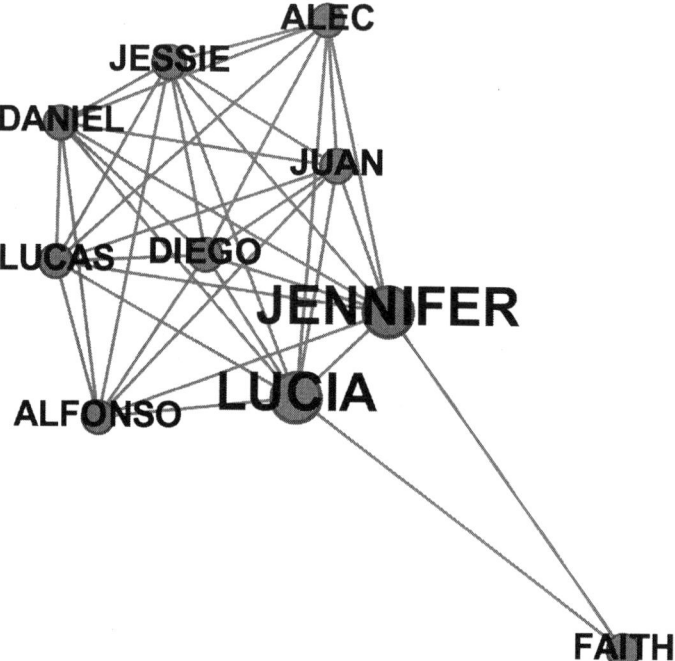

FIGURE 5.2. Jennifer's friendship networks, Dartmouth year two (above) and at graduation (on the next page). Note: asterisks indicate they remained friends.

to make friends here" because she had this already-made friendship group. Lucia's friends became Jennifer's friends, as shown in figure 5.2.[15] Jennifer described Lucia's friends as "really excited to meet me because I was Latina from LA and they're like, 'Oh my god, me too.'" Lucia also lived in the Latinx House on campus, which helped Jennifer feel immediately at home there.

Jennifer lit up when she told me about the intellectual discussions she had with friends. She called her friends "brilliant," commenting that "they know so much." She described how "all my most important learning has happened outside of the classroom, through conferences or discussions with friends." Jennifer noted that "a lot of it happens naturally . . . just because my friends are so passionate about what I'm passionate about. It's something that's on our minds." So they discuss it.

They also just enjoy each other's company. For example, when I asked Jennifer about the last time she spent with a friend, it was with Lucia the previous night. Jennifer told how "I was about to go to bed, and then my friend Lucia texted me, 'Do you want to go to McDonald's?'" Lucia said that another friend in the Latinx House would drive them in forty minutes. Jennifer explained, "I was like, 'Ugh, I'm in bed, but I want McDonald's. Okay.'

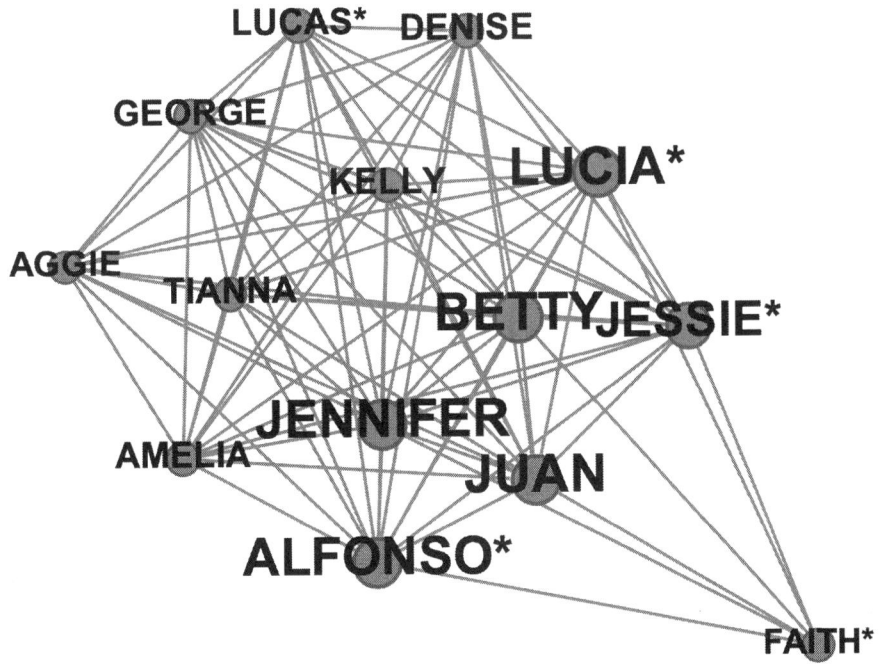

FIGURE 5.2. (continued)

I got up, I got dressed, I went downstairs, and they were doing homework. Four other friends, too. And then we all just went to McDonald's at 1:00 a.m. It was great." Jennifer described herself as someone who "need[s] to be around people . . . I tend to put my social stuff first because I know that's what keeps me going, mentally, and keeps me okay here." She explained that being social and being with friends is "how I feel better." Later in the interview, she said, "I cannot imagine a whole day where I don't go and hang out with my friends." Jennifer experienced joy from her friendships.[16]

Jennifer described a tremendous amount of social support from her friends. Along with the emotional support of knowing what it is like to be from a marginalized background ("they understand that"), she detailed the practical ways they support each other: "We all try to support each other. We see when each other are struggling. Yeah. Like, I've had a difficult last week, and then last week my friends have been, like, 'Do you need me to bring you tea?' 'If you have the flu, I can bring you tea. Just text me, and I'll go to Novack and I'll bring it to you.' Or, 'Do you want me to bring you food?' 'Do you need me to come upstairs?' 'Do you need to talk?' So I think that that's what we have in my friendship group." She summed it up by saying, "I have a group of people that I can depend on, who I can call if

I need them." Jennifer added: "The academics here make it impossible for people to survive without having close friends... friendship is the one thing that keeps people going. Especially minorities. People who are not used to this type of environment and who are so closely connected to home, where there's a lot of pressure. You're here because your family worked so hard for you to come here." Her friends encourage each other through "knowing that we're all struggling together. That we all have that same feeling of like, 'I want to go home. I don't know if I want to be here.' Or, 'I'm scared. What if I don't get a job after this?' Like, all those same fears that we can all relate on, so we know it's not just us."

Friends also provide that support academically. Jennifer described how her friends "check in on each other, like, Are you okay? If you're struggling in this class, let me help you. If you need to talk to your prof, you can do that." Jennifer also explained that "in my friend group we encourage each other to get our work done. Because we know how rigorous it is." She went on to say, "A real friend would [laughs] not let you just not do your work." Academic pressure—positive (as described here) or negative—is most powerful in tight-knit networks like Jennifer's. Friends are more able to exert control when it comes from a group rather than just one (or a few) individuals.[17]

Throughout her time at Dartmouth, both race and class have been identities in which Jennifer has felt marginalized, and she processed those experiences and found support for them with friends. Jennifer remarked that racial or ethnic similarity does not mean that someone will be able to support her—for example, not all Latinos will be able to "relate to [her] financial struggles," it depends "on what class you come from." While Jennifer's friendship group started with Lucia and participating in Latinx organizations on campus, it also includes a group of low-income, first-generation students who work at one of the cafés on campus. Jennifer mentioned that "those groups overlap a lot, so all my friends know each other." These dense ties are shown visually in both sociograms in figure 5.2.

Like Jennifer and Danica, Nella recognized how both race and class influence her friendship ties. Nella, a Black and Latinx first-generation college student, formed a tight-knit friendship group at UNH with other students from marginalized backgrounds. Nella noted that she met most of these friends in campus programs for low-income, first-generation, or students of color. These happened during the initial friendship market, specifically at UNH's two-week orientation program for these groups, as well as the secondary friendship market, at the multicultural center on campus and in an organization for Black engineering students. Nella described one of these friendships, with Sammy, as being one where we can "relate" and "we talk a lot about our experience being first gen and underrepresented." Nella felt that these similarities "made our friendship really develop faster because we could connect in that way and be stronger because we relate and we have so many same experiences." Jennifer, Danica, and Nella all have high levels of bonding social capital in their friendships.

Bonding social capital helps students deal with microaggressions. Research has documented the importance for "self-preservation" of students of color and other minoritized groups of bonding together in what may appear to be "self-segregation."[18] Troy, a Black student at Dartmouth, explained the support that other Black students provide: "We can offer that support . . . because a lot of us have gone through the experience of either failing or having to work three times as hard" because of the high schools they went to before, and hearing their White peers say things like, "It's not that you're not smart. It's that you're smart in different things than what other people are smart in." Like many other microaggressions, this is presented as a compliment but implies that their intelligence is unusual and perhaps unexpected. Troy noted that his Black friends were able to understand this feeling and offer empathy without him needing to explain. The "sense of home" such ties provided were crucial to students' feeling a sense of belonging on campus. They also countered the "exhaustion" of always having to explain yourself, as Danica put it, with a sense of comfort and ease.

Among the students I interviewed, some did make close friendships across difference. Although these friendships were important and meaningful, they often were not comfortable or easy. During our interview, they also expressed wishing that they had homophilous ties with others from minoritized backgrounds. One example was Kira, a Black student at Dartmouth, who brought up how she did not have a group of Black women friends. Kira lamented: "I wish that I'd made more friends that were Black women when I came into Dartmouth." She described how for the class below her (juniors) and "I'm sure for other classes as well, they all know each other and are friends with each other. . . . I wish I had had that because that's not something I have ever had: a group of Black female friends. So I guess it's not something that I necessarily missed, so much as it's just that I never had it and [it] would be interesting to know what it's like." In our interview, Kira described how she joined clubs and organizations, including a sorority, to make friends, but did not intentionally seek out Black women friends.[19]

Bonding social capital can bring students together based on a variety of interests and identities, not only in response to the isolation experienced by marginalized groups. As mentioned in chapter 1, homophily based on interests as well as identities bonds students together and facilitates the formation of friendships. Dani, an upper-class White and Jewish woman at Dartmouth, described the role that identities play in her friendships:

> I think that it's really hard to admit that, because I don't think it happens consciously, but I look at my friends and a lot of them are upper-class, Jewish, White girls. I went to a diverse high school, and my two best friends are upper-class, Jewish, White girls. I think that it's just, like, finding similarities and cultural similarities. I think one of the biggest connections for me is actually Judaism. So I'm Jewish, and I found that a lot of my friends here are Jewish. And not that I can only be friends with Jews because of the religion, I just think that the cultural way that we're brought up, our values, our tendencies, just the way we act towards other people: very outgoing, inquisitive, very open, sharing. And they, along those lines, tend to be more privileged and White girls. Yeah. But I would never say that it's impossible to make friends that are not that. And I do think that naturally people gravitate towards certain things.

Similarity brings a sense of comfort and home for many students, such as Dani. Rather than having different identity-based groups as the clusters, Dani was a compartmentalizer with two clusters of friends that both consisted primarily of other upper-class White, Jewish women. One cluster she met at Dartmouth, and another was formed eight to ten years earlier at summer camp. While Dani's experience of bonding is not based on feelings of not belonging, she was nonetheless able to feel more comfortable and connected by the sense of familiarity with friends.

## Bridging Social Capital

Researchers distinguish between the support provided by bonding social capital and the new information and perspectives provided by bridging social capital.[20] Some students have both bridging and bonding social capital in their friendship networks. Tight-knitters have high levels of bonding social capital, but vary in their levels of bridging social capital. Samplers have high levels of bridging social capital, and most have low levels of bonding social capital. Thus, samplers often have bridging social capital to facilitate new opportunities, yet they also feel isolation and lack of belonging on campus.

The high levels of bonding social capital and varying levels of bridging social capital are illustrated through the experiences of Troy and Jennifer.

Both Troy and Jennifer are tight-knitters, and both described the strong sense of support they felt from their friendship networks in line with high levels of bonding social capital.[21] Both have predominantly, but not exclusively, same-race friends: 84 percent of Troy's friends are other Black students, and 89 percent of Jennifer's friends are other Latinx students. Troy's high levels of bonding social capital, however, are complemented by high levels of bridging social capital, while Jennifer has lower levels of the latter. Along with talking about their "closer friends" during the interview, I asked students about the number of friends in their "next level" of friendships. Troy estimates that would include sixty friends, compared to Jennifer's ten. This meant that Troy had lots of ties on campus that he could reach out to for information about classes, internships, and many other issues.

Concerned about the insularity of bonding social capital, some people express alarm that people from marginalized groups are "sticking together" at a high cost for themselves and society. Some worry that these college students, by only hanging out with students in their own group, are not getting the benefits of connecting with more highly resourced individuals on campus, including peers.[22] Among the students I interviewed, there were a handful of students who had high levels of bonding social capital at the cost of low levels of bridging social capital. Jennifer would be one example. Like many others, Jennifer did not view this as a conscious decision, but as the way she felt comfortable on campus.

A challenge that students from marginalized groups face when building bridging social capital comes from issues with interracial interactions. Danica spoke about this, as we saw earlier, when she described interactions with White upper-class students as "exhausting." Other research backs this up, documenting difficulties that students from minoritized groups face in navigating cross-racial friendships, including facing microaggressions from White friends, and the need for institutional support so that the burden to educate their peers does not fall to them and increase their marginalization.[23] For example, Yingyi Ma discusses how Chinese international students often feel they do not have access to diverse networks, which keeps them from more deeply integrating into American campuses.[24] Having friends does not mean that students feel a sense of belonging on campus.[25]

As they make friends on campus, students find that balancing a sense of comfort with not being isolated within just one group is a challenge. It is a challenge not only for students but also for the administrators, professors, and parents who support them. As Dawn, an Asian middle-class student at Dartmouth, described the support among her group of Asian and Asian American friends: "We all mostly come from the same place and it's nice to have that familiarity and comfort, but it's also dangerous in a way [laughter] to not be exposed to new ideas and, like, other cultures." She explained that it is not "a bad thing necessarily but just that it sort of narrows your world and you don't get to see as much or hear as much."

## Hostile Ignorance from Friends

Forming friendships based on marginalized identities or interest in diversity does not mean that these relationships will always be supportive. In making such an assumption, students' identities are placed as one-dimensional, which they are not. Students hold intersectional identities, which vary over time and in different settings in their salience. In a study of working-class students at two universities, Sherelle Ferguson and Annette Lareau identify "class-based antagonism" that students experience from their same-race friendships, which they refer to as "hostile ignorance." Alongside this class-based hostile ignorance, these same-race friendships also provided a "source of sanctuary from racial isolation on campus."[26] The researchers point out that these alienating comments from close friends may be an underexplored mechanism harming students' sense of belonging, and their academic and social integration on campus. Building on their work, I find hostile ignorance among friends in terms of class as well as other identities.

One striking example of hostile ignorance around race comes from Patrice's experience with friends in the cultural exchange club at MCC. Patrice described herself to me as "mixed," half Black and half White. She mentioned how, when she was growing up, most of her friends were White, which was "definitely hard" because "there's a lot of things that they thought was okay to say to me, but they really weren't.'" She said, "I'm not afraid to speak out," not to be rude, but "more to educate them." Patrice told about an incident that happened when she was president of the MCC cultural exchange club, noting that the other members were of different racial backgrounds than hers, some working-class and some middle-class. They were brainstorming ideas for Black History Month programming, and the other members, her friends, "made a comment saying that we should go to Walmart and get fried chicken. We should get Kool-Aid and watermelon. It wasn't the first time that I've heard jokes like that, but honestly, I just looked at them, and I was like, out of all times, why would you think that that would be funny, especially talking about this month [Black History Month]? And they said, 'It's a joke, it's just a joke, I'm not racist.' I'm like, 'Saying a racist joke makes you racist.'" While Patrice had considered these people to be her friends, she remarked that she could no longer be friends with them after this incident. She explained:

They think it's okay, but it's not. It's really not okay. It really hurts my feelings, and I don't like it at all, and I'm gonna say something about it. And they thought it was really funny, and I was just like, "Yeah, that's not really funny at all. I'm really sorry that you feel that way. I'm not really sure if you know what the struggle was of African Americans growing up." I start talking about slavery. I start talking about the civil rights movement. I start talking about lynching. And people get really uncomfortable, and they don't say anything else. And for me, I just walked out. I left. I took my stuff with me. I did cry, because it's very hard to talk about that kinda stuff. And I'm like, in this day and age, this still is a problem, and people think that it's not, but I have run-ins more than people would think. And it's very bad, especially coming from people that I consider my friends.

Patrice got tears in her eyes as she related this to me. This experience would have been challenging coming from anyone, but it felt even harder coming from people she considered to be friends. She also explained feeling "confused" that the head of the cultural exchange center and the advisor for the club was present during the event, but he did not take a stand. Patrice observed: "The head of the center, my advisor, he just kinda sat there, and I was confused because I thought he had my back, and I know that he does, but he didn't say anything." She described how she is still friends with the advisor, talking with him right before our interview, yet she is "still kinda hurt" and "confused 'cause I thought he would've said something, but he didn't say anything."

Not only her trust in her advisor, but her trust in the mission of the club was shaken through this experience: "The club was really about reaching out and bringing cultural awareness in, breaking down walls and barriers that people have, so that kind of stuff doesn't happen. I really believed in the club. I did. I want to help. I've always wanted to help with stuff like that, but that was too much for me." Like the "hostile ignorance" discussed in other research, the microaggressions Patrice experienced came from friends. Such experiences have not only individual consequences, but also interactional ones because hostile ignorance from friends has implications for trust, comfort, and reciprocity as they are all key to friendship.[27]

Unlike the students in the previous section, Patrice lacks an emotionally supportive network of same-race friends or other people of color to turn to and debrief after a racist incident. Patrice mentioned friends of color in the cultural exchange club and outside of it, noting one friend who is half Black and "the same ethnicity as me" as "really important to me." Yet, she did not turn to any of these friends when the experience happened. Of the seven friends shown in figure 5.3, only one is White (Dawson). The three friends

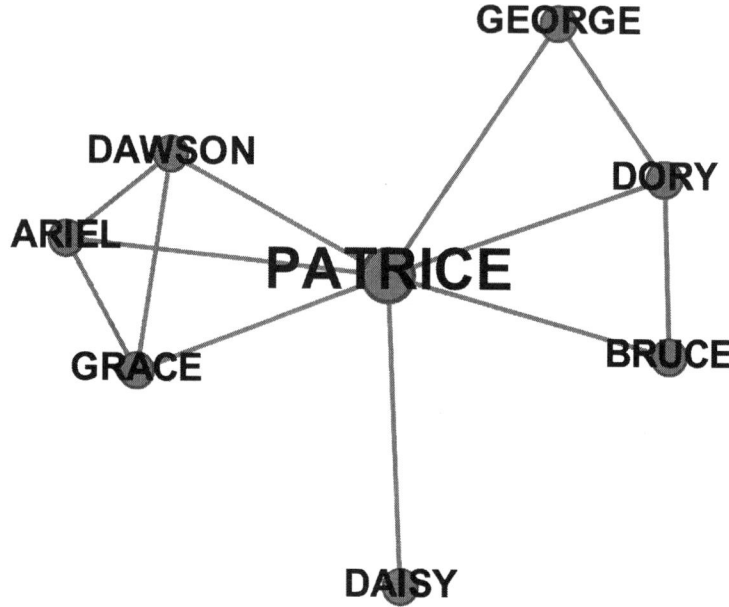

FIGURE 5.3. Patrice's friendship network, MCC year two.

on the righthand side and Daisy, listed at the bottom of the sociogram, were all friends she made at MCC, while Dawson, Ariel, and Grace were friends she had had for six or seven years. Patrice did not participate in a second interview, so it is not clear if she developed friendships that provided race-based solidarity when she moved to a four-year university.[28] At MCC, clubs and organizations are less powerful in shaping students' friendship networks, and there are fewer identity-based clubs, so MCC students do not have this avenue for finding the support based on same-race or same-class bonds.

While Patrice described her friendships as emotionally supportive, the examples she gave me all involved her providing support to her friends. She observed that she tends to bond with people who have similar challenges, like Grace, who has a similar family structure, and Ariel, who "overthinks a lot" of things. Patrice provided a mothering kind of support to these friends, worrying about them and their safety when she is not with them and being "proud" of them when they do well. She notes, "I'm kind of a mom."[29] Patrice does not directly mention receiving or wanting emotional support from her friends. Yet, her comment that "I wish I had more stable friends" and that her friends are "struggling," suggests they may not be able to provide much emotional support.

Instead of getting support from her friends, either one on one or in the clusters shown in figure 5.3, Patrice described getting most of her emotional support from her mother. She described different groups of friends, noting, "I stay away from one group. That's too much drama. I learned that last year, the hard way." Many compartmentalizers found emotional support from one (or more) clusters of friends, but Patrice did not find that support from any of hers.

Like Danica, Patrice remarked that friendships with White students can be hard, because there are things "they don't get," meaning issues and situations they do not understand, even after Patrice tries to explain. Neither of them has "given up on" forming friendships across difference, as Danica put it, yet they both also struggle to find same-race friends who provide the sense of comfort they desire.

While students from marginalized backgrounds often bond together into tight-knit groups, this is not universal. In fact, students of color did not overall have higher network densities than White students. Across all three campuses, I find the lowest network density in my sample among Black students (45 percent of their friends know each other), followed by Latinx (51 percent) and White (52 percent) students, with the most dense networks for Native American (61 percent) and Asian (63 percent) students. At Dartmouth, the racial differences are even smaller, with groups ranging from 48 to 61 percent density.[30] Moreover, race and gender intersect such that women of color tend to have less dense networks than White women.[31] Black and Latina women often find a friend or two to support them, which results in less dense networks, whereas Black and Latino men find groups more often, and their friendship networks consist of one group of friends or two dense groups. Not only tight-knit networks but also sampler networks can be a reaction to greater marginalization on campus.

## "Money Plays a Big Part in Friendships"

In addition to hostile ignorance that occurs when students are friends across class lines, there are other ways that class backgrounds shape friendships. Some students bond based on their shared class backgrounds. Relatedly, students told me that it is not common to form friendships or get to know each other well across class lines.

Sharing a class background can bring friends together, sometimes implicitly and other times explicitly. Friendships form based on class similarities implicitly when similarities in interests, experiences, and spending money make doing things together feel easy. Other times, this happens explicitly, particularly for low-income students at an elite school, who feel different from their peers. Bonding with other low-income students can help students feel less alone. As Safiya, a Black lower-middle-class Dartmouth student, explained, "Having a similar background creates a common understanding. Some things can go on that we won't have to explain." Another Dartmouth student, Jorge, a Latinx student from a working-class background, told me how class is the biggest obstacle he faces at Dartmouth. He described: "I come from a low socioeconomic background and it's not necessarily in overt ways, it's subtle things, [such as peers] talking about what they did, like, 'Oh, this summer I went on vacation.' It's just, like, I just went back home. So sometimes I feel like I can't talk about that or stuff like that. Just in general, it's different experiences, so you're obviously not going to have the same things to talk about with other people."[32] The experiences that lower-income students share with each other create bonding social capital, while also leading to feelings of separation with regard to peers from more advantaged backgrounds.

Safiya was quite direct in noting how class background "creates a common understanding," and it also "divides people," inhibiting relationships across differences in class background. As Safiya noted, while class-based similarities facilitate some friendship ties, they limit the development of other ties and opportunities that may come with bridging social capital. This fits with Ferguson and Lareau's insights about the "feelings of discomfort" that often came from interactions with affluent students, such that working-class students "avoided certain opportunities—opportunities that might have broadened and deepened their ties," like sororities. Ferguson and Lareau refer to working-class students' avoidance as acts of "self-exclusion."[33]

Even if not as extreme as "self-exclusion," the distance that lower-class students may keep from their upper-class peers can make it difficult for them to feel that they fully belong on campus. Austin, a White student from a lower-class background at Dartmouth, told me: "I think money doesn't play a huge part, but it definitely plays a big part in friendships. I think that's actually something that's always driven a bit of a wedge in my friendships." He described growing up: "We've always been like a paycheck-to-paycheck type [of] family. We've definitely had a lot of hard struggles that come from being financially unstable. Sometimes people don't have that same awareness as you do. And I'm somebody who bases a lot of hard decisions off of, 'Can I afford that? Can I do that?' That's just always something that's been in the back of my mind. I think it distances me from some people." Often, especially at Dartmouth, where 21 percent of students come from the top 1 percent of family income,[34] I heard students from lower-class backgrounds describe navigating everyday activities with their friends, such as going to dinner in town or taking a trip together. Austin explained how figuring out if he can do these things with friends is "something that very much affects me." He expanded: "Even when I'm doing okay financially, it's still something that I've just been so conditioned to just want to consult it [finances] in that way. I just can't bring myself to spend that amount of money. I always think I have that holding me back." The easy way that some of his friends spend money on food, clothes, and activities drives a wedge in their friendships. Austin found this was easier to navigate in close friendships when they talked about this difference; however, it required attention even when friends knew about Austin's financial situation. This comes up more for Austin than for some of the other respondents because he regularly interacts with friends across class lines in his fraternity and varsity sports team; propinquity brings them into regular contact, where he must again and again navigate this situation.

Class also shapes the types of interactions that feel comfortable. As noted in chapter 1, students from less privileged backgrounds whom I spoke with expressed less comfort overall in academic and social spaces on campus than did those from privileged backgrounds. Other research concludes that privileged students find collaborating with peers in classrooms to be easier, while less privileged students exhibit a sense of constraint in seeking or accepting help.[35] Because working together in courses can lead to friendships, less privileged students may also be missing out on forming more friendships in classroom settings, including cross-class friendships.

Students notice a lack of interaction across class limiting their ability to form cross-class friendships. While students sit side by side in class, they may not talk to each other. Or if they do, they may not talk about class inequality. This echoes other research that identified difficulties students had in managing cross-class friendships, including the tendency to not talk about class inequality in these relationships.[36] Dawn, a compartmentalizer, described Dartmouth this way: "You hear this is the place for trust fund babies or so-called trust fund babies. And that kind of rich elite class exists, but I personally, I feel like I haven't met anyone—that probably isn't true. I've probably been in class with someone, I just didn't realize. But we're just not friends. And we're not friends because we don't frequent the same social spaces. It sort of happens that way." She goes on to explain that they do not frequent the same sorority houses and the same major (that is, "econ"), so "I just naturally don't meet them that way." Dawn concludes, "It's not like an open criteri[on], but it just sort of happens." On all three campuses, close friendships across class do not happen frequently, and they are more challenging to navigate than those based on class similarities.

## Gender Stereotypes, Gender Inequalities, and Gendered Support

While students from marginalized race and class backgrounds find themselves as a numerical minority on each of these campuses, gender operates differently. Women and men make up roughly equal numbers of the student body, and nonbinary and trans students are growing in numbers and visibility. Even with segregation and clustering in some majors and extracurriculars, the opportunities and patterns of interaction across gender are quite different from those based on race and class.

In sum, gender impacts friendship in different ways than do race and class. Six main themes come up. These themes conflict with each other, and frequently I heard more than one from the same respondent, so they are not mutually exclusive. The first is that men are "easier" to be friends with because they are more "laid-back" compared to women, who are more "dramatic." The second is that women are "better communicators," so students of all genders seek out women friends for conversations, especially "serious conversations." The third relates to the "mom" role that women often play within friendships. The fourth relates to the unique support women can provide to other women. In these first four themes, students are positioning women and men as different sorts of friends, reflecting cultural beliefs about gender.[37] The fifth theme contrasts with this: some students I spoke with remarked that there is not a difference in having women or men as friends. And the sixth theme relates to differences in friendship network structure and content of the women and men in my sample. Networks are more integrated across gender than they are across race and class, and most students have more experience interacting across gender than across these other identities.

One theme that frequently came up was that men are more "laid-back" and women are more "dramatic" in their friendships. When explaining why they had men friends or felt comfortable with them, students would use this cultural frame. For example, MCC student Monika reported that her men friends are "more open-minded" and "more understanding, less judgmental." Violet, another MCC student, concurred, adding, "I find it so much harder to connect with girls" because "women, just in general . . . aren't very laid-back." Violet found that with women friends, "there's drama. But I've never had that with a guy," noting that "it's easier, simpler, to hold a relationship with a guy." Similarly, MCC student Ciara noted that "girls are very dramatic. They can go behind your back easier than a guy would. Even though I have a lot of girlfriends, I always have that sense in the back of my mind that they are going to betray me somehow." Some students brought up that it is easier to connect with men friends, without offering much explanation. Ciara is one example, remarking that she "definitely" feels a "connection with males." Dartmouth student Sasha also commented, "Socially, it's easier for me to connect with guys, which is really weird." Kevin, a UNH student, mentioned that he finds it easier to connect with guys because they like to do the same things, such as going to the gym to lift weights.

While some of the statements above highlight strengths that both genders bring to their friendship, others mark men's "laid-back" attitude as preferable to women's "overreactive, super sensitive" one. Melinda, a UNH student, remarked, "I love having the contrast between guy friends and girlfriends, and just how they handle situations, and how they go about things." She explained that her guy friends "just avoid kind of the whole drama, and overreactive, super-sensitive, stereotypical-girl reactions to things. I think that is refreshing, that's how I see them differ socially."[38] MCC student Patrice observed: "Some females can be more sensitive when I need them to be. Males provide a lot less drama, which makes me very happy." When reflecting on his friends, Dartmouth student Austin noticed: "Definitely a lot more laid-back, I've noticed, among my guy friends versus my girl friends." He added: "My guy friends tend to be more laid-back about academics. Even when they have a lot going on, they don't get as stressed about it." Piper, an MCC student, remarked: "I can joke a lot more with my male friends. They're really funny. We laugh a lot." Clearly, these differences both reflect and contribute to gender stereotypes.[39] I focus on them here to acknowledge that students experience these differences as meaningful in how they form and keep friendships during the college years.

A second theme that came up in students' accounts is that they seek out and appreciate their women friends because women are "better communicators." Dartmouth student Safiya elaborated: "So if you want to talk about serious things, it's not a struggle to get there" with women, noting that it can be a struggle to get men engaged in such conversations. Similarly, another Dartmouth student, Luz, commented that her women friends "just generally listen" to her, and Jennifer noted that "my female friends are a lot more open to talk" and have "serious conversations," whereas male friends talk "more jokingly." MCC student Mindy remarked that women "are better communicators" and so "I have never really had close male friends." Heidi, a UNH student, noted, "I have a lot of guy friends, but I feel, like, they're all just such guys. You can't really talk to them about anything really. So [I wish I had] more guy friends who understood more and were easier to talk to, weren't just someone you're kind of surface-level with." Men also mention and value the communication skills of their women friends. UNH student Will remarked that it is "easier for me to talk with them," referring to his women friends. Communication skills are valuable, yet they add to the emotional labor women are doing within relationships. Similar to online gaming, where women communicate more frequently and with more people, while men have better connected communication partners, communication skills come with costs as well as benefits for women in their friendships.[40] To be clear, many of the men I interviewed appeared to be good communicators in their friendships. However, this theme does resonate with research finding that high school and college-age boys often have a hard time expressing vulnerability in their friendships with other boys.[41] Gender schemas constrain men's and boys' expressions of intimacy and emotions.

The third difference is the "mom" role that women friends play. The type of support women provide as the "mom" within their friendship group is a burdensome and unequal one, where they give more emotional support than they receive. Some students, such as Patrice, described themselves as the "mom" in their friend group, while others used this descriptor for a friend. Lafayette, a gay man in a mixed-gender friendship group at MCC, described his friend Violet as "the mothering type in our group." Violet works to maintain contact between their friends after they leave MCC, he said, and this is not something he would do. This highlights women's emotional labor in relationships. Elyse described a friend as "my school mom" at MCC, and when I asked what she meant, she responded that "she would listen to my problems and give me advice and yell at me if I wasn't doing something [laughter]." Elyse added that she has done these things for other people "probably my whole life. I was always the one that, if people went out drinking, I would stay the most sober to make sure everybody's safe." Similarly, Patrice noted that "I'm kind of a mom" who "watches" her friends: "I have eyes on her, so she's safe." Abigail, a UNH student, told me: "They refer to me as mom of the group. It's not really a bad thing, so it's all right." One of her "mom" tasks is encouraging her friends to study and do their homework. Abigail exclaimed, "My boyfriend says, 'If I wouldn't have met you last year, I don't think I would be in school anymore. He thinks he would've seriously dropped out and not be coming back. Even his parents are like, 'We're very glad that you're in his life' [laughs]." Abigail's comment that "it's not really a bad thing, so it's all right" reflects the ambivalence or lack of prestige accompanying this role. While being the friend "mom" may seem like a valuable role in students' friend groups, it is an unequal one.[42] As "mom," women give more emotional support than they receive, and they expend energy taking care of others, often at the expense of caring for themselves.

While the previous themes came up in interviews with both women and men, only women emphasized the important support women friends could provide. This support by women friends is the fourth theme. Similar to the support that homophilous friends provide for students historically marginalized by race or class, some women spoke about the unique support they received academically and socially from other women. Dartmouth student Savannah noted how she was more comfortable talking with women about school: "it's easier for me because we know that we can struggle through this together because we're the same." This came up earlier in this chapter with Kira's "wish" to have more Black women friends. It also came up in Melanie's experiences (see chapter 1), where she spoke of the importance of women's friendships, particularly given the male-dominated social space on Dartmouth's campus. Dani explained, "I definitely try to model my friendships" on the "huge support network my mom has" through her "two groups of girlfriends." Dani remarked, "I have always valued women friends" and "I love my girlfriends." She explained, "I think women understand more, even if simply [that] men just look at things differently," adding, "women are just very empathetic towards each other. At least my friends are." These sentiments echo the findings by Ana Martinez Alemán from two decades ago about the safe space in women's same-gender friendships.[43] Some respondents also mentioned that women provided unique academic support as well as social support. MCC student Monika noted that "girls are more supportive with school than guys." She added, "I feel like the relationships I have with a girl are more based around school, so we just push each other that way." The academic support women provide each other remains relevant in contemporary classrooms, which research continues to find "chilly" for women.[44]

Gender divisions on campus and in society also shape whether students are friends. Underlying some students' comments about the importance of having women friends is that this minimizes the sexual tension or pressure that can come up in friendships between heterosexual or bisexual women and men. Students describe maintaining some distance with cross-gender friendships when those friends have partners. Otto, a UNH student, remarked that with his women friends, "it's hard to maintain the friendships with them at times," noting that "they also have, like, boyfriends, too. So, I don't want to get too, too close to them where I feel like their boyfriends will think I'm overstepping the boundaries. It's just like a respectable distance." Danica observed that she feels safer with women friends. She characterized her experience at Dartmouth by noting that "being a girl here is pretty dangerous. Girls plus alcohol plus [fraternity] basement. No, thank you. I would rather not put myself in that predicament" because "it's usually someone that you know. A friend." While men friends are potentially dangerous in this setting, she describes women as empathetic. Danica noted, "It's so ridiculous how any time I ever share with someone that this happened [to me] in that situation, [women say,] 'It also happened to me.'" Consequently, Danica is distrustful of men as friends. Other students point to the dominance of the gender-segregated Greek system on campus as challenging the formation of close friendships across gender. Dustin, who was a member of a fraternity at Dartmouth, commented that he has "only a lot of male friends." Sydney, who is in a sorority, explained, "My mom told me, you don't really need a boyfriend but you need male friends. . . . Dartmouth is super gendered, the campus, especially with the frats and sororities, so I don't really have any" male friends. Heteronormativity and societal gender divisions both can limit friendships across gender, or at least make them more challenging to maintain.[45]

Fifth, although most respondents discuss differences between their men and women friends or their motivations for having friends of a specific gender, some students remark that there are no differences in having women or men as friends. Dartmouth student Melvin stated, "It's about the same . . . I don't think there's anything gendered" about my friendships. Dawn, another Dartmouth student, told me, "It's not really different. Really, we just sort of all do the same things together." Some students (men and women) mentioned that friendships with men and women are different academically but not socially, while others noted the opposite. And some students documented differences between men and women friends alongside stating in the same interview that there are no gender differences. These themes are not mutually exclusive.

The sixth theme relates to the gender differences in the friendship networks of students in my sample, rather than the experiences students recounted during the interviews. Three differences are particularly notable.[46] The first is that, on average, women's networks include significantly more same-gender friends than men's networks, which also means that women are more often included as friends by all genders. While women's close friends include 74 percent women friends and 26 percent men friends, men's networks include 65 percent men friends and 35 percent women friends. At Dartmouth and UNH, women are more often named as friends compared to men,[47] resembling patterns in other research.[48] As noted in the "mom" theme earlier and other research documenting that men and boys struggle to be vulnerable in their same-gender friendships,[49] this suggests that women may be doing more of the emotional labor of friendship both for other women and for men.

The other differences are more about network structure than composition: during college, women have smaller networks and are more likely to be samplers. In other words, women have smaller and less connected networks. Overall, women name 10.7 friends, and men name 12.6. Although this is not a huge difference, it appears on each campus: at MCC women named 8.6 friends compared to 9.4 named by men; at Dartmouth, it was 11 compared to 14; and at UNH, 12 compared to 13.7. Also notable is that this gender difference reverses after graduation, both in my interviews and in other research. Among the nineteen UNH students I interviewed a second time, women reported 9.2 friends and men reported 8.2.[50] The larger network size for women I interviewed after college parallels what research finds among network size of adults.[51] During college, propinquity helps everyone maintain friendships. Without propinquity, after college, men seemed to struggle more to maintain their networks, so their networks shrank more after college than did those of women. Women's additional emotional labor related to friendships was practice for maintaining more ties after graduation.

Overall, women's networks are also less closely connected. As mentioned in earlier chapters, the most common network type on each campus is compartmentalizers. This is true of both men and women. However, more men in my sample are tight-knitters and more women are samplers. For example, of the nine men at Dartmouth, 33 percent are tight-knitters and none are samplers, compared to 19 percent of the twenty-six women who are tight-knitters and another 19 percent who are samplers.[52] Men have more dense networks across most racial groups, including Latinx and Black students. Latino men's average density is 68 percent compared to Latinas' 50 percent density, and Black men's average density is 64 percent compared to 36 percent for Black women. Given the greater emotional labor that women, on average, put into their friendships, it is striking that this does not translate to more connected networks.

Although most students I spoke with carefully point out that women and men are equal when they discuss ways they differ as friends, their explanations reflect widely shared, hegemonic cultural beliefs about gender, which shape social interactions. Moreover, these cultural rules about gender, including ones that highlight women's strengths in communication, matter because they assign greater competence and statusworthiness at "what counts" to men more often than to women.[53] It matters even though most students I spoke with hold sentiments similar to Terrence, an MCC student, who noted that "men and women are different. I mean, we're equal, but we're different." Sociologist Cecilia Ridgeway explains that this is how gender inequality persists: gender status beliefs maintain patriarchal hierarchies and influence people's behaviors.[54] People can verbally affirm gender equality alongside beliefs that reinforce the traits associated with men as more valuable than those of women. This is illustrated, for example, by students who state "we're equal" yet stress their appreciation for men friends' "laid-back" demeanor compared to women's drama.

Race, gender, and class all impact how students make, keep, and lose friends, and they do so differently.[55] Race and gender are more visible markers than is class. Each of these identities, as well as other identities, however, are also differently salient in different contexts; for example, the outdoorsy culture of Dartmouth helps to hide these class differences more than in other elite spaces, although they are more visible in some settings, such as high-status sororities.[56] Most students have lots of experience forming and keeping relationships across gender in their families and prior schools, whereas race and class are often more homogeneous in settings and in ties within those settings. Race, class, and gender differences in friendships also contribute to differing experiences of isolation, again showing how connections among students' friends are important to our loneliness epidemic.

## Takeaways

For students:

1. A common challenge for students is feeling a sense of comfort while also not feeling isolated within just one group. Do you have friends who provide you with social support and a sense of home? This support is particularly important for students from marginalized groups who may form strong homophilous bonds to find belonging in the face of microaggressions. Do you also have friends who expand your world through connecting you to new ideas or new people? Both bonding and bridging social capital are important resources.
2. Ask yourself: What identities do you share with friends? Are there identities that are important to you that your friends do not reflect? If so, consider expanding your network through clubs or activities related to this identity.
3. Do not assume that your friends will always be supportive just because they share an identity with you. Identities are intersectional, and hostile ignorance can happen.
4. Be aware that cultural beliefs about gender shape interactions and may encourage stereotyped views of your friendships. Consider whether your women friends may be carrying an outsized burden of emotional labor, and redistribute it as needed.

For parents and other supporters:

1. Do not assume that your child's friends can relate to them because they share an identity. Ask them if they have friends who provide social support and a sense of home (or comfort).
2. A challenge for parents—along with college administrators—is to help their child feel a sense of comfort while also not feeling isolated within just one group. Do not assume that self-segregation of students from marginalized identities is bad. It is more nuanced, as these homophilous ties can provide important feelings of belonging.
3. Your child's identities are intersectional, so they may need multiple groups of friends as different identities become salient. They may have these multiple groups of friends at the same time, or they may gain some and lose others.

For colleges:

1. A challenge for administrators, staff, and professors is to help students feel a sense of comfort, while also not feeling isolated within just one group. Joining a club or organization could be a way to encourage these new connections.
2. Recognize that students from marginalized backgrounds often form dense friendship networks that serve as a source of belonging and support. Other research has noted that these homophilous bonds are important sources of self-preservation.
3. Do not assume that homophilous friendships are always supportive. When students share an identity, their identities are intersectional and multiple, and they can still face microaggressions and hostile ignorance from friends.
4. Students can also face a bind in a supportive but insular network. Supporting a range of clubs and organizations where students can expand their networks helps overcome this bind. Maintaining expansive initial friendship markets and a range of secondary friendship markets allows students to more easily make friends who offer both support and new opportunities.
5. Be aware that cultural beliefs about gender shape interactions and may encourage stereotyped views of students' friendships. Help students reflect on and name when they (or their women friends) may be carrying an outsized burden of emotional labor, and redistribute it as needed.

[ CONCLUSION ]

# Points of Intervention

Making friends is one of the main joys and one of the main challenges of students' time at college. As UNH student Liahna told me, "I love my two roommates now, but we butt heads. They're still some of my best friends, but sometimes it's nice to have space and to have other friends, because I wouldn't want to be spending all my time with them." Prevailing wisdom suggests that "college are the best years of your life" and that having friends will keep loneliness away. As this book details, making friends is not a one-time event. And having friends does not inoculate people from feeling lonely. Instead, these processes are more complex. Students are making friends throughout their time in college, keeping some friends, and losing others along the way, sometimes regaining lost ties. Importantly, friendships are not just between two people, but are experienced within a broader campus context and a network of friends, as Liahna's comment suggests.

Gaining a deeper understanding of the processes of making, keeping, and losing friends has the potential to benefit students and colleges. It also drives forward scholarship on friendship and the sociology of education. By intervening at strategic times, students and college administrators can minimize loneliness and isolation, and maximize success. MCC student Monika explained that her friends have a "huge impact:" without them, "I become sad and just lonely, then I just become unmotivated" academically. The solution to our current loneliness epidemic is not just collecting friends, but making and keeping a network of friends that feels supportive. It is also knowing that these friendships will change over time, thus there will be a need to lose friends and make new friends along the way. As discussed throughout this book, students' identities impact processes of making, keeping, and losing friends, as do features of campus environments.

# Points of Intervention

At the end of each chapter, I have offered specific takeaways for students, their supporters, and colleges. Here, in conclusion, I focus on four broader points of intervention. While there are many reforms I could advocate for society and at colleges, I chose these four because they are supported by the evidence I present here, they lend themselves to actionable steps, and they have the potential to impact students individually and to have broader impacts. Specifically, they offer concrete possibilities for supporting individual students in crafting meaningful friendships, as well as supporting a society where loneliness is not an epidemic and where high amounts of both bridging and bonding social capital abound.

The first point of intervention targets students in their transition to college, advocating for colleges to keep or institute roommate assignments rather than letting incoming students choose their own roommate. While not all roommate assignments lead to students becoming best friends, they do tend to place students in close proximity with someone different from them. As the senior associate dean of students at Bates College said in a *New York Times* article, "Roommate experiences are an intense learning experience.... They're fun and they're hard."[1] The roommate matches that most UNH students made themselves were based on people they knew before college, particularly those from their high school, a friend of a friend, or someone they met on a Facebook group for incoming UNH students. These tend to result in homophilous ties. In contrast, students' first-year roommates at Dartmouth, which are assigned, resulted in interactions across difference in terms of class, race, region, and many other identity markers. Rather than being completely random, the assignments are based on characteristics that matter for roommate compatibility, such as students' preferences for tidiness, studying in their room, and whether they wake up early or stay up late. Other studies of assigned roommates at Dartmouth find that they impact not only students' interactions but also a range of academic and social outcomes, including GPA and the fraternity they join.[2]

It is not enough, however, to put students into contact with others with different backgrounds or values. Students, staff, and others on campus must also be equipped with the skills to have meaningful and respectful interactions. Without these skills in place, students from marginalized groups find themselves in the position of having either to educate others or to just put up with microaggressions. As education researcher Tara Hudson puts it, "Expecting students from minoritized groups to educate their 'ignorant' peers is a heavy—and unjust—burden to place upon them and exacerbates

TABLE 6.1. Points of Intervention for Students and Colleges

| INTERVENTIONS | FOR STUDENTS | FOR COLLEGES |
| --- | --- | --- |
| *Intervention 1*: Roommate selection for incoming students | Get to know your assigned roommate. And if you have a choice, opt for an assigned roommate. | Assign first-year roommates, and provide education and training to students and staff on intercultural dialogue. |
| *Intervention 2*: Initial friendship market | Remain open to making friends, even after you have some. Keep this time period in mind, knowing that making new friends is easier in the first few weeks. | Increase awareness of its existence to staff who can bring it up at orientation and thus among students. Extend the market through LLCs and residential colleges. |
| *Intervention 3*: Secondary friendship market | Know that these "pop-up markets" happen. Seek out these opportunities if you are looking to expand your network. Interact with peers in these environments, which means being present and not on your phone. | Support a range of campus organizations, especially those that provide students time together regularly, to interact, and to deepen their connections with each other. In classes, students form friendships when they can regularly interact and work together, as on group projects. |
| *Intervention 4*: Opportunities for students regardless of network type | Each network type experiences challenges to keeping friends. Which type are you? Socially, tight-knitters benefit from high levels of social support from friends, but find it difficult to exit the network. Compartmentalizers have multiple friendship groups and may struggle to balance them and navigate between them. Samplers can find social support from one-on-one friendships, yet this network type can lead to loneliness and isolation. | Because students on every campus have a range of network types—tight-knitters, compartmentalizers, and samplers—offer activities and spaces that appeal to each type. For example, tight-knitters often want to attend activities, grab meals, and hang out with a large group, whereas samplers more frequently attend activities and spend time by themselves or with one friend. Spaces and activities should accommodate and appeal to all friendship network types. |

the marginalization they struggle against."[3] Just as we would not simply hope students would learn because they are in classrooms, Hudson advises that we not just put diverse peers together, assuming they will benefit from these interactions.[4] Staff need training, and students need facilitated and repeated opportunities to engage in "honest and meaningful" conversations in supportive settings.[5] I summarize this advice for students and colleges in Table 6.1.

The second point of intervention involves extending the initial friendship market and increasing awareness of how it works. Since these first weeks of the students' first term are a time when students are particularly open to making friends, students should be careful not to close off these opportunities too early. When students feel they have achieved their goal of making friends, some "opt out" of the market after a few days (or even a few hours). Students need to spend time with friends to maintain them, as chapter 2 details. To be sure, neglecting these new friendships could lead them to end. However, balancing time with these new friends while remaining open to making new friends throughout the initial friendship market allows students to more effectively build supportive ties and remain connected across multiple groups on campus, developing both bonding and bridging social capital, as I explain in more detail below.

As discussed in chapter 1, the initial friendship markets in orientation and pre-orientation programs help students transition to campus, including making friends. However, like roommate self-selection, they can lead to insular and homophilous networks. For example, Troy had a close-knit group of friends, mostly made up of other Black men whom he met during the orientation for first-generation students at Dartmouth, and Timothy made most of his friends at a backpacking pre-orientation program at UNH. Both Troy and Timothy described how support flowed through these dense and homophilous ties, whether based on race and class identities or shared interests, like outdoor activities.

Broader and more diverse ties are also supported by colleges creating spaces where students live and learn together and build community. Residential colleges and living-learning communities are types of campus structure that particularly support these meaningful ties. These can be more interest-based organizations, such as themed living-learning centers.[6] They can also be random assignments of larger groups of students, such as residential colleges. The residential college system is an old one, used at the universities of Oxford and Cambridge, for example, and defined as "a small, cross-sectional, social and academic unit within a large university." Advocates note that "because they are small, diverse, and fundamentally decentralized communities ... residential colleges provide the kind of stable and challenging social and intellectual environment that everyone in a university deserves."[7] Dartmouth began a residential college system in 2016, shortly after I started my interviews at Dartmouth. The students I spoke with were well into their college careers by the time the residential colleges were set up, so they had little interaction with the system. As random cross-sections of the undergraduates, graduate students, postdoctoral fellows, and faculty on campus, as well as diverse groups of staff, the "house communities" are unlike most other groups on campus, which are based on homophily of interests or identities. Because students live together by house and house members regularly encounter each other in house common spaces during unstructured time and at formal events, these communities have the potential to build and sustain connections among diverse individuals. At other residential colleges, dining halls are another important place where students regularly encounter each other.[8] Like other programs in the initial friendship market, propinquity brings students together; however, the stability and continuity of the house communities over students' college years provide structure to keep friendships together and to spark new ones over time.

The third point of intervention is in secondary friendship markets. By providing and supporting a range of campus groups, campuses facilitate students' maintaining meaningful friendships and seeking out new ties. Colleges already invest in a range of campus activities, and my findings suggest particularly investing in those programs, clubs, and organizations that provide students time together regularly, to interact, and to deepen their connections with each other. For example, UNH student Will saw his friendship group "quadruple in size" when he joined the Programming Board club, noting that the format of the club helped friendships form and deepen. They plan big events, like concerts, and they "hang out" at the concerts together. The regular time they spent together at meetings and events, and actively working on projects together, made student organizations with these features especially powerful in crafting meaningful friendship networks. More basically, students would benefit from knowing that secondary friendship markets exist. Institutions would be wise to invest in secondary markets; they can make a difference for students—both for those who do not make friends in the initial market, and for those who later find that their friends are not a good fit. Secondary friendship markets provide opportunities to make new friends and expand students' networks.

Prioritize investing in those that bring together diverse individuals as well as those that provide connections for marginalized identities. A range of research documents the difficulties students from marginalized backgrounds can have on college campuses.[9] Providing space to regularly meet and connect with people around these difficult experiences is an important investment in secondary friendship markets. Evaluate which clubs and organizations have consistently "owned space" on campus, in line with Melanie's earlier comments about how such spaces made her sorority connections easier than those in the "alternative social space" she sought to create in her Coffee Club. Space is limited on campuses, so being deliberate about the use of shared spaces as well as "owned spaces" on campus would support meaningful friendships. Certainly, colleges should provide other institutional resources, such as counselors and trained staff, so that friends are not solely responsible for this support. Numerous students in this study described the important support of friends they had met in identity-based groups in the secondary friendship market. Troy told me that in a club for Black students, he connected with friends who "can offer that support . . . because a lot of us have gone through the experiences of either failing or having to work three times as hard." Students from marginalized groups often found a sense of belonging or "sense of home" through such organizations.[10] In contrast, high-status activities, such as sororities and fraternities, can be troublesome secondary markets. Students often saw the possibility of forming friendships there (that is, they act as strong secondary markets); however, this often did not solve students' friendships problems. Because they are exclusive organizations, students experienced rejection, which amplifies feelings of loneliness and not belonging, especially when their friends and peers are included, and they are not.

As someone who teaches college classes, I hoped that classes would be a more central place where meaningful friendships form than what I found on any of the three campuses. When they form, three elements facilitate their formation, as discussed in chapter 1. Here, I focus on the second element, which is the most within instructors' control. At each college, students described friends they made through projects in class. Spending more time together, working together, and getting to know each other more closely facilitates a secondary friendship market in classes. For example, at the community college, Mira described two friends she made through doing group projects, and Alexa highlighted the friendships she made in her creative writing class because the instructor required them to organize a "poetry slam night, where anybody in the school could participate."

The fourth point of intervention is in recognizing that students have different friendship network types and in offering opportunities suited to all three types: samplers, compartmentalizers, and tight-knitters. Some students may feel comfortable approaching others whom they do not know in campus activities, including those in the initial and secondary friendship markets. This is particularly common for samplers. Other students, however, may only attend activities once they already have a group of friends. Or, if they attend on their own, they do not feel comfortable reaching out to peers they do not know unless it is structured into the activity. Jennifer, a tight-knitter at Dartmouth, told me how attending with friends makes her more comfortable in classes and other places around campus: "I would much rather go with a friend. I feel less awkward walking into a big room full of people." Allowing students to bring friends to events would make some students more likely to attend, particularly tight-knitters and some compartmentalizers. Tight-knitters and compartmentalizers will likely interact more with people they do not know when those activities have the criteria mentioned earlier of regular interaction and working toward a collective goal. In contrast, groups that allow for unstructured interaction with nonfriends appeal more to samplers. Along with providing a range of opportunities, enabling students to know which type of friendship network they have also helps students better understand themselves. When they better understand the benefits and barriers of their network type, they are enabled to see the patterns behind it rather than thinking it is a personal flaw that they are not able to make friends or participate in the expected way. Thus, this is another way to combat feelings of loneliness on campus.

## Driving Forward Scholarship on Friendship and Sociology of Education

Along with those practical and policy implications, this book also has implications for scholarship. I focus on two areas: friendship and the sociology of education. These findings particularly contribute to our understandings of friendship as a process, a dynamic one that is shaped by individuals, their networks, and the institutions they attend. In line with relational sociology, this research provides an example of agency and structure, and their duality,[11] specifically, the relationships between people and the meanings of these relationships in particular networks and campus structures. Students come to college with individual preferences for friendship and prior experiences, yet the campus they attend shapes how they make friends, as well as how they keep and lose them, throughout their time on campus.

My findings bolster and refine several key concepts in prior scholarship. Students' experiences on these three campuses reinforce that propinquity and homophily shape who students become friends with. Moreover, they refine these concepts by showing ways that campus structures shape these processes. On campuses with weaker initial friendship markets, such as the community college compared to the residential campuses, propinquity and homophily operate less strongly. On campuses with weaker secondary friendship markets, such as UNH compared to Dartmouth, the initial patterns of propinquity and homophily not only bring friends together but keep them together, even when the relationships are not meaningful for students.

Students' experiences support the benefits of both bonding and bridging social capital. While bonding social capital is based on similarities and is inward looking, bridging social capital can bring in different resources and is outward looking. Rather than advocating for one or the other, my findings show that both types of social capital can bring valuable resources. Arguing that people have become increasingly disconnected from each other over the past few decades, political scientist Robert Putnam advocates for increasing society's stock of both bridging and bonding social capital.[12] Orientation and pre-orientation programs, for example, can lead to insular networks, yet also have opportunities to develop bridging social capital.

The points of intervention above can support and encourage students to develop bonding social capital as well as bridging social capital. For example, Troy told me how he appreciated how he and his friends "found a community, we found fellowship," but he also recognized the limits of having only bonding social capital. He put into action the friendship advice he received to "branch out" and "explore what's out there." Troy noted that this was spurred by hearing his friendship group described as "being exclusive." While it can be an individual decision to seek out both the bonding social capital of "community" and "fellowship" as well as the bridging social capital involved with "branching out," it also can be structured into the campus environment. By providing and supporting a range of student groups, campuses facilitate students maintaining bonds and seeking out new ones.[13] In other words, these investments support the development of both forms of valuable social capital on campus.

My findings also support several of Mario Small's findings in his innovative look at whom people turn to for support when they are facing difficulties. Students' experiences across the three campuses echo Small's conclusion about the importance of "the contexts in which people spend their lives" and "the fluid nature of their decisions in those contexts."[14] For example, whether their campus has a strong initial friendship market and a strong secondary friendship market will shape their ties, similar to how they shaped whom people confide in, in Small's research. My findings provide further support for Small's conclusion that "even in the midst of a strong support network, people may experience profound isolation."[15] Students in each of the three network types experienced loneliness; however, they experienced it differently. Bringing these findings back to the forms of social capital discussed above, Small's findings point to the important role that bridging ties play as confidants. My findings show how both bridging and bonding social capital are valuable resources for college students in combating loneliness.

A growing body of research has uncovered many inequalities in the experiences of students across college campuses. This book fills an important gap in centering the experiences of community college students and demonstrating the important role of social ties in these settings. It also fits with a growing body of work using an institutional approach to understand how features of colleges impact students' experiences.[16] Institutional decisions involving roommates, for example, shape not only friendship processes but also students' racial scripts and behaviors,[17] as well as students' sexual options and experiences on campus.[18] By using a mixed-methods design with case studies on multiple campuses, I am able to leverage the benefits of quantitative network analysis to document patterns with the benefits of qualitative interviews to understand the meaning of these patterns for participants. While my previous book also used a mixed-methods design to document networks and how friends support students academically and socially, this book adds to our understanding of processes and the role of institutions. Thus, I add to work on college friendships, much of which is on the composition of networks,[19] by detailing processes of making, keeping, and losing friends.

There remains much we do not yet know about friendship networks. Are there campuses that have different distributions of the three friendship network types or additional network types? How do these networks change as students graduate and go through other stages of the life course? Along with cross-campus comparisons, longitudinal studies of students' friendships are needed to allow researchers to better understand the dynamics, benefits, and drawbacks of these relationships for student success. Other network researchers have "advocat[ed] for more regular longitudinal studies of college student networks that examine change over time."[20] Better understanding the experiences of making friends, keeping friends, and losing friends over time for a wide range of students would enable greater support for people through these experiences.

As students and their families consider where they will attend college, the quality of the classes is not the only important factor. Perhaps one benefit of the COVID-19 pandemic was the way it highlighted the importance for students of engaging in social aspects of college life, including friendship ties.[21] This also illustrates the importance of campus structures in not just providing friendships but also shaping how students make friends and how easily they can keep the meaningful friendships they form. Friendships matter for students' emotional support and belonging, and the ways they matter is different when students are in a tight-knit network than when they have multiple clusters of friends or mostly one-on-one friendships. In other words, their friendship network type influences their experiences on campus, including feelings of support or loneliness. In this way, the loneliness epidemic on college campuses is not about individual students unable to make friends, but about the structure of their networks, the structure of the institutions they attend, and how their identities matter in each of these places. As illustrated by a quote from Yusef in the introduction, students can feel lonely surrounded by thousands of people. Making not just friends, but meaningful friendships is a way to keep loneliness from remaining at epidemic levels. As MCC student Erin remarked, "The friendships I've made are what turned it [community college] into an experience. . . . They renew my energy. They inspire me, and help me figure things out and learn new things about myself and them." Across all three institutions, meaningful friendships embedded in a network are the key to helping students feel socially connected.

# Acknowledgments

I am immensely thankful for the multiple communities I am part of that shaped this book. One such community consists of the many scholars and colleagues who have read parts of the manuscript, listened to talks, and discussed ideas with me. My impetus to conduct this research came from the questions that repeatedly came up as I gave talks on my previous book, *Connecting in College*, particularly questions about how much of what I found was specific to that one institution. This fueled my curiosity about the role of institutional structures in shaping friendship and how much larger cultural changes, such as those related to technology, generational change, and gender inequality, may shape friendship networks. I particularly thank audiences at Boston College, Dartmouth College, the Sociology of Education Association, and the author-meets-critic session for *Connecting in College* at the American Sociological Association. The arguments I make in this book benefited from the conversations I had with multiple audiences, including college students, their parents, alumni, and college staff, administrators, and faculty. Donna Eder and Brian Powell have been consistently wonderful mentors. My writing group at Dartmouth—Jason Houle, Emily Walton, and Kim Rogers—encouraged my weekly updates about the book and offered constructive comments on drafts of various pieces. The participants at my manuscript review session—Annette Lareau, Lisa Nunn, Scott Pauls, and Eric Ramsey—provided insightful feedback and discussion on an early draft of this book, and the "Takeaways" at the end of each chapter are the result of them nudging me to better articulate these implications.

I am fortunate to have an outstanding editorial team at the University of Chicago Press. I especially thank Elizabeth Branch Dyson for her support and incisive questions at key junctures in this project. Assistant editor Mollie McFee also helped immensely in this process with a range of logistics.

This project benefited from the former Dartmouth College students who served as research assistants in this project over the years: Alexis Castillo, Amber Strock, Arvind Shankar, Claire Marshall, Ellie Wilson, Hailey Noronha, Hannah Nam, Jennifer Jiwon Lee, Jessica Cortez, Kelly Zeilman, Olivia Goodwin, Ramya Chilappa, and Sam Selleck. They played important roles in organizing, collecting, and analyzing the multiple waves and types of data on which this book is based.

Dartmouth College helped to fund this research in many ways, including grants from the Nelson A. Rockefeller Center for Public Policy and the Social Sciences, for aspects of data collection and my manuscript review seminar; Dartmouth Undergraduate Advising and Research, for funding undergraduate research assistance; and the Walter and Constance Burke Research Funds.

I have learned so much about friendship from my own friends. I'm thankful to have had a variety of communities of support, people who have shared joys and sorrows with me over the years, through many walks, cups of tea, glasses of wine, and long talks. There are too many people who have touched my life in this way to note them all, but I especially want to call out the support of Abby Neely, Alicia Suarez, Amy Bergholz, Belinda Chiu, Emily Fairchild, Lauren Oliver, and Sienna Craig. These are some of the meaningful friendships that inspired this book, and I appreciate the ways you showed this, whether through listening to me talk through ideas, bringing me dinner when I was finishing edits, or cheering me on. And there is one friend who provided this support through phone calls, writing retreats, and many other points of meaningful connection through multiple decades; I am so fortunate to have Sarah Rainey Smithback in my life.

My family also supported the creation of this book. I thank them for asking about the book—but not too often—and for their unwavering belief in me through the path that took me to this project. Throughout my life, my parents, Mark and Marilyn McCabe, encouraged me to find good evidence to back up the hunches that I had and to make connections with lots of people, even those whom others thought were "difficult"; both lessons are reflected in this book. My children Kallen and Cole have eaten many takeout meals and even made dinner so I could write for a few more minutes, and they provided much joy throughout this project. I thought of them and their future often as I wrote, and I hope that the experiences and advice in this book support them and other young people to feel connection and belonging.

Finally, my deep appreciation to my participants, who shared slices of their lives with me, detailing their experiences of making, keeping, and losing friends. I remain interested in how friendships change and how our friendships change us throughout our lives. Continuing to talk to a researcher every few years about something as personal as friendship is a big ask. Thank you for trusting me with your joys and your challenges. My hope is that this book accurately reflects your experiences and helps others to have more meaningful friendships and support in college and throughout their lives.

# Appendix A
Researching Students' Networks on Three Campuses

## The Origins of This Project

I had been at Dartmouth College for four years as a faculty member in sociology when I started to interview students on campus about their friendships for this project. That year, my first book, *Connecting in College*, was published. In that book, I developed the typology of friendship networks (tight-knitters, compartmentalizers, and samplers) discussed here and addressed how students' friendship networks encourage academic and social success, and how they get in the way of this success. As I was writing the book and giving talks about it, audience members often asked questions about what would be similar and what would be different about students' friendship networks on other campuses. I found these questions challenging to answer, and they brought up more questions of my own.

As I was teaching classes at Dartmouth, especially those on sociology of education and sociology of youth, I was sharing my findings with students and getting their opinions. I was intrigued by many things about the Dartmouth experience, including the D-plan schedule, why so many students joined Greek organizations, how local Greek organizations differed from national ones, and how co-ed fraternities (as they were called at the time) differed from traditional fraternities for men and sororities for women. In explaining the dominance of Greek life, students often brought up how Dartmouth was the inspiration for the 1978 film, *National Lampoon's Animal House*.[1] Dartmouth students often talked about how, by the time they had built strong friendships at the end of their first year, they moved that summer, often back home, and might not be in the same location as their friends again for more than a year, when they returned to campus for "sophomore summer." I was also struck by the difference of being a Dartmouth student on a campus of 4,000 undergraduates compared to my two previous institutions, Florida State University and Indiana University—Bloomington,[2] each of which had more than 30,000 undergraduates, or the university I attended, Tulane University, a campus that was embedded in a city. In other words, I started thinking about how the ways that campuses are structured impact how students make and keep friends. I also found Dartmouth to be an interesting site to look at friendship networks, given that it is more racially diverse than the Big Ten school that was the site for *Connecting in College*.

When I arrived at Dartmouth in 2012, the student life that students had been used to seemed uncertain. An exposé had just come out in *Rolling Stone* magazine, detailing one student's experiences in the Greek system with hazing.[3] Students were vocal and divided about Greek life, about sexual assault, and about racial tensions on campus. In 2015, the Dartmouth president announced a plan called "Moving Dartmouth Forward" that sought to end high-risk drinking and sexual assault on campus and to give students a greater sense of community and inclusivity on campus.[4] This plan also established "house communities" on campus, a residential college system to which undergraduates were randomly assigned upon admission and which served as a microcosm of campus to help establish continuity in their campus experience and increase community and intellectual engagement.[5] A few years later, I came to lead one of one of these house communities, which allowed me to facilitate students' sense of belonging and meaningful connections on campus through a range of social, intellectual, and cultural activities.[6]

It became clear to me that Dartmouth would be an illuminating site for a comparative case study of students' friendships at three types of postsecondary institutions. Along with Dartmouth, a small elite private college, I wanted to include a large public university and a nonresidential community college. Community colleges are particularly understudied in sociological research on students' experiences, especially given the large number of students who attend this type of institution. Choosing a nonresidential community college would also allow me to explore the role of residential life in students' friendships. As I started to investigate other campuses, I considered quite a few in the Northeast, including some in Massachusetts, Vermont, Maine, and upstate New York. Choosing institutions in similar locations that differ in size, selectivity, residential life, and campus culture leverages strengths of case study design.[7] Ultimately, I landed on two more institutions in New Hampshire: the University of New Hampshire and Manchester Community College.

My focus on three campuses builds on a range of sociological and educational research that examines students' experiences of colleges across different types of institutions. For example, in analyzing how social class shapes students' experiences, Jenny Stuber and Ann Mullen both compare a large public institution (Stuber's is flagship, Mullen's is regional) with a small elite private institution. These two types of institutions are also the comparison of Sherelle Ferguson and Annette Lareau, in their investigation of classist interactions in working-class students' same-race friendships; of Amy Binder and Kate Wood, in their focus on how campus culture shapes political styles; and of Lisa Nunn's investigation of how first-generation college students create belonging. In a three-institution comparison, which includes regional and flagship public universities and a liberal arts college, Daisy Reyes shows how campuses shape the ways students interact and understand their Latino identities on campus.[8] My analysis and design are unique in comparing a community college to residential ones—both an elite liberal arts college and a public flagship university.

## Access to the Three Campuses

I gained access differently at each of the institutions. Getting access to Dartmouth was relatively easy. I knew the campus, so I knew where to put up flyers in spots that were visible to students, and it was easier to find the student leaders of campus organizations, to contact them and invite their members into the study. My position as a faculty member in sociology gave me legitimacy with the students that I believe helped their willingness to share my flyer with their organizations and friends. However, I also was cautious that students might view me as an authority figure, so might not be as open to share their experiences with me. To address this in part, I did not interview students who were currently taking a class with me or who I expected would take a class with me. I did end up with three students in my sample who later enrolled in a class with me. All three participated in follow-up interviews after that class ended, and they appeared to be as open with me as they were in the first interview. Of course, it is not possible to know what they may not have told me.

At UNH, I knew a couple of faculty and staff members, whom I spoke with to better understand the campus culture. These individuals served as informal sponsors who helped me gain access to and information about the campus, including how and when to best sample at the institution. I hired a student to put up flyers on campus; this not only saved me time in driving to and from campus (four hours, round-trip) but also ensured that flyers were placed where students would see them.[9] This student knew the campus better than I did, so she knew, for example, to put up flyers in the commuters' parking lot, in dorms, and in academic buildings. I found that most students who contacted me from flyers were White, so I reached out to two staff members who worked with students from marginalized groups.

I sent several emails with no response. When I mentioned a specific time that I would be near their offices and stop by, I received a reply from both staff members. Upon meeting in person, I explained the study. Both staff members allowed me to put up flyers, and they also volunteered to introduce me to students in their study space at that visit.

I did not have any personal contacts at MCC at the start of the study, so I began by reaching out to staff members who worked directly with students. As discussed in my field notes in chapter 1, the staff members were willing to meet with me and show me around campus. At the time, I did not yet have a full-time daycare spot for my ten-month-old son, so he came with me to some of these meetings. Although it was not my intention, having him with me seemed to help me connect with some of the women staff members, who enjoyed playing peek-a-boo and other activities with my son, and it also humanized me in their eyes, particularly when my status as a faculty member at an Ivy League institution could have felt like a barrier.

What was hardest about MCC was gaining Institutional Review Board (IRB) permission. Because it is not a research institution, unlike UNH and Dartmouth, MCC did not have a standing IRB committee or a web portal to submit applications. I reached out to the head of the IRB listed on the MCC website, who was an instructor in math. He asked that I meet with him, so I came to campus twice for that purpose. On the second visit, he said that he would need to confer with the president of MCC before going further. Accordingly, I also had two visits with the president, where I explained my sociological approach and the study's goals. It was clear that she cared about students and about MCC's reputation. On the second visit, she said that her concerns had been addressed, and I submitted my IRB application. After some additional clarifications with the head of the IRB about my protocols, the study was approved at MCC. In contrast, UNH accepted Dartmouth's IRB approval and did not require its own. Dartmouth's approval did not involve any in-person meetings or phone calls, although it did require one point of clarification after my original application.

## The Case Study Design

As part of the case study design, I considered the historical, institutional, and demographic contexts[10] of these three institutions. Two undergraduate research assistants helped me to collect archival information about the institutions. We focused on collecting articles written by and about the institutions in local papers, the student newspapers at UNH and Dartmouth,[11] the *Princeton Review*, and so on, ending up with nearly 300 articles and web pages. We also collected data about the institutions from the Common Data Set and any internal surveys and reports that are publicly available. My data also include field notes from my observations in public spaces on these campuses, particularly in libraries and cafeterias. Most times that I traveled to do an interview, I would spend an extra couple of hours at the campus in these public spaces, taking field notes. My approach was not to initiate conversations with people, but to respond when they engaged me. Only at MCC did anyone invite me to sit with them in the cafeteria or library. This happened multiple times and was initiated by respondents, staff members at the college, and two people I had never met (on separate occasions). As I jotted in my field notes, "there is a community feel here and a feeling of care." By drawing on these multiple sources of evidence, along with the interviews and network data that constitute the bulk of my data, I was able to maximize reliability by triangulation as well as to construct fuller cases of friendship on these three campuses.

My approach in sampling was on identifying patterns within and across institutions, rather than being generalizable to specific populations.[12] I recruited interview participants through a range of clubs and organizations (for example, identity-based clubs for racial groups and first-generation college students, academic clubs, and Greek organizations), by posting flyers on and near each campus, and through asking participants for suggestions of individual students to speak with, noting that I was particularly interested in speaking with people who might have different experiences or opinions than the participant. I obtained participants through each of these recruitment strategies, although the numbers differed by site. At Dartmouth, I recruited 15 through clubs, 8 through flyers, and 12 through snowball sampling. At UNH, I recruited fewer through clubs (5) and more through flyers (18), with a similar number through snowball sampling (11). At MCC, I recruited primarily through tabling at the club fair, where I was able to get a table and have students sign up if they were interested,[13] and I also explained my study in three classes, one each in the nursing, HVAC, and business programs. Of my 26 participants, 9 came from the club fair, 9 from my visits to classes, 5 from flyers, and 3 from snowball sampling.

My original goal was to recruit 7–10 White, Asian, Black, Latina/o, and Native American students at each institution. In doing so, I would have 21–30 students from each racial/ethnic group and 40 from each institution. I was able to come close to this at Dartmouth, but not at the other two institutions. When I met with the president of MCC, she noted that she could "count the number of Native American students on one hand," so that would be an impossible goal. I aimed for as much racial diversity as possible in my samples from each of the three institutions.

I received funding from the Nelson A. Rockefeller Center at Dartmouth College for this project. This allowed me to pay my participants on each campus ($20 for the first interview while they were in college, $40 for the second); get each of us a cup of coffee, pastry, or sandwich when we met in a coffee shop or cafeteria; pay a professional transcription service; and cover my travel costs to and from the research sites. I did the interviews mostly in the fall term, from September to December, when I was not teaching.[14]

I wanted to do all the initial interviews myself, rather than hiring a research team or training students to do them. This meant that I needed to stagger my data collection. I started with Dartmouth College. In 2016–17, I interviewed 95 students: 35 from Dartmouth, 34 from UNH, and 26 from MCC. At Dartmouth and UNH, most students whom I interviewed were finishing up their second year or starting their third year in college; at MCC, most interviews were with students in at least their second year in college. I gave students several options of where we could conduct the interviews. At Dartmouth, most students chose my office in the sociology department, but eight chose a reservable room in the library and two chose a common space in their dorm. At UNH, most students chose either a coffee shop off campus or a favorite spot in the student union. These spaces worked well because, even though they were not private, they were places where others were talking, so they were not too quiet or too loud. In a few instances, students chose a cafeteria, in which case we found a quiet corner to talk so that we could hear each other well and my recorder would pick up our conversation. At MCC, administrators gave me access to a couple of private rooms, where I could schedule the interviews. I offered to meet students at an off-campus restaurant or coffee shop, but only two students chose that option. The others met me in the conference room or study room that I had access to at MCC. I scheduled these interviews at times most convenient for the respondents; however, no-shows and last-minute cancellations were more of a problem at MCC and UNH, given that I had driven one or two hours, respectively, to get to these campuses. On two occasions, I spent the night at UNH so that I could complete evening and early-morning interviews. When possible, I tried to schedule two interviews for the same trip so that at least one would work out. However, being able to take field notes on campus and to replenish flyers made my trips useful even when the interviews did not work out.

The interviews lasted 75 minutes on average, although they varied from about 50 minutes to 2 hours and 20 minutes. I asked students many open-ended questions about their friendships and experiences on campus, including their decision to attend that campus, what it was like to first make friends there, the activities they currently did with friends, what had been most helpful for them at college socially and academically (as separate questions), the biggest barrier for them socially and academically at college (also as separate questions), and advice they had for other students on their campus. Most students seemed to open up to me quickly. This was true for students on all three campuses. Perhaps their cultural frames of women as being "easy to talk to" and good communicators, as discussed in chapter 5, helped them feel comfortable talking with me. Many of them noted that they think a lot about their friendships, and appreciated the space to talk about them with someone. A few students told me that our conversation felt like therapy, which I considered to be a sign of their openness and degree of comfort. Of course, my identities as a faculty member and a White woman impacted how students related to me. Snowball sampling was particularly helpful for recruiting students of color in all three settings; while no one said it directly, my sense is that students were more likely to trust me with their stories when a same-race peer recommended the study.

Participants completed two short surveys along with the interview. The first one was a screening survey that asked how many years they had been enrolled at the school, their racial background, and which clubs and organizations, if any, they belonged to, and which were most important to them. At the beginning of the interview, students completed a longer survey with more demographic questions and identity scales, including the academic-social one discussed in chapter 4. Summaries of many of these survey responses appear in Table B.2 in Appendix B.

Along with participants' stories about their friendships, I systematically collected a list of each participant's friends and their perception of whether each friend knew each other friend. Because it is from the perspective of the participant, this is referred to as "egocentric" network data. Rather than limiting the number[15] or types of friends that participants could name—for example, to those attending the same college—I allowed students to name all closer friends. I attended to power dynamics in and across networks[16] by understanding not just the structure of students' networks, but how students experience them. The in-depth interviews enabled this approach. As they mentioned specific friends throughout the interview, I added them to a list. Toward the end of the interview, I shared this list with the participant and asked if they had other friends to add or anyone on the list whom they would not currently consider a closer friend. I also checked the demographic information that I had been recording about their friends, including gender (using pronouns), race, which college (if any) they attended, how long they had been friends, where they met, and how they usually stay in touch. I also collected their perceptions of which of their friends knew each other, collecting information on many ties. For example, 3 ties for networks of 3 friends, 55 ties for networks of 11 friends, and 528 ties for networks of 33 friends. By collecting this information, I elicited stories about students' friendships, and I also was able to compute measures of homophily, including those in Table B.1 in Appendix B. I used these techniques in my earlier research in *Connecting in College*, which enables comparisons to those data.

I interviewed 54 of the 95 students again near the time they graduated from college or should have graduated. This was timed well for Dartmouth students, with most of those interviews happening in 2019. Of the 35 Dartmouth students in the first wave, 34 gave me permission to contact them for follow-up interviews, and 27 of those participated in a wave two interview. No one turned me down for wave two, but several either did not respond to my initial outreach or follow through with an interview. The COVID-19 pandemic interrupted my planned interviews in spring 2020 with students at the other two campuses. Instead, in 2021 I interviewed the UNH and MCC students, which was three and a half to four years after their original interview with me. Of the 34 UNH students in wave one, 33 gave permission to contact them again, and 21 participated in wave two. Of the 26 MCC students in wave one, 7 participated in wave two.[17] The 2021 interviews were conducted over Zoom and by telephone, and two undergraduate research assistants conducted 22 of these interviews with me. Both students had taken a research methods course with me and had been involved in previous social science research. Prior to doing interviews, they read transcripts from earlier interviews from this project, contributed to memos, and conducted two practice interviews. We met weekly throughout the two terms, planning and debriefing interviews, and discussing emerging findings. Both research assistants were young women in their early twenties; one was White and one was a student of color who identifies as Indian. I sent the initial email or text to participants to set up the interviews, introducing them to and putting them in touch with the research assistant who would conduct their interview. My participants from UNH seemed to connect especially well with the research assistants, as they were similar in age and had experienced the COVID-19 pandemic disrupting their schooling as well. I interviewed most of the MCC participants myself because they were more varied in age and two had expressed a preference to talk with me. I plan to continue to interview participants every five years to assess how institutional factors and friendship networks impact their long-term success; these follow-up interviews will happen next with Dartmouth students in 2025.

## Analysis

After each interview, I wrote field notes, describing the participant and key themes from the interview.[18] After the interview was transcribed, I wrote memos and had undergraduate research assistants write memos across the multiple interviews for each participant and across emerging themes. I added insights from the archival data into these memos. I read and reread these memos as I was coding the interviews and drafting this book.

After entering my field notes and transcribed interviews into Atlas.ti, I used the constant comparative method[19] to pursue confirming patterns and negative cases. For example, I coded for the role of propinquity and homophily in students' experiences, constantly returning to the data to compare across patterns and categories, including campuses and students' identities. Inductive coding involved the creation of new codes from the data—such as friendship funneling and friendship expansion. As I continued to read over the quotes attached to these codes by institution, by friendship network type (sampler, compartmentalizer, and tight-knitter), and by students' identity group, I memoed about patterns in how students described making friends, keeping friends, and losing friends, as well as how these varied by institution and identities. These patterns became the structure of the chapters of this book.

Using the network analysis software Gephi, I generated the friendship network maps and quantitative measures—such as density, betweenness centrality, and modularity. Network researchers refer to the visual network maps as "sociograms" and the individuals shown in them as "nodes." Density is the network measure I report most frequently throughout this book; it captures the number of ties present out of the possible ties. For ego networks, this measure excludes all ties connected to the person interviewed. As with *Connecting in College*, networks with density of 0–0.33 are considered "samplers"; 0.34–0.66 are considered "compartmentalizers"; and 0.67–1 are considered "tight-knitters." Along with density, betweenness centrality and modularity scores helped to decide on these cut points. Betweenness centrality scores measure how central someone is in a network by how many nodes are connected only through that individual, with higher scores indicating a person is more central in connecting others.[20] Because these are egocentric networks, I focus only on the students I interviewed, computing betweenness centrality scores for each respondent. As expected, these are highest for samplers (0.66) and lowest for tight-knitters (0.07), with compartmentalizers in the middle (0.36).[21] Modularity patterns also exist between these three types. Modularity measures communities in a network, calculated by comparing the number of edges (i.e., ties between friends) that are present compared to those that are expected.[22] Modularity scores are again highest for samplers (0.39) and lowest for tight-knitters (0.02), with compartmentalizers in the middle (0.22).[23]

The sociograms I present in this book use the Yifan Hu algorithm in Gephi.[24] I partition the nodes by modularity class.[25] I also indicate betweenness centrality with size of the node, with bigger nodes indicating that the person is more central to the network. The participant is always the biggest node because they are connected to all their friends; however, sometimes other friends are equally central, meaning that they also are connected to everyone in the network, which is shown visually by the node size. In other words, the nodes' size and position as well as the ties are not placed randomly, but systematically and according to the underlying dimensions of the networks.

Data from both surveys along with Gephi were entered into Stata by undergraduate research assistants. I used Stata to generate descriptive statistics to compare across institutions and network types.

Most of the data presented in this book come from the interviews and friendship networks; however, the other methodological approaches often helped me arrive at the understandings presented here. In sum, the approach I take here is a mixed-method, longitudinal, case study design focused on better understanding students' friendship networks on these campuses. As I continue the data collection, I focus on how college friendship matters for people in later stages of the life course and how processes of making, keeping, and losing friends are similar and different than in college.

# Appendix B

Tables Describing Study Participants and the Campuses

TABLE B.1. Characteristics of College Friends

|  | DC (N=35) | UNH (N=34) | MCC (N=26) | Overall Sample (N=95) | Range |
|---|---|---|---|---|---|
| Number of friends | 11.9 | 12.3 | 8.2 | 11.0 | 2-39 |
| Range of number of friends | 2-25 | 4-39 | 3-16 | 2-39 | — |
| % Friends at their college | 72 | 75 | 44 | 65 | 0-100 |
| Range | 40-100 | 22-100 | 0-100 | 0-100 | — |
| % Friends from home | 29 | 32 | 67 | 40 | 0-100 |
| Range | 0-60 | 0-78 | 0-100 | 0-100 | — |
| % Friends from home who also attend their college | 1 | 7 | 9 | 5 | 0-50 |
| Range | 0-10 | 0-50 | 0-43 | 0-50 | — |
| % Same-race friends | 58 | 79 | 65 | 68 | 0-100 |
| % Same-gender friends | 70 | 71 | 66 | 69 | 0-100 |
| Density (mean) | 0.53 | 0.58 | 0.43 | 0.52 | 0.10-1 |
| Modularity (mean) | 0.20 | 0.18 | 0.24 | 0.21 | 0-0.67 |
| Betweenness centrality (mean) | 0.33 | 0.27 | 0.47 | 0.35 | 0-.89 |
| % Same friends across interviews[a] | 43 | 42 | 9 | 39 | 0-100 |

[a] This is based only on students who participated in both waves of network data, which is 27 students at Dartmouth, 21 at UNH, and 7 at MCC. For Dartmouth, the two waves are two years apart and both are during college. For UNH and MCC, the waves are 3.5–4 years apart.

TABLE B.2. Characteristics of Sample by Campus

| | DC (N=35) | UNH (N=34) | MCC (N=26) | Overall Sample (N=95) | Range |
|---|---|---|---|---|---|
| **Background** | | | | | |
| Age | 19.7 | 20.0 | 26.2 | 21.6 | 18–51 |
| Gender | | | | | |
| % Women | 74 | 68 | 71 | 71 | — |
| % Men | 26 | 30 | 26 | 26 | — |
| % Nonbinary | 0 | 3 | 4 | 3 | — |
| % Lesbian, gay, bisexual, or pansexual | 17 | 12 | 27 | 18 | — |
| % in a romantic relationship[a] | 23 | 32 | 38 | 31 | — |
| **Race** | | | | | |
| % White | 23 | 76 | 65 | 55 | — |
| % Asian | 17 | 9 | 8 | 12 | — |
| % Black | 20 | 9 | 12 | 14 | — |
| % Latinx | 31 | 6 | 15 | 18 | — |
| % Native American | 9 | 0 | 0 | 3 | — |
| % Multiracial | 14 | 6 | 6 | 9 | — |
| % International student | 23 | 0 | 8 | 11 | — |
| % In-state resident | 0 | 35 | 85 | 36 | — |
| *Population*: % In-state resident | 3 | 41 | 98 | | — |
| Mean ACT score | 31 | 25 | 25[b] | 28 | 18–36 |
| *Population*: ACT scores at the 25th & 75th percentiles | 30–34 | 23–28 | NA | — | — |
| % First-generation | 43 | 21 | 39 | 39 | — |
| **Class** | | | | | |
| % Upper | 34 | 26 | 12 | 25 | — |
| % Middle | 37 | 65 | 54 | 53 | — |
| % Lower | 29 | 6 | 35 | 22 | — |
| Household income[c] | 103K | 142K | 71K | 110K | |
| **Campus experiences** | | | | | |
| Years at that college | 2.3 | 2.7 | 2 | 2.4 | 0.5–5 |
| Years at any college | 2.3 | 3 | 3.1 | | |
| GPA | 3.4 | 3.3 | 3.2 | 3.3 | 1.7–4.0 |
| % Living on campus[d] | 91 | 56 | 0 | 47 | |

TABLE B.2. *(continued)*

| | DC (N=35) | UNH (N=34) | MCC (N=26) | Overall Sample (N=95) | Range |
|---|---|---|---|---|---|
| *Population*: % living on campus | 88 | 56 | 0 | — | — |
| % Employed | 80 | 53 | 85 | 72 | — |
| Hours/week, if employed | 13 | 12 | 23 | 16 | 2–50 |
| Academic-social scale[e] | 5.0 | 5.1 | 4.7 | 5.0 | 0–9 |
| Lots of friends–few friends scale | 5.7 | 5.8 | 7.1 | 6.1 | 0–10 |
| Partier–never party scale | 5.9 | 5.7 | 8.0 | 6.4 | 0–10 |
| Academically serious–academically unengaged | 3.1 | 2.1 | 2.0 | 2.5 | 0–8 |

[a] "In a relationship" includes those who chose this category as well as those who chose engaged or cohabitating. It does not include those who listed themselves as single, separated, or dating (unless they also indicated they were in a relationship).

[b] Because ACT or SAT scores are not required at MCC, only 5 students reported scores. Most had transferred from four-year schools to MCC, so it is likely a select group.

[c] Like other categories, this is based on students' self-report; however, it had more missing data than other categories (91% of Dartmouth students, 94% of UNH students, and 81% of MCC students reported their household income).

[d] Following how the campus classifies these, living in most sororities and fraternities is considered on-campus at Dartmouth but considered off-campus at UNH. On-campus includes dorms and apartments located on campus and owned by the university.

[e] For each of the scales, 0 is the first word or phrase; 10 is the second. For example, 0 = academic and 10 = social; 0 = lots of friends and 10 = few friends.

TABLE B.3. Characteristics of the Three Institutions

| Institution | Dartmouth College | University of New Hampshire | Manchester Community College |
|---|---|---|---|
| State | New Hampshire | New Hampshire | New Hampshire |
| Location[a] | Hanover, rural town (population=9,078) | Durham, rural town (population=11,147) | Manchester, mid-size city (population=115,644) |
| Type | 4-year liberal arts college | 4-year public flagship university | 2-year public community college |
| Size of undergraduate population | 4,000[b] | 11,000[c] | 3,500 |
| % Admitted who applied | 12% | 80% | 100% |
| ACT scores at the 25th & 75th percentiles (reported above) | 30–4 | 23–28 | NA |
| % Graduated[d] | 95% | 76% | 15% 21% transfer |
| Clubs and organizations on campus | Over 150 | Over 250 | Over 30 |
| % in fraternities or sororities | 50% (70% of eligible students)[e] | 10% | 0 |
| % Students living on campus[f] | 88% | 56% | 0 |
| % Students attending full time | 99% | 96% | 33% |
| % Students from in-state | 3% | 41% | 98% |
| Traditional age (% 24 and under) | 99% | 97% | 57% |
| Tuition and fees (2014–2015) | $48,108 | $16,552 in-state $29,532 out-of-state | $6,848 in-state $15,008 out-of-state |
| Tuition and fees (2020–2021) | $60,648 | $18,938 in-state $36,278 out-of-state | $7,090 $15,340 out-of-state |
| % Students receiving Pell Grants[g] | 14% | 22% | 37% |
| % of students from top 1% of family income ($630K+)[h] | 20.7% | 1.8% | <1% |

TABLE B.3. *(continued)*

| Institution | Dartmouth College | University of New Hampshire | Manchester Community College |
|---|---|---|---|
| % of students from Bottom 60% of family income (<65K) | 14.4% | 21.8% | 43.0% |
| Racial composition[i] | | | |
| % White | 47% | 80% | 76% |
| % Asian | 14% | 2% | 2% |
| % Black | 7% | 1% | 3% |
| % Latinx | 8% | 3% | 4% |
| % Native American | 2% | <1% | <1% |

Note: Information is from US Department of Education's NCES College Navigator (available at https://nces.ed.gov/collegenavigator/) or each school's Common Core Data in 2016, unless otherwise noted.

[a] US Census, 2020. All three locations had slight increases in population from 2010 to 2020.

[b] 6,000 students, including those attending graduate and professional schools.

[c] 14,000 students on the main campus in Durham, including those attending graduate and professional schools.

[d] Includes graduation rates within 150% of time to degree, which is six years for Dartmouth and UNH, and three years for MCC.

[e] Because first-year students are not eligible, when they are removed from the denominator, the percentage of affiliated students rises from half to 70%.

[f] Among only first-year students, 100% live on campus at Dartmouth and 91% at UNH. MCC is nonresidential; it has no dorms.

[g] Pell Grant receipt indicates low income, and rates have become more similar between Dartmouth and UNH over time. For the financial aid in 2021–22, 16% of students at Dartmouth and 17% at UNH received Pell grants. At MCC, 33% of students received Pell grants in 2021–22.

[h] Opportunity Insights, "Mobility Report Cards."

[i] Unlike MCC, Dartmouth and UNH also have administrative initiatives to increase racial diversity. See https://d7admin.unh.edu/cspc/commission; http://www.dartmouth.edu/~president/forward/.

TABLE B.4. Participant Key Characteristics

| Name | Campus | Age | Year in School at First Interview | Race | Social Class | First Gen | Gender | Participated in Second Interview |
|---|---|---|---|---|---|---|---|---|
| Abigail | UNH | 19 | 2 | Latinx | LMC | Yes | W | Yes |
| Alexa | MCC | 21 | 1 | White | LMC | No | NB | Yes |
| Amanda | DC | 19 | 2 | Latinx | MC | No | W | Yes |
| Amber | UNH | 20 | 3 | White | UMC | No | W | Yes |
| Anjali | MCC | 21 | 3 | Asian | MC | Yes | W | No |
| Austin | DC | 21 | 2 | White | WC | Yes | M | Yes |
| Bill | DC | 18 | 2 | Asian | MC | No | M | Yes |
| Bobby | UNH | 18 | 1 | White | UC | No | M | Yes |
| Calvin | DC | 20 | 2 | Asian | WC | Yes | M | Yes |
| Chandra | UNH | 20 | 4 | Asian | MC | No | W | Yes |
| Chris | UNH | 22 | 4 | White | LMC | No | NB | Yes |
| Ciara | MCC | 18 | 1 | Latinx | P | Yes | W | No |
| Cindy | UNH | 21 | 4 | Asian & White | MC | Yes | NB | Yes |
| Cynthia | DC | 18 | 2 | Asian | UMC | No | W | Yes |
| Daisy | UNH | 20 | 2 | White | LMC | No | W | Yes |
| Dani | DC | 20 | 2 | White | UC | No | W | No |
| Danica | DC | 19 | 2 | Latinx | P | Yes | W | Yes |
| David | MCC | 21 | 2 | White | LMC | No | M | No |
| Dawn | DC | 20 | 2 | Asian | MC | No | W | Yes |
| Dory | MCC | 24 | 1 | Black | P | Yes | W | No |
| Dustin | DC | 20 | 3 | White | UMC | No | M | Yes |
| Elizabeth | DC | 23 | 5 | Native American | LMC | Yes | W | No |
| Ella | DC | 19 | 2 | White | UC | No | W | Yes |
| Elyse | MCC | 26 | 4 | White | MC | No | W | No |
| Emma | MCC | 34 | 4 | White | MC | No | W | No |
| Erin | MCC | 34 | 2 | White | WC | Yes | W | No |
| Grace | UNH | 19 | 2 | White | MC | No | W | No |
| Hazel | MCC | 22 | 3 | White | MC | Yes | W | No |
| Heidi | UNH | 22 | 4 | White | MC | Yes | W | No |

TABLE B.4. *(continued)*

| Name | Campus | Age | Year in School at First Interview | Race | Social Class | First Gen | Gender | Participated in Second Interview |
|---|---|---|---|---|---|---|---|---|
| Irina | UNH | 18 | 1 | Black | MC | No | W | No |
| Jane | UNH | 21 | 4 | White | UMC | No | W | No |
| Jenna | DC | 19 | 3 | Asian | MC | No | W | Yes |
| Jennifer | DC | 20 | 2 | Latinx | LMC | No | W | Yes |
| Jill | UNH | 19 | 2 | White | MC | No | W | Yes |
| Jodi | DC | 19 | 2 | White | UMC | No | W | No |
| Jorge | DC | 21 | 3 | Latinx | WC | Yes | M | No |
| Kari | MCC | 45 | 2 | White | WC | No | W | Yes |
| Kate | DC | 19 | 2 | Black | MC | No | W | No |
| Kelly | UNH | 20 | 3 | White | MC | No | W | No |
| Kevin | UNH | 20 | 3 | White | UMC | No | M | No |
| Kira | DC | 19 | 2 | Black | MC | No | W | Yes |
| Kris | MCC | 20 | 1 | Black | WC | Yes | M | No |
| Kylie | UNH | 22 | 2 | White | P | No | W | Yes |
| Lafayette | MCC | 22 | 2 | Latinx | UC | No | M | Yes |
| Layla | DC | 19 | 2 | Latinx | WC | Yes | W | Yes |
| Lev | MCC | 27 | 4 | White | MC | No | M | No |
| Liahna | UNH | 21 | 4 | White | UMC | No | W | No |
| Libby | DC | 22 | 5 | Latinx | UMC | No | W | Yes |
| Lindsay | UNH | 18 | 1 | White | LMC | Yes | W | Yes |
| Lori | UNH | 21 | 4 | White | MC | No | W | Yes |
| Luz | DC | 20 | 2 | Latinx | LMC | Yes | W | No |
| May | UNH | 20 | 3 | White | MC | No | W | Yes |
| Melanie | DC | 19 | 2 | White | UMC | No | W | Yes |
| Melinda | UNH | 20 | 2 | White | UMC | No | W | No |
| Melvin | DC | 20 | 2 | Black | UMC | Yes | M | Yes |
| Mindy | MCC | 30 | 3 | White | MC | Yes | W | No |
| Mira | MCC | 20 | 1 | Latinx | LMC | Yes | W | No |
| Monika | MCC | 18 | 1 | Latinx | WC | Yes | W | Yes |
| Morgan | UNH | 18 | 1 | White | UMC | No | W | No |
| Nancy | UNH | 19 | 2 | White | MC | No | W | Yes |
| Natalie | UNH | 21 | 3 | White | UMC | No | W | Yes |

*(continued)*

TABLE B.4. *(continued)*

| Name | Campus | Age | Year in School at First Interview | Race | Social Class | First Gen | Gender | Participated in Second Interview |
|---|---|---|---|---|---|---|---|---|
| Nella | UNH | 21 | 4 | Latinx | P | Yes | W | Yes |
| Nicole | DC | 19 | 2 | White | WC | Yes | W | Yes |
| Olivia | DC | 21 | 2 | Latinx | WC | Yes | W | Yes |
| Otto | UNH | 23 | 3 | Black | LMC | Yes | M | Yes |
| Paige | DC | 20 | 2 | Latinx & White | UC | No | W | No |
| Patrice | MCC | 18 | 2 | Black & White | MC | Yes | W | No |
| Paul | DC | 19 | 2 | Black | LMC | Yes | M | No |
| Pauline | MCC | 49 | 1 | White | P | Yes | W | Yes |
| Piper | MCC | 20 | 2.5 | White | MC | No | W | No |
| Rachel | UNH | 20 | 3 | White | MC | Yes | W | No |
| Renata | DC | 19 | 2 | Latinx | P | Yes | W | Yes |
| Robbie | UNH | 20 | 3 | Asian | MC | No | M | Yes |
| Ruben | MCC | 31 | 4 | Asian | MC | No | M | No |
| Safiya | DC | 21 | 2 | Black | LMC | No | W | Yes |
| Sarah | MCC | 24 | 2 | White | UMC | Yes | W | No |
| Sasha | DC | 19 | 2 | White | MC | No | W | Yes |
| Savannah | DC | 19 | 2 | Native American | WC | Yes | W | Yes |
| Shirley | MCC | 19 | 2 | White | UMC | No | W | Yes |
| Skip | MCC | 51 | 2 | White | MC | Yes | M | No |
| Sophia | UNH | 20 | 3 | White | UMC | No | W | No |
| Susan | UNH | 21 | 3 | White | MC | No | W | Yes |
| Sydney | DC | 20 | 2 | Black | UMC | No | W | Yes |
| Tania | MCC | 23 | 2 | White | MC | No | W | Yes |
| Teddy | UNH | 19 | 2 | White | LMC | No | M | Yes |
| Terrence | MCC | 24 | 2 | White | WC | Yes | M | No |
| Timothy | UNH | 18 | 1 | White | LMC | No | M | No |
| Tom | DC | 21 | 3 | Latinx | UC | No | M | Yes |

TABLE B.4. *(continued)*

| Name | Campus | Age | Year in School at First Interview | Race | Social Class | First Gen | Gender | Participated in Second Interview |
|---|---|---|---|---|---|---|---|---|
| Troy | DC | 20 | 2 | Black | P | Yes | M | Yes |
| Tyler | UNH | 20 | 3 | White | LMC | No | M | Yes |
| Uma | DC | 19 | 3 | Asian & White | UMC | No | W | Yes |
| Victoria | DC | 20 | 2 | Native American | MC | Yes | W | Yes |
| Violet | MCC | 20 | 2 | White | WC | Yes | W | No |
| Will | UNH | 19 | 2 | White | MC | No | M | Yes |
| Yusef | UNH | 21 | 3 | Black | MC | No | M | No |

Note: Social class is students' self-identified social class, along with their parents' income and occupations, categorized as: P = poor; WC = working class; LMC = lower middle class; MC = middle class; UMC = upper middle class; and UC = upper class.

# Notes

INTRODUCTION

1. Students' names, including those of my interviewees and their friends, are all pseudonyms.

2. This is shown in individual studies as well as meta-analyses. For example, the Harvard Study of Adult Development, "the longest scientific study of happiness ever conducted," demonstrates that the strength of people's relationships predicts their health and happiness (i.e., whether they live "the good life"), and a study with 100,000 participants in Britain found that frequency of confiding in others was the strongest of 106 factors, and one of only two that were protective against depression. In addition, meta-analyses show that having multiple high-quality relationships improves mental health and reduces morbidity and mortality. Waldinger and Schulz, *The Good Life*; Choi et al., "An Exposure-Wide and Mendelian Randomization Approach to Identifying Modifiable Factors for the Prevention of Depression"; Holt-Lunstad et al., "Loneliness and Social Isolation as Risk Factors for Mortality"; Holt-Lunstad, Smith, and Layton, "Social Relationships and Mortality Risk: A Meta-analytic Review."

3. In this study of 4,500 students at 19 college campuses, the quality of interpersonal relationships with other students had a significant effect on all six dimensions of psychological well-being that were studied. Bowman, "The Development of Psychological Well-Being among First-Year College Students."

4. In other words, "friendships may reach their peak of functional significance" during young adulthood. Arnett et al., *Debating Emerging Adulthood*, 27.

5. For example, a study of 4,500 people in the U.S. ages ten to ninety-seven finds that loneliness peaks at age nineteen, and another study of more than 20,000 adults finds that loneliness decreases with age, with the oldest category being sixty-five and older. Shovestul et al., "Risk Factors for Loneliness"; Bruce et al., "Loneliness in the United States."

6. For example, see Flannery, "The Mental Health Crisis on College Campuses"; Sanchez, "The Worst of the Pandemic Is Behind Us."

7. About half of US adults report loneliness compared to 12.5% for smoking, 14.7% for diabetes, and 41.9% for obesity. Office of the Surgeon General, *Our Epidemic of Loneliness and Isolation*, 9.

8. Not to suggest that loneliness has not been a concern in earlier time periods. Sociologists have long been concerned with questions of social integration, including in influential books like Emile Durkheim's *Suicide*, Georg Simmel's *Conflict* and *The Web*

*of Group-Affiliations*, and David Risman, Nathan Glazer, and Reuel Denney's *The Lonely Crowd*.

9. ACHA, *American College Health Association—National College Health Assessment III*.

10. Franco, *Platonic*; Goldfarb, *Modern Friendship*; Sow and Friedman, *Big Friendship*. See also Flora's *Friendfluence* on how friends influence us, and Liming's *Hanging Out* for insightful reflections on spending unstructured time with friends as well as strangers.

11. Prior research has looked at network structure and loneliness in a different way, specifically identifying how loneliness spreads in social networks. I examine a different question here; however, I looked through my interview transcripts and did not find evidence of loneliness spreading within friendship networks. Future research with diverse samples and focused specifically on this question could do more to address this empirical question. Cacioppo, Fowler, and Christakis, "Alone in the Crowd."

12. Network density for tight-knitters ranges from 0.67 to 1, and tight-knitters have the lowest mean betweenness centrality scores (0.07) and modularity scores (0.02) of the three types. Samplers have network density between 0 and 0.33, with the highest betweenness centrality scores (0.66) and modularity scores (0.39). Compartmentalizers are in the middle for all three of these measures, with density of 0.34 to 0.66, betweenness centrality scores of 0.36 and modularity scores of 0.22. The values for betweenness centrality and modularity are means. See the methodological appendix for more details about the network data.

13. Chapter 4 focuses on the differences across campuses. For more details about these three network types, see McCabe, *Connecting in College*.

14. More on Dartmouth's scheduling, referred to as "The D-Plan," will be found in later chapters, especially chapter 4.

15. For example, see Astin, *What Matters in College?*; Kuh et al., *Student Success in College*; Nunn, *College Belonging*; Pascarella and Terenzini, *How College Affects Students*; Strayhorn, *College Students' Sense of Belonging*.

16. Description is from the publisher's website.

17. Astin, *What Matters in College*, 398.

18. The gaps remain despite several wonderful recent books, including Syed Ali and Margaret Chin's *The Peer Effect*.

19. Chambliss and Takacs, *How College Works*, 89.

20. Felten et al., *Connections Are Everything*, 47. Also see Felten and Lambert, *Relationship-Rich Education*.

21. "Social capital" refers to the resources embedded within ties, resources that must be activated in order to be useful. Portes, "Social Capital."

22. McCabe, *Connecting in College*.

23. There are many too many examples to list them all. For an in-depth look at Black students' same-race friendships, see Gilkes Borr, "The Strategic Pursuit of Black Homophily on a Predominantly White Campus"; Johnson, "'I can turn it on when I need to'"; Leath et al., "'I can be unapologetically who I am.'" For friendships among women students and women of color, see Martínez Alemán, "Understanding and Investigating Female Friendship's Educative Value"; Winkle-Wagner et al., "Instrumental or Meaningful Friendships."

24. In network terms, clubs are "foci," putting people into contact with each other through focused group activity. Feld, "The Focused Organization of Organizational Ties."

25. For example, antonio, "When Does Race Matter in College Friendships?"; Nenga, Alvarado, and Blyth, "'I kind of found my people'"; Park, "Clubs and the Campus Racial Climate"; Reyes, *Learning to Be Latino*.
26. Silver, "On the Margins of College Life."
27. For example, antonio, "When Does Race Matter in College Friendships?"; Fischer, "Does Campus Diversity Promote Friendship Diversity?"; Stearns, Buchmann, and Bonneau, "Interracial Friendships in the Transition to College."
28. Cherng, Calarco, and Kao, "Along for the Ride"; Flashman, "Academic Achievement and Its Impact on Friend Dynamics."
29. Stearns, Buchmann, and Bonneau, "Interracial Friendships in the Transition to College."
30. Stevens, Armstrong, and Arum, "Sieve, Incubator, Temple, Hub," 134.
31. Katz et al., *Gen Z, Explained*.
32. As sociologist danah boyd put it in the title of her book, *It's Complicated*. Social media's impact on teens brings both challenges and opportunities.
33. Bonsaksen et al., "Associations between Social Media Use and Loneliness in a Cross-National Population," 1.
34. Arnett et al., "Debating Emerging Adulthood."
35. Anthony and McCabe, "Friendship Talk as Identity Work."
36. Silver, *The Cost of Inclusion*.
37. Lu, "Everyone Is Talking about 'Belonging.'"
38. NCES, "Digest of Education Statistics."
39. For example, at public four-year institutions—which most students who begin at four-year colleges attend—about 67% White and Asian students graduate within six years, compared to 58% of Latina/o, 46% of Black, and 42% of Native American students. NCES, "Digest of Education Statistics," Table 326.20.
40. For example, see Jack, *Class Dismissed*; Jackson, *Brotherhood University*; Lee, *Class and Campus Life*; Reyes, *Learning to Be Latino*; Tichavakunda, *Black Campus Life*.
41. For example, see Labaree, "A System without a Plan"; Schudde and Goldrick-Rab, "On Second Chances and Stratification."
42. This point is made by Armstrong and Massé, "The Sociology of Higher Education"; Stevens, Armstrong, and Arum, "Sieve, Incubator, Temple, Hub." For exceptions, see the excellent sociological work on students' experiences at two-year colleges by Deil-Amen, "Socio-Academic Integrative Moments"; Deterding, "Instrumental and Expressive Education"; Nielsen, "'Fake it 'til you make it'"; Schudde and Goldrick-Rab, "On Second Chances and Stratification."
43. NCES, "Digest of Education Statistics," Table 321.20.
44. For example, one study found that community college students experience social and academic integration differently than four-year residential students, and they expect fewer friendships on campus. Deil-Amen, "Socio-Academic Integrative Moments."
45. Karp, Hughes, and O'Gara, "An Exploration of Tinto's Integration Framework for Community College Students," 78.
46. Nelson et al., "Saving Face While (Not) Talking about Race," 470. See also Armstrong and Hamilton, *Paying for the Party*; Binder, Davis, and Bloom, "Career Funneling"; Binder and Wood, *Becoming Right*; Hirsch and Khan, *Sexual Citizens*; Reyes, *Learning to Be Latino*.
47. Binder, Davis, and Bloom, "Career Funneling," 22. For more on capital, see Bourdieu, "The Forms of Capital."

48. Hirsch and Khan, *Sexual Citizens*, xx.

49. This is also in line with a relational approach, which focuses on structure and agency. Emirbayer, "Manifesto for a Relational Sociology"; Erikson, "Formalist and Relationalist Theory in Social Network Analysis"; Finn, *Personal Life, Young Women and Higher Education*; McCabe, "Why Study with Friends?"

50. The research discussed already in this introduction demonstrates these trends. For example, Chambliss and Takacs, *How College Works*; Gilkes Borr, "The Strategic Pursuit of Black Homophily on a Predominantly White Campus"; Johnson, "'I can turn it on when I need to'"; Stuber, *Inside the College Gates*.

51. NCES, "Digest of Education Statistics," Table 303.25.

52. An *Annual Review of Sociology* article that describes research on the sociology of education advocates for more work on what the authors call the "experiential core" of college. Stevens, Armstrong, and Arum, "Sieve, Incubator, Temple, Hub."

53. Examples of multi-campus research that demonstrates how campus structures shape students' experiences include Ann Mullen's *Degrees of Inequality*, Daisy Reyes's *Learning to be Latino*, and Jenny Stuber's *Inside the College Gates*.

54. Small, "'How many cases do I need?'"

55. Johnson, "New Hampshire Demographic Trends in an Era of Economic Turbulence."

56. Table B.2 in Appendix B describes these and other characteristics of my sample.

57. For details about the case study design, see Yin, *Case Study Research and Applications*.

58. I interviewed most Dartmouth participants in the summer after their second year, a time they refer to as "sophomore summer," when most students were taking classes. I interviewed most UNH participants in the fall of their third year, and most MCC participants in the fall of their second year. As shown in Table B.3 in Appendix B, some students had been in school for periods shorter or longer than these times; my interviewees varied from students who had been in college at least one term to those who were at least one term before graduation. For the second wave, I interviewed most Dartmouth participants within a few weeks of their graduation; this was enabled by being on the same campus and by yearly rhythms. In early 2020, I was gearing up to interview the UNH and MCC students in May, which would have been two years later and when most were set to graduate; however, the COVID-19 pandemic delayed those interviews until 2021. See Appendix A for more details.

59. The enthusiasm from parents and prospective students at seeing the hockey arena reminded me of the reaction to basketball at Indiana University when I was there and football at Florida State University. The draw of NCAA Division I sports on these campuses feels like a distinguishing feature of many state flagship campuses.

60. Indeed, it was modeled after Independence Hall in Philadelphia: https://www.dartmouth.edu/library/bakerberry/general/AboutBaker-BerryLibrary.html.

61. At MCC, only students in the nursing program referred to their program as intense, but they distinguished this from the campus environment. Their program was intense, MCC was not.

62. A survey that included more than 2,300 students at multiple colleges and universities found that students reported spending 51% of their time "socializing, recreating, and other," compared to 9% attending class or lab, 7% studying, 9% working, volunteering, participating in fraternities/sororities and student clubs, and 24% sleeping. Some jobs or volunteer positions are not with same-age peers. However,

when students have a roommate, all of these, including sleeping, may happen alongside peers. Arum and Roksa, *Academically Adrift*, 97.

63. In this book, particularly at the end of chapter 1, I describe the experiences of students who do not have meaningful friendships.

64. They also resonate with the network types of expansionists, brokers, and conveners in a more recent book on patterns of connections. King, *Social Chemistry*.

65. Unlike the three campuses I focus on in this book, I used a pseudonym, "Midwest University" (MU), in *Connecting in College*. The MU data were collected in 2004–5. Data were collected for the other three campuses in 2016–17.

66. Average networks have shrunk dramatically over the past twenty years. For example, the number of Americans who reported three or fewer close friends went from 27% in 1990 to 49% in 2021. In other words, around half of Americans report having no more than three close friends. Office of the Surgeon General, *Our Epidemic of Loneliness and Isolation*, 13.

67. He writes, "The people in the 15-layer consist of five close friends whom you see often and what look like two more groups of five friends whom you see somewhat less often." Dunbar, *Friends*, 71.

68. I also thought that distance from home might matter, but when I calculated the miles from their hometown to college, this did not have a clear relationship to the percentage of friends from home in their friendship network.

CHAPTER ONE

1. Student names, including those of their friends, in the text and sociograms are pseudonyms. Some identifying details about students, such as hometowns and specific names of clubs, were altered as needed to protect confidentiality.

2. I use the term "dorm" rather than "residence hall" throughout because it is the term that students themselves used. "Residence hall" is the more formal term used by staff, researchers, and academics.

3. New Student Orientation at Dartmouth lists its mission as "support[ing] new students as they transition to both academic and co-curricular life at Dartmouth." https://www.dartmouth.edu/orientation/.

4. For more details on the social hierarchy among sororities and fraternities at Dartmouth, see Sam Hussey's honors thesis, which focuses on students' perceptions of this hierarchy in 2019–20. Dartmouth has a clear hierarchy of houses, and students largely agree on which ones are "A-side" (or high status) versus "B-side," and on a specific ranking within tiers. I advised this thesis. Hussey, "A System for All?"

5. Martínez Alemán, "Understanding and Investigating Female Friendship's Educative Value."

6. See chapter 5 for more detail about how gender and other identities influence students' friendships.

7. Melanie and Simone were not close friends at the second interview. Simone was not in Melanie's friendship list, and Melanie told me that "we don't talk" but "I don't think it's as full on as a friendship breakup, but we'll see. I'll let you know in five years." By "five years," she was referencing the prospective time for our next interview.

8. Melanie also did not list Cameron as a friend in the second interview. She said, "I ended that relationship, and I think that was a really good choice for me."

9. The Coffee Club did not continue to exist as a club at Dartmouth after Melanie graduated, so the "alternative social space" she sought to build did not persist beyond her time at Dartmouth.

10. In their research on sexual relationships among students at Columbia, Jennifer Hirsch and Shamus Khan highlight the importance of space. They posit that "sexual geographies" facilitate meaningful sexual encounters as well as sexual assault, depending on how campus spaces are configured. Similarly, I find that space matters for creating meaningful friendship relationships. Hirsch and Khan, *Sexual Citizens*.

11. Several of my participants told stories of friends who experienced sexual assault in fraternity basements at Dartmouth. These dangers are also the topic of sociological research. See, for example, Ispa-Landa and Thomas, "Navigating the Risks of Party Rape in Historically White Greek Life at an Elite College"; and Armstrong, Hamilton, and Sweeney, "Sexual Assault on Campus."

12. Cuba et al., *Practice for Life*.

13. For more detail on the differences between campuses, see chapter 4.

14. Cuba et al., *Practice for Life*, 54.

15. These temporal patterns are reinforced by findings from a nationally representative survey of more than 4,000 US college graduates. In response to a question asking graduates when they got to know their closest friend in college, 61% said in the first semester, 18% second semester, 16% middle of college, and only 5% late in college. Covington, "Elon Poll."

16. In my descriptions, I use the more inclusive language of "first-year" and "gender-inclusive" that is more common now (as I'm writing this book) than when I was conducting my interviews, but to accurately convey what the respondents said, I use their language, including "freshman" and "co-ed," in direct quotations.

17. Grace's strategies also echo advice in books on adult friendship. Her question about Francis's shorts is strikingly similar to the "statement + question conversation starter" exercise in Goldfarb's *Modern Friendship*, 241.

18. This research was among men at the University of Michigan, and specifically measured "attraction relationships" or liking, including among floormates and roommates. Newcomb, *The Acquaintance Process*.

19. As mentioned in the introduction, Dartmouth students take classes during the full year (fall, winter, and spring terms) during their first and last years, but during their second and third year they are required to take two of these terms away from campus. This means that students may make friends in their first year and be together, but they may not be on campus during the same terms during their second or third year.

20. See chapter 2 for more about why students keep friends and how this varies across institutions.

21. The other 10% who do not participate may be participating in varsity athletics that conflict or may choose not to do an outdoor activity. At the start of my research, there were fewer options that did not involve camping than there are currently; now, students can explore local museums or cook together and stay in their dorm room as part of Trips.

22. More details about Trips can be found at https://outdoors.dartmouth.edu/prospstudent.html. While UNH's outdoor trips program is a pre-orientation activity, the one at Dartmouth is considered an orientation program.

23. For more information about the First Year Summer Enrichment Program (FYSEP), see https://students.dartmouth.edu/fgo/programs/first-year-student-enrichment-program.

24. For more information about the International Student Pre-Orientation Program (ISPOP), see https://students.dartmouth.edu/opal/community-leadership/orientation-pre-orientation-programming/international-student-pre-orientation.

25. While it was comforting, it was often not completely comfortable. As Anthony Abraham Jack found in his research on an elite campus, low-income students had a harder time adjusting to peers (and other aspects of college life) when their high schools were different culturally (i.e., the "doubly disadvantaged" who attended disadvantaged high schools) than when they had prior experience at elite schools (i.e., the "privileged poor"). Jack, *The Privileged Poor*.

26. Troy's friendship network appears in chapter 2 on friendship funneling. See figure 2.3.

27. When the specific country could be identifying and not crucial to the narrative, I refer to the continent rather than the country throughout this manuscript.

28. Propinquity works during the program when students are living together. Once classes start, however, students live throughout campus.

29. Lazarsfeld and Merton, "Friendship as Social Process." It has been documented in a range of social settings, as shown in McPherson, Smith-Lovin, and Cook, "Birds of a Feather."

30. For example, see discussions and examples in Gilkes Borr, "The Strategic Pursuit of Black Homophily on a Predominantly White Campus"; Leath et al., "'I can be unapologetically who I am'"; Leath et al., "'Our community is so small'"; Martínez Alemán, "Race Talks"; McCabe, "Racial and Gender Microaggressions on a Predominantly-White Campus"; McCabe, "'That's what makes our friendships stronger'"; Nenga et al., "'I kind of found my people'"; Tichavakunda, *Black Campus Life*; Villalpando, "Self-Segregation or Self-Preservation?"

31. antonio, "The Influence of Friendship Groups on Intellectual Self-Confidence and Educational Aspirations in College"; Gilkes Borr, "The Strategic Pursuit of Black Homophily on a Predominantly White Campus"; McCabe, "'That's what makes our friendships stronger.'"

32. The bottom cluster are her three friends from home.

33. For example, see Marmaros and Sacerdote, "How Do Friendships Form?"; Newcomb, *The Acquaintance Process*.

34. Marmaros and Sacerdote, "How Do Friendships Form?" discuss this among roommates; Newcomb, *The Acquaintance Process*, for housemates; and Moffatt, *Coming of Age in New Jersey*, for floormates. These tendencies are also noted in resources on campus environments, including the nice review in Strange and Banning, *Designing for Learning*.

35. This was not always a good way to find a compatible roommate. Several students I interviewed who became roommates after connecting on Facebook found that they had different studying, sleeping, and cleaning habits, and that living together was tense; they did not consider each other friends or opt to live with each other in the next housing cycle.

36. I expand on this in chapter 4 when discussing how institutions influence friendships.

37. See, for example, the ethnographic accounts in Moffatt, *Coming of Age in New Jersey*; Nathan, *My Freshman Year*.

38. Admitted students day is referred to as "Dimensions" at Dartmouth. See https://admissions.dartmouth.edu/apply/admitted-students/dimensions-dartmouth.

39. Resident advisors (RAs) are students who receive several days of training on college policies, communication strategies, and crisis management. They are employed by the college, serving in exchange for room and board or a stipend. At Dartmouth, this position is referred to as a UGA or undergraduate advisor, but I refer to this position as an RA throughout for consistency with how it is used at most postsecondary institutions.

40. Notably, in a study at a liberal arts college, the highest academic outcomes were not among those who did not work, but among those students who worked ten to nineteen hours per week. Students working ten to nineteen hours per week had higher grades and reported more hours studying than those working longer hours or fewer hours, including nonworking students. Dundes and Marx, "Balancing Work and Academics in College."

41. Gilkes Borr, "The Strategic Pursuit of Black Homophily on a Predominantly White Campus."

42. See, for example, antonio, "The Influence of Friendship Groups on Intellectual Self-Confidence and Educational Aspirations in College"; Leath et al., "'I can be unapologetically who I am'": McCabe, *Connecting in College*; Nenga et al., "'I kind of found my people'"; Reyes, *Learning to Be Latino*.

43. See Park and Kim, "Interracial Friendship and Structural Diversity"; and Park, "Clubs and the Campus Racial Climate," for examples of quantitative studies. See McCabe, "Doing Multiculturalism," for a qualitative study documenting these interracial friendships.

44. Chambliss and Takacs, *How College Works*; Nunn, *College Belonging*; Tinto, *Leaving College*.

45. In 2017–18, there were 889 NCAA varsity athletes among 4,410 undergraduates. Some of these students (159) participated in more than one of the thirty-five varsity teams. Dartmouth publicizes that more than three-quarters of students are involved with athletics, but this covers club and intramural sports as well. As a member of the Ivy League, Dartmouth does not offer athletic scholarships to students. In contrast, UNH has Division 1 athletics and offers athletic scholarships.

46. For example, Bowdoin College has approximately 1,800 students, and 36% of those are varsity athletes. Nelson et al., "Saving Face While (Not) Talking about Race," 461.

47. Most teams are explicitly separated by gender. And numerous studies note how sports tend to be segregated by race and class, including at colleges and universities, something that is often tied to racial and socioeconomic segregation in housing, where specific sports are offered, and the different financial investments required, which tends to make teams more homophilous. On segregation among athletic teams at college and universities, see, for example, Nelson et al., "Saving Face While (Not) Talking about Race"; and Hextrum, "Segregation, Innocence, and Protection."

48. The exception is Danica, and I discuss her experience at the beginning of chapter 5.

49. Smith et al., "Patterns of Undergraduate Student Interpersonal Interaction Network Change during the COVID-19 Pandemic," 13.

50. Nunn, *College Belonging*.

51. Including both sororities and fraternities, there are twenty chapters at UNH and twenty-eight chapters at Dartmouth.

52. On clubs and organizations as social capital, see Putnam, *Bowling Alone*.

53. Silver, *The Cost of Inclusion*.

54. A nationally representative survey of more than 4,000 US college graduates asked where students met the "one close friend who had the biggest impact," and found that 30% said they had met in a classroom and 27% in a dorm. Covington, "Elon Poll"; Lambert et al., "Mentors Play Critical Role in Quality of College Experience, New Poll Suggests."

55. Johnson also discusses how students' perceptions of their peers differ by whether they are seen as "good" collaborators or "bad" collaborators. Johnson, "Collaborating in Class."

56. For similar experiences, see Johnson, "'I can turn it on when I need to'"; Johnson, "Collaborating in Class"; Tichavakunda, *Black Campus Life*.

57. Johnson, "Collaborating in Class"; McCabe, *Connecting in College*.

58. For example, see Grant and Ashford, "The Dynamics of Proactivity at Work."

59. The authors write: "Our friends and family serve as conduits for us to be influenced by hundreds or even thousands of other people" because "we are all connected." Christakas and Fowler, *Connected*, 30.

60. The term "weak ties" comes from Mark Granovetter. He focuses on their benefits for job seeking. Mario Small also focuses on the benefits of these weak ties for mothers in terms of reciprocal obligations and favors, and graduate students talking about a range of important topics, including those related to health and relationships. Granovetter, "The Strength of Weak Ties." Small, *Unanticipated Gains*. Small, *Someone to Talk to*.

61. Robert Putnam popularized the notions of bridging and bonding social capital. He discusses bonding social capital as inward-looking and often based on similarities. Bridging social capital is outward looking and can bring in diverse and different resources. Both types can contain valuable resources. Putnam, *Bowling Alone*.

62. For example, books on adult friendship offer strategies for "how to turn strangers into friends" and "six hard truths about modern friendship," including "It's on us to look for opportunities for connection." Franco, *Platonic*, 61. Goldfarb, *Modern Friendship*, 37.

63. A recent *New York Times* op-ed argued for the United States to have a minister of loneliness because "if the researchers are correct, social isolation probably kills far more people in the West each year than terrorists and murderers, and it costs the public enormous sums in unnecessary health costs. Countermeasures can make a huge difference: One review of 148 studies concluded that social connections increase the odds of an individual's surviving over roughly the next seven years by about 50 percent." Kristof, "We Know the Cure for Loneliness."

64. I talk about Danica's struggles with making friends in the opening of chapter 5.

### CHAPTER TWO

1. Kuwabara, Luo, and Sheldon, "Multiplex Exchange Relations"; Verbrugge, "Multiplexity in Adult Friendships."

2. See chapter 4 for more on these differences across institutions.

3. Hall, "How Many Hours Does It Take to Make a Friend?"

4. Hall uses the term "striving episodes" to capture these more meaningful interactions. "Striving episodes were measured using 5 items (i.e., "Catch up by talking about events that have occurred since you last saw each other," "Talk about what's up and about what happened to you during the day," "Have serious conversations where both of you are involved in the conversation," "Engage in playful talk to have fun or

release tension," "Talk in ways that express love and give attention and affection")." Hall, "How Many Hours Does It Take to Make a Friend?" 1288.

5. It is unclear if Heidi's best friend also would name Heidi as her best friend. Other research shows that it is quite common for students' friends to not name them as friends, including best friends. See, for example, Almaatouq et al., "Are You Your Friends' Friend?"

6. Newport, *Deep Work*, 198.

7. Chambliss and Takacs, *How College Works*, 21.

8. Waldinger and Schulz, *The Good Life*.

9. Felton et al., *Connections Are Everything*, 58. Also see Felton and Lambert, *Relationship-Rich Education*.

10. Sandelson, *My Girls*, xiii.

11. Other work has explored this issue in much more depth than I do here. See for example, boyd, *It's Complicated*; Katz et al., *Gen Z, Explained*.

12. During each interview, I systematically asked how they kept in touch with each of their friends, and technology was important for each participant. While not important for every tie, it was important for some ties in every interview.

13. In these two experiments, in each way participant students perceived the slant—verbally, visually, or haptically—they rated it as less steep when they had a friend with them and when thinking about a friend than when they were alone. See Schnall et al., "Social Support and the Perception of Geographical Slant."

14. McCabe, *Connecting in College*; Winkle-Wagner et al., "Instrumental or Meaningful Friendships."

15. See examples in Brooks, "Friends, Peers, and Higher Education"; McCabe, *Connecting in College*.

16. Sow and Friedman, *Big Friendship*.

17. McCabe, *Connecting in College*.

18. This shows up in other work on friendship as well. Michelle Obama, for example, noted that relationships are not fifty-fifty all the time, but over time they achieve that balance. Obama, *The Light We Carry*.

19. Other research reports this language as well; see Leath et al., "'Our community is so small,'" 16; McCabe, *Connecting in College*; Winkle-Wagner et al., "Instrumental or Meaningful Friendships."

20. antonio, "Diversity and the Influence of Friendship Groups in College"; Brooks, "Friends, Peers, and Higher Education"; Finn, *Personal Life, Young Women and Higher Education*; Martínez Alemán, "College Women's Friendships" and "Race Talks"; McCabe, *Connecting in College*.

21. This is also discussed in McCabe, *Connecting in College*; Smith, "Magnets and Seekers."

22. See McCabe, "Why Study with Friends?" for more detail on why students study with friends, even when they know it is not the most productive use of their study time.

23. Dueñas and Gloria, "Para honrar los sacrificios de mi familia: Motivating Persons and Processes of Latinx Undergraduates Attending a Predominantly White Institution"; McCabe, *Connecting in College*.

24. In her study of high school girls' friendships in a poor neighborhood, Jasmin Sandelson stressed how friends have fun together and how that helps the girls avoid the boredom and tedium of everyday life. Sandelson, *My Girls*.

25. Arnett et al., "Debating Emerging Adulthood"; Pahl, *On Friendship*.

26. This resonates with the three strategies of friendship talk as identity work, particularly the strategy of "envisioning self through others." Anthony and McCabe, "Friendship Talk as Identity Work."

27. Office of the Surgeon General, *Our Epidemic of Loneliness and Isolation*, 8.

28. Tight-knitters face the same challenges at UNH, Dartmouth, and MCC that I found at "Midwest University," suggesting that these challenges are common among tight-knitters. Also supporting this is a range of social network findings showing that dense networks increase social support, social control, and the spreading of redundant information. See McCabe, *Connecting in College*, chap. 3.

29. McCabe, *Connecting in College*, 49. Also see examples in Armstrong and Hamilton, *Paying for the Party*; Moffatt, *Coming of Age in New Jersey*.

30. McCabe, *Connecting in College*, 64.

31. The numbers of students in each network type are relatively small in my Dartmouth sample, which is the sample designed best to get at change during college. Therefore, it is wise not to put too much weight into the exact numbers. Future research on representative and larger samples can better document the specific patterns of similarity and change over time in network type.

32. Troy characterized these friends from home as friends but not "closer friends" in our first interview, so they are not in the sociogram.

33. The structure of term scheduling at Dartmouth shapes when students are on and off campus, which is often a different pattern than those of their friends. See chapter 4 for more on the D-Plan.

34. See advice in Ginsburg, "Strategic Group Selection—By Teachers, Not Students."

CHAPTER THREE

1. Bill's other two clusters were friends he made before Dartmouth. The larger cluster includes friends from home, whom he met from elementary school to high school, who all attend other colleges. The smaller cluster includes friends he made in his gap year between high school and Dartmouth.

2. Novack Café is well known on campus for the community built there among student workers and as a space for marginalized students on campus. See, for example, these articles in the student newspaper, *The Dartmouth*: Beilstein, "A Soundtrack to Go with Your Latte?"; Rojas, "Student Workers Find Community within On- and Off-Campus Jobs."

3. Office of the Surgeon General, *Our Epidemic of Loneliness and Isolation*.

4. College students' friendships show some similarities with and some differences from Matt Desmond's concept of "disposable ties." Like the "disposable ties" that Desmond discusses among people who had experienced an eviction, the friendships that students rapidly form are characterized by high levels of propinquity. These relationships are "important resources," in which people provide each other with emotional and instrumental support. They also frequently ended; there was much turnover in both samples. Yet, the "short duration" was central to Desmond's conceptualization, and some of students' ties lasted, so I do not conceptualize college students' friendships as "disposable." Desmond, "Disposable Ties and the Urban Poor," 1329.

5. Smith et al., "The Value of Interpersonal Network Continuity for College Students in Disruptive Times"; Smith et al., "Patterns of Undergraduate Student Interpersonal Interaction Network Change during the COVID-19 Pandemic."

6. Arnett, *Emerging Adulthood*; Arnett et al., *Debating Emerging Adulthood*. For more detail, see the review by Schwartz and colleagues, "Identity in Emerging Adulthood." Identity exploration is also important to theories of student development, such as that of Chickering and Reisser, *Education and Identity*.

7. Cooley, for example, talks about the looking-glass self and Mead about "taking the role of the other." Cooley, *Human Nature and the Social Order*; Mead, *Mind, Self and Society*.

8. Anthony and McCabe, "Friendship Talk as Identity Work."

9. This resonates with writing about "failures of reciprocity," including one recent piece on friends who break your heart. Senior, "It's Your Friends Who Break Your Heart."

10. Silver, *The Cost of Inclusion*.

11. Wade, *American Hookup*, 186.

## CHAPTER FOUR

1. According to the Dartmouth Admissions website, "the term 'D-Plan' refers to the flexibility Dartmouth gives its students in choosing when they take classes and when they're on break. But the plan isn't about Dartmouth, it's about each individual student. Within a few guidelines, students have the autonomy to schedule their classes and breaks around their academic, research, and professional interests." https://admissions.dartmouth.edu/glossary-term/d-plan.

2. See the introduction for a longer discussion of these three network types.

3. MCC highlighted its "transfer partners" as well as "Transfer Pathways," where students in particular majors could transition to an associated major at a nearby four-year college. See, for example, https://www.mccnh.edu/pdf/studentservices/NH_Transfer_Partners.pdf.

4. Karp, Hughes, and O'Gara, "An Exploration of Tinto's Integration Framework for Community College Students," 83.

5. Violet reported thirty and Ruben forty "less close" friends.

6. On bridging social capital, see Putnam, *Bowling Alone*. For more on the benefits of weak ties, including for job seeking, see Granovetter, "The Strength of Weak Ties."

7. Patrice's network is included in chapter 5. See figure 5.3.

8. See the section of chapter 1 on classes as secondary friendship markets for more detail about these processes.

9. Chambliss and Takacs, *How College Works*; Felten and Lambert, *Relationship-Rich Education*; Felton et al., *Connections Are Everything*.

10. In 2016, when I started this study, 56% of UNH students lived on campus, including 91% of first-year students. These numbers are higher now because starting in the fall of 2023, new first-year students who are under twenty-one are required to live on campus for their first two years.

11. Anthony and McCabe, "Friendship Talk as Identity Work."

12. See Table B.1 in Appendix B for the other identity scales. Means range from 3.1 on "academically serious to academically unengaged" to 5.9 on "partier to never party."

13. *U.S. News & World Report* lists the fall 2021 undergraduate enrollment at Arizona State University as 64,716. The University of Central Florida is a close second at 60,075. UNH has far fewer at 11,480 undergraduates and approximately 13,000 students in total. See https://www.usnews.com/education/best-colleges/the-short-list-college/articles/

colleges-with-the-most-undergraduates on the largest undergraduate populations, and https://www.usnews.com/best-colleges/university-of-new-hampshire-2589, for UNH.

14. Armstrong, Hamilton, and Sweeney, "Sexual Assault on Campus"; Ispa-Landa and Thomas, "Navigating the Risks of Party Rape in Historically White Greek Life at an Elite College"; Ray and Rosow, "Two Different Worlds of Black and White Fraternity Men."

15. Lisa Nunn discusses these multiple realms of belonging. Samplers at UNH were more likely to feel what Nunn calls "academic belonging" than "campus-community belonging" or "social belonging" within friendships. Nunn, *College Belonging*.

16. In the 2022–23 edition of *Best Colleges by U.S. News & World Report*, Dartmouth was ranked twelfth among "National Universities." In 2016, when I started my research, it was also ranked twelfth overall, and second for "Strong Commitment to Undergraduate Teaching." A Dartmouth News announcement added: "Other rankings that distinguish Dartmouth in this year's "Best Colleges" list include a No. 2 ranking for alumni giving; a No. 5 ranking for graduation and retention rate; and a No. 8 ranking for selectivity. Princeton is the only university listed ahead of Dartmouth in undergraduate teaching this year." https://home.dartmouth.edu/news/2015/09/2016-best-colleges-rankings-us-news-world-report.

17. For example, an article on the Class of 2021 highlights that 96% graduated among the top 10% of their high school class and more than one in four were valedictorian or salutatorian. https://home.dartmouth.edu/news/2017/03/2092-students-are-offered-admission-class-2021.

18. The original motto is in Latin: "Vox clamantis in deserto."

19. See, for example, the opportunities students have to make friends at other colleges and in the surrounding urban area of New York City, described by Hirsch and Khan, *Sexual Citizens*.

20. Cortez, *A Perfect Storm*.

21. House communities were established in 2015 at Dartmouth as a way to establish continuity and community for all students. My interviews with students are not timed well to capture the impact this has had on students. I discuss this in a bit more detail in Appendix A.

22. In response to the question, "Whom you would talk to, if you were experiencing serious emotional distress?" 32% of Dartmouth students said "no one" compared to 10% on campuses overall. Compare Dartmouth's results posted at https://provost.dartmouth.edu/news/2023/02/jed-campus-update-and-healthy-minds-study-survey-results; *The Healthy Minds Study*, 17.

23. Armstrong and Hamilton, *Paying for the Party*.

24. Binder, Davis, and Bloom, "Career Funneling."

25. Uppaluri, "Quality over Quantity."

26. In addition to coming up in many interviews, the term is also referenced in the student newspaper. See Wood, "Dark Side or Light Side? Deconstructing the Athlete and NARP Divide."

27. While there is some variation in which organizations are the highest status, often Greek organizations and varsity sports are toward the top of the status hierarchy. See, for example, Ispa-Landa and Thomas, "Navigating the Risks of Party Rape in Historically White Greek Life at an Elite College"; Nelson et al., "Saving Face While (Not) Talking about Race."

28. Putnam, *Bowling Alone*.

29. They also noted that the housing policies "failed to disrupt segregation more broadly due to the outsized influence of varsity athletics," which at Dartmouth would be centered instead on Greek life. Nelson, Graham, and Rudin, "Saving Face While (Not) Talking about Race," 464.

30. Certainly, UNH students' involvement faded and intensified over time, but there was less change overall, in line with the weaker secondary friendship market there.

CHAPTER FIVE

1. The discussion of "culture shock" at Dartmouth for those who attended public schools in impoverished areas with mainly Black or Latinx students echoes that in Anthony Abraham Jack's work. See Jack, *The Privileged Poor*.

2. Throughout this chapter and the book, I use the terms students themselves used. No students I interviewed used the term "Latine," so I do not use it here. I alternate between Latinx (for all genders), Latina, and Latino.

3. The boundary work that Danica experienced echoes that in research on how Latinx students create and negotiate belonging at a predominantly white institution (PWI) both within and outside of ethnic-based organizations. Marín and McCabe, "Is Belonging What You Do, Who You're With, Or Who You Are?"

4. As described in chapter 1, there were "pop up markets" throughout college where students were more easily able to make friends, such as student clubs and sororities. As described in chapter 4, these secondary markets are stronger at Dartmouth than at the other two campuses.

5. Danica's "dabbling" resembles the "partitioning" strategy of managing extracurricular involvement that Blake Silver found in his study of race, class, and gender patterns in how students get involved in extracurricular activities. Like the "partitioning" strategy, characteristic of more advantaged female or racially/ethnically minoritized students, Danica strategically selected a few activities to join, experienced marginalization in these settings, and varied in her participation to avoid mistreatment. Silver, "Inequality in the Extracurriculum."

6. Most students attending summer term at Dartmouth are the class who just finished their second year, which is why it is called "sophomore summer." This means that most leaders of the Greek organizations are those second-year students, and second-year students fill the Greek houses, since most upper-division students are not around. Both the leadership roles and the living arrangements of second-year students lead to those students bonding within these organizations, which also increases the sense of ostracism for those who do not fit in.

7. This seems like an accurate estimate. When I checked in December 2023, the price for Canada Goose jackets started at $950. https://www.canadagoose.com/us/en/shop/jackets/?srule=price-low-to-high.

8. These markers echo those that researchers have documented on other campuses. See, for example, Ferguson and Lareau, "Hostile Ignorance, Class, and Same-Race Friendships"; Jack, *The Privileged Poor*; Lee, *Class and Campus Life*; Stuber, *Inside the College Gates*; Thornton, "Lucky Me."

9. Colleges are racialized organizations, as Ingrid Nelson and colleagues discuss in their research on how elite colleges are structurally diverse yet segregated in many aspects of students' social experiences. Nelson, Graham, and Rudin, "Saving Face While (Not) Talking about Race."

10. Because of the D-Plan, Danica took the spring and summer of her third year away from campus. She spent those two terms at home in another state, working and "helping support my single mother and my autistic younger brother," noting that it felt "worthwhile." She also explained: "I got in a relationship with a wonderful girl for about four months."

11. After our first interview, I wrote in my field notes, "This is the hardest interview I've done," noting that Danica felt "socially isolated on campus." She had two close friends, but struggled to name others, and ended up including her brother and her therapist among the seven she listed. The second interview was also intense, and it felt like Danica had grown a lot. Looking back, she said, "I was not in a good place" the term when we did our first interview.

12. In their research on another elite liberal arts college (Bowdoin), Nelson and colleagues juxtapose students' and institutions' claims to value diversity for how it could enhance learning with the few places on campus where they found meaningful connections structured into students' experiences across difference. While they noted that first-year housing assignments "seeded some lasting friendships," they concluded that "after students' first year, the student-driven nature of housing enabled residential segregation along extracurricular, and thus demographic, lines, with Whiteness acting as a credential in high status social spaces," notably varsity athletics. Nelson, Graham, and Rudin, "Saving Face While (Not) Talking about Race," 464.

13. Tatum, *"Why Are All the Black Kids Sitting Together in the Cafeteria?"*

14. Putnam, *Bowling Alone*.

15. The algorithms used to generate the sociograms connect node size to centrality, so Jennifer and Lucia are the two largest circles (i.e., nodes) in Jennifer's year two network because they both are connected to each person in Jennifer's friendship network. In Jennifer's year four network, four other friends were equally central in the network (two of whom, Jessie and Alfonso, were in Jennifer's year two network).

16. Jennifer's positive emotions from friendships that share her ethnic identity echoes that of many students I interviewed, and the concept of "Black joy" on campus. Tichavakunda, "Black Joy on White Campuses."

17. See chapter 3 of *Connecting in College* for a broader discussion of the positive and negative pressure in tight-knit networks. Tight-knit networks can pull students up academically when their friend group provides academic support, such as studying together and checking in with each other, and they push students down academically when their friend group distracts them from academics. McCabe, *Connecting in College*.

18. Villalpando, "Self-Segregation or Self-Preservation?"

19. For an excellent discussion of the processes through which Black students seek out same-race ties on a campus where they are a numerical minority, see Gilkes Borr, "The Strategic Pursuit of Black Homophily on a Predominantly White Campus."

20. Putnam, *Bowling Alone*. Smith and Vonhoff, "Problematizing Community."

21. Troy's network density was 86% among his nineteen friends, and Jennifer's was 78% among her nine friends.

22. See, for example, Khan, "Legacy Admissions Don't Work the Way You Think They Do."

23. Hudson, "Random Roommates."

24. Ma, *Ambitious and Anxious*.

25. Sense of belonging is dynamic, changing over time, and multi-dimensional, including connections to the institutions as well as smaller groups, such as campus organizations. Nunn, *College Belonging*.

26. Ferguson and Lareau discuss hostile ignorance as a type of microaggression, but one that is specific to peer interactions. Like researchers studying microaggressions, they do not seek to "adjudicate each individual's intention," noting that hostile ignorance could be, but is not necessarily, intended to be hurtful. Ferguson and Lareau, "Hostile Ignorance, Class, and Same-Race Friendships," 3.

27. Ferguson and Lareau, "Hostile Ignorance, Class, and Same-Race Friendships."

28. I know that she received a bachelor's and a master's degree, but we were not able to connect for a follow-up interview so that I could get details about her friendships.

29. Patrice's mom-like friendships are very different from the mom-like friendships of women in *Connecting in College*. At MU, when students acted like each other's mom, they were making sure their friends did their homework. McCabe, *Connecting in College*.

30. From least to most dense: Black students' mean network density is 48%, Latinx students 50%, Asian students 55%, White students 57%, and Native American students 61%. In interpreting these density scores, it is important to keep in mind that my samples for specific race and gender groups are small, some extremely small (for example, I had no Native American men in my sample), and the samples were not drawn to be representative. Future research using larger and representative samples should investigate these patterns.

31. On average, Black women have networks with 36% density, while Latinas have 50% density, Native American women 61%, and Asian women 62%. In contrast to other groups, Asian women had higher network densities than men (62% compared to 41%). As I have noted above, these sample are extremely small and not representative, so should be interpreted cautiously.

32. In chapter 2, I discuss further how these common interests help maintain friendships.

33. Ferguson and Lareau, "Hostile Ignorance, Class, and Same-Race Friendships," 11–12.

34. Opportunity Insights, "Mobility Report Cards."

35. Johnson, "Collaborating in Class."

36. Lee, *Class and Campus Life*.

37. Ridgeway, *Framed by Gender*.

38. This came up in our interview when Melinda noted that in her second year at UNH, eight of her ten closer friends were women. Melinda told me, "I had a lot of really, really great guy friends in high school" and "that's really important to me to have close guy friends, and I haven't yet found a lot of that here, I guess."

39. These differences echo the "cookie-cutter identities" and gender inequalities sociologist Blake Silver finds in *The Cost of Inclusion*.

40. These findings are based on an online-game society of 300,000 players. Szell and Thurner, "How Women Organize Social Networks Different from Men."

41. See Way, *Deep Secrets*; and review in Fox, "Toward a Sociological Perspective on the Gender and Sexuality of Friendship."

42. In his detailed ethnography of how college students fit in with their peers, Blake Silver discusses the downsides of the "mom" role clearly, explaining how it was a "labor-intensive task. Not only did they commit to a kind and supportive style of self-presentation, but they were also proactive. Ready to anticipate and respond to needs, they were prepared and vigilant. Relinquishing claims to authority, they inquired about

needs, offered praise, and sought to provide physical and emotional comfort to their peers. These kinds of contributions requires that caregivers demonstrate their kindness by putting others' needs before their own." Silver, *The Cost of Inclusion*, 32–33.

43. Martinez Alemán, "Understanding and Investigating Female Friendship's Educative Value."

44. For example, men speak 1.6 times as often as women, and they use more assertive language while women use more hesitant and apologetic styles. Lee and McCabe, "Who Speaks and Who Listens."

45. A review summarizes much research as "impl[ying] that close friendships between men and women are inevitably complicated by romantic and sexual feelings." Fox "Toward a Sociological Perspective on the Gender and Sexuality of Friendship," 4.

46. These differences stand out in my sample, although it is important to keep in mind that my sample is not representative and there are small numbers of students in some groups when combining race and gender.

47. At Dartmouth, women report 74% same-gender friends (compared to 58% same-gender friends among men), 78% at UNH (compared to 66%) and 68% at MCC (compared to 73%). Only at MCC did men have more same-gender friendships than women.

48. In a survey of college students, men had more significantly fewer same-sex friends than women: 65% compared to 70%. Reeder, "The Effect of Gender Role Orientation on Same- and Cross-Sex Friendship Formation."

49. When boys are children, they frequently confide in each other, but they do so less often as they become teenagers. Way, *Deep Secrets*.

50. The UNH wave two sample includes 13 women, average of 9.2 friends, and 6 men, average of 8.2 friends. Among the 7 MCC students in wave two, there was only 1 man, 1 nonbinary student, and 5 women, so I do not present findings across gender.

51. Life stage seems to influence the relationship between gender and social network size. Women's networks are larger in early adulthood into midlife; however, starting in midlife, men's networks expand relative to women. Ajrouch, Blandon, and Antonucci, "Social Networks among Men and Women." However, conflicting results about how life stage matters come from an earlier study of fifty communities in Northern California that finds that elderly women have larger networks than middle-aged women. Fischer, *To Dwell among Friends*.

52. Interestingly, these patterns do not hold at UNH, where men's density is 59% and women's 58%, with the two nonbinary individuals having more dense networks at 67%.

53. Ridgeway, *Framed by Gender*, 57.

54. Ridgeway, *Framed by Gender*; Ridgeway and Correll, "Unpacking the Gender System."

55. Although I focus on these three, other identities certainly matter. Future research should explore additional identities, such as LGBTQ+, immigrant, and religious, following up on research noting, for example, "the importance of supportive friendships with other Black students who validated her ethnic and sexual experiences as a queer African woman." Leath et al., "'Our community is so small,'" 18.

56. For example, students talked about status symbols, such as Moncler coats and Van Cleef & Arpels necklaces, which cost thousands of dollars but do not stand out until they know to look for them.

## CONCLUSION

1. Paul, "What Is Lost When Freshmen Choose Their Roommates."
2. For example, economist Bruce Sacerdote concludes, "When I limit the sample to rooms of two where both roommates have joined a fraternity, I find that 27 percent of the roommate pairs join the same house," compared to an expected value of 5 percent. Sacerdote, "Peer Effects with Random Assignment," 699–700. Also see Marmaros and Sacerdote, "How Do Friendships Form?"
3. Hudson, "Random Roommates," 19. She comes to similar conclusions about friendships across differences in religion, spirituality, or other "guiding life principles." Hudson, Rockenbach, and Mayhew, "Campus Conditions and College Experiences That Facilitate Friendship across Worldview Differences."
4. Hudson, "Random Roommates," 21.
5. One example is intergroup dialogue. Zúñiga, "Bridging Differences through Dialogue," 12.
6. For a discussion of best practices in different types of living-learning communities, see Inkelas, Benjamin, and Jessup-Anger, *Living-Learning Communities in Practice*.
7. O'Hara, "How to Build a Residential College," 52–53.
8. Dartmouth does not have house-based dining halls. For a discussion of their role in residential colleges, see O'Hara, "How to Build a Residential College."
9. For example, see Jack, *Class Dismissed*; Jack, *The Privileged Poor*; Silver, *The Cost of Inclusion*; Solórzano, Ceja, and Yosso, "Critical Race Theory, Racial Microaggressions, and Campus Racial Climate"; Thornton, "Lucky Me"; Tichavakunda, *Black Campus Life*.
10. This resonates with "social belonging," one of three realms of belonging identified by Lisa Nunn, *College Belonging*.
11. Emirbayer, "Manifesto for a Relational Sociology"; Erikson, "Formalist and Relationalist Theory in Social Network Analysis."
12. Putnam, *Bowling Alone*. Similarly, Smith and Vonhoff advocate for the creation of communities that provide students with "both bonding and exploratory experiences" through high-impact practices like learning communities. Smith and Vonhoff, "Problematizing Community," 268.
13. Existing research tends to focus on the value of one type over another. In a network analysis of ties among 322 first-year students at a private liberal arts college, Scott Thomas concludes that "a broader discussion network is better" for academic performance and persistence. The type of broader network Thomas describes fits with bridging social capital. Thomas, "Ties That Bind," 609.
14. Small, *Someone to Talk to*, 173.
15. Small, *Someone to Talk to*, 174.
16. For example, see Armstrong and Hamilton, *Paying for the Party*; Binder and Wood, *Becoming Right*.
17. Nelson et al., "Saving Face While (Not) Talking about Race."
18. Hirsch and Khan, *Sexual Citizens*.
19. For example, see Fischer, "Does Campus Diversity Promote Friendship Diversity?"; Stearns, Buchmann, and Bonneau, "Interracial Friendships in the Transition to College."
20. Smith et al., "The Value of Interpersonal Network Continuity for College Students in Disruptive Times," 14.
21. Lu, "Everyone Is Talking about 'Belonging.'"

## APPENDIX A

1. Indeed, the film was co-written by Dartmouth alumnus Chris Miller, Class of 1963, who was a member of a fraternity at Dartmouth that later became un-recognized for a variety of violations around the time I arrived on campus.
2. As of fall 2022, Florida State University had 33,000 undergraduates, and Indiana University—Bloomington had nearly 36,000 undergraduates.
3. Reitman, "Confessions of an Ivy League Frat Boy."
4. See "Past Initiatives," Dartmouth website, accessed February 2, 2025, https://sites.dartmouth.edu/teaaa/about-the-plan/past-initiatives/.
5. O'Hara, "How to Build a Residential College."
6. This came after my initial round of interviews. When the house communities were established, but before I became involved, I thought a great natural experiment could involve studying a cohort of students before and after the house communities to see if they were successful in their goals. My role in the communities and the COVID-19 pandemic disrupted this plan. The pandemic changed too much about students' connections and social experiences on campus to make that comparison work; in other words, it would be impossible to disentangle the effects of the house communities from those related to pandemic policies and practices. Moreover, it affected my ability to be and be seen as a neutral observer about the impact that the house communities had on students' connections on campus. As house professor, I live on campus, in a single-family home with my children and pets, for eight years and frequent the dining halls since my compensation includes a meal plan. All of this means that I interact much more frequently with undergraduates and in more informal ways than I did as just a regular faculty member.
7. Yin, *Case Study Research and Applications*.
8. Stuber, *Inside the College Gates*; Mullen, *Degrees of Inequality*; Ferguson and Lareau, "Hostile Ignorance, Class, and Same-Race Friendships"; Binder and Wood, *Becoming Right*; Nunn, *College Belonging*; Reyes, *Learning to Be Latino*.
9. This student was the daughter of my co-worker.
10. Yin, *Case Study Research and Applications*.
11. MCC does not have a student newspaper.
12. Small, "'How many cases do I need?'"
13. Although I collected nearly thirty signatures, about half of those individuals never responded to my emails, texts, or phone calls, and after the initial screening survey I discovered that some were not appropriate for the study because this was their first term at MCC.
14. At Dartmouth, faculty usually teach two terms and must be in residence for advising during a third term. During this research project, I taught my classes in the winter and spring terms, which freed up summer and fall for interviewing.
15. An important concern is to not artificially constrain network size, and my approach seeks to address this concern and to maximize validity through attention to participants' own meanings of "friendship." On concerns about artificially constraining network size, see Marsden, "Network Data and Measurement."
16. Bourdieu and Wacquant, *An Invitation to Reflexive Sociology*.
17. The MCC students were harder to get in touch with than the other students as their contact information changed more frequently than that of the UNH and Dartmouth students, including the multiple email addresses, phone numbers, and mailing addresses they shared with me at the end of the first interview.

18. Lareau, *Listening to People*.

19. Glaser and Strauss, *The Discovery of Grounded Theory*.

20. Freeman, "A Set of Measures of Centrality Based on Betweenness"; Marsden, "Network Data and Measurement."

21. These scores are similar to those presented in *Connecting in College*, which are also highest for samplers (0.62) and lowest for tight-knitters (0.04), with compartmentalizers in the middle (0.25). Smith and Vonhoff discuss how higher betweenness centrality both indicates that someone spans disconnected groups and is associated with higher feelings of loneliness. Smith and Vonhoff, "Problematizing Community."

22. Newman, "Modularity and Community Structure in Networks."

23. In *Connecting in College*, tight-knitters' average modularity score was also 0.02, with scores following a similar order but not as wide a range for the other groups: 0.19 for compartmentalizers and 0.25 for samplers.

24. Hu, "Efficient and High Quality Force-Directed Graph Drawing."

25. While the sociograms are shown in black and white in this book, I used color in previous analyses to indicate different clusters within the network by setting color to indicate strength of tie between nodes.

# Bibliography

ACHA (American College Health Association). *American College Health Association—National College Health Assessment III: Undergraduate Student Reference Group Data Report Spring 2022*. Silver Spring, MD: American College Health Association, 2022.

Ajrouch, Kristine, Alysia Y. Blandon, and Toni C. Antonucci. "Social Networks among Men and Women: The Effects of Age and Socioeconomic Status." *Journals of Gerontology: Series B* 60, no. 6 (2005): S311–17.

Ali, Syed, and Margaret M. Chin. *The Peer Effect: How Your Peers Shape Who You Are and Who You Will Become*. New York: NYU Press, 2023.

Almaatouq, Abdullah, Laura Radaelli, Alex Pentland, and Erez Shmueli. "Are You Your Friends' Friend? Poor Perception of Friendship Ties Limits the Ability to Promote Behavioral Change." *PLoS ONE* 11, no. 3 (2016): e0151588.

Anthony, Amanda Koontz, and Janice McCabe. "Friendship Talk as Identity Work: Defining the Self through Friend Relationships." *Symbolic Interaction* 38, no. 1 (2015): 64–82.

antonio, anthony lising. "Diversity and the Influence of Friendship Groups in College." *Review of Higher Education* 25, no. 1 (2001): 63–89.

———. "The Influence of Friendship Groups on Intellectual Self-Confidence and Educational Aspirations in College." *Journal of Higher Education* 75, no. 4 (2004): 446–71.

———. "When Does Race Matter in College Friendships: Explaining Men's Diverse and Homogeneous Friendship Groups." *Review of Higher Education* 27, no. 4 (2004): 553–75.

Armstrong, Elizabeth A., and Laura T. Hamilton. *Paying for the Party: How College Maintains Inequality*. Cambridge, MA: Harvard University Press, 2013.

Armstrong, Elizabeth A., Laura Hamilton, and Brian Sweeney. "Sexual Assault on Campus: A Multilevel, Integrative Approach to Party Rape." *Social Problems* 53, no. 4 (2006): 483–99.

Armstrong, Elizabeth A., with Johanna C. Massé. "The Sociology of Higher Education: Contributions and New Directions." *Contemporary Sociology* 43, no. 6 (2014): 801–11.

Arnett, Jeffrey Jensen. *Emerging Adulthood: The Winding Road from the Late Teens through the Twenties*. New York: Oxford, 2004.

Arnett, Jeffrey Jensen, Marion Kloep, Leo B. Hendry, and Jennifer L. Tanner. *Debating Emerging Adulthood: Stage or Process*. New York: Oxford, 2011.

Arum, Richard, and Josipa Roksa. *Aspiring Adults Adrift: Tentative Transitions of College Graduates*. Chicago: University of Chicago Press, 2014.

Astin, Alexander W. *What Matters in College? Four Critical Years Revisited*. San Francisco: Jossey-Bass, 1993.

Beilstein, Grace. "A Soundtrack to Go with Your Latte?" *The Dartmouth*, October 19, 2022. https://www.thedartmouth.com/article/2022/10/a-soundtrack-to-go-with-your-latte.

Binder, Amy J., Daniel B. Davis, and Nick Bloom. "Career Funneling: How Elite Students Learn to Define and Desire 'Prestigious' Jobs." *Sociology of Education* 89, no. 1 (2016): 20–39.

Binder, Amy J., and Kate Wood. 2013. *Becoming Right: How Campuses Shape Young Conservatives*. Princeton: Princeton University Press.

Bonsaksen, Tore, Mary Ruffolo, Daicia Price, Janni Leung, Hilde Thygesen, Gary Lamph, Isaac Kabelenga, and Amy Østertun Geirdal. "Associations between Social Media Use and Loneliness in a Cross-National Population." *Health Psychology and Behavioral Medicine* 11, no. 1 (2023): 2158089.

Bourdieu, Pierre. "The Forms of Capital." In *Handbook of Theory and Research for the Sociology of Education*, edited by John Richardson, 241–58. New York: Greenwood, 1986.

Bourdieu, Pierre, and Loïc J. D. Wacquant. *An Invitation to Reflexive Sociology*. Chicago: University of Chicago Press, 1992.

Bowman, Nicholas A. "The Development of Psychological Well-Being among First-Year College Students." *Journal of College Student Development* 51, no. 2 (2010): 180–200.

boyd, danah. *It's Complicated: The Social Lives of Networked Teens*. New Haven: Yale University Press, 2014.

Brooks, Rachel. "Friends, Peers, and Higher Education." *British Journal of Sociology of Education* 28 (2007): 693–707.

Bruce, Liana DesHarnais, Joshua S. Wu, Stuart L. Lustig, Daniel W. Russell, and Douglas A. Nemecek. "Loneliness in the United States: A 2018 National Panel Survey of Demographic, Structural, Cognitive, and Behavioral Characteristics." *American Journal of Health Promotion* 33, no. 8 (2019): 1123–33.

Cacioppo, John T., James H. Fowler, and Nicholas A. Christakis. "Alone in the Crowd: The Structure and Spread of Loneliness in a Large Social Network." *Journal of Personality and Social Psychology* 97, no. 6 (2009): 977–91.

Chambliss, Daniel F., and Christopher G. Takacs. *How College Works*. Cambridge, MA: Harvard University Press, 2014.

Cherng, Hua-Yu Sebastian, Jessica McCrory Calarco, and Grace Kao. "Along for the Ride: Best Friends' Resources and Adolescents' College Completion." *American Educational Research Journal* 50, no. 1 (2013): 76–106.

Chickering, Arthur W., and Linda Reisser. *Education and Identity*. 2nd ed. San Francisco: Jossey-Bass, 1993.

Choi, Karmel W., Murray B. Stein, Kristen M. Nishimi, Tian Ge, Jonathan R. I. Coleman, Chia-Yen Chen, Andrew Ratanatharathorn, Amanda B. Zheutlin, Erin C. Dunn, 23andMe Research Team, Major Depressive Disorder Working Group of the Psychiatric Genomics Consortium, Gerome Breen, Karestan C. Koenen, and Jordan W. Smoller. "An Exposure-Wide and Mendelian Randomization Approach to

Identifying Modifiable Factors for the Prevention of Depression." *American Journal of Psychiatry* 177 (2020): 944–54.
Christakis, Nicholas A., and James H. Fowler. *Connected: The Surprising Power of Our Social Networks and How They Shape Our Lives*. New York: Little, Brown, 2009.
Cooley, Charles Horton. *Human Nature and the Social Order*. New York: Schocken, 2009 [1902].
Cortez, Jessica. "A Perfect Storm: College Community Cultural-Structural Vulnerability to Suicide." BA thesis, Dartmouth College, 2023.
Covington, Owen. 2018. "Elon Poll." https://www.elon.edu/u/news/2018/08/22/elon-poll-relationships-with-mentors-friends-have-powerful-impact-on-college-experience/.
Cuba, Lee, Nancy Jennings, Suzanne Lovett, and Joseph Swingle. *Practice for Life: Making Decisions in College*. Cambridge, MA: Harvard University Press, 2016.
Deil-Amen, Regina. "Socio-Academic Integrative Moments: Rethinking Academic and Social Integration among Two-Year College Students in Career-Related Programs." *Journal of Higher Education* 82, no. 1 (2011): 44–91.
Desmond, Matthew. "Disposable Ties and the Urban Poor." *American Journal of Sociology* 117, no. 5 (2012): 1295–1335.
Deterding, Nicole M. "Instrumental and Expressive Education: College Planning in the Face of Poverty." *Sociology of Education* 88, no. 4 (2015): 284–301.
Dueñas, Mary, and Alberta M. Gloria. "Para honrar los sacrificios de mi familia: Motivating Persons and Processes of Latinx Undergraduates Attending a Predominantly White Institution." *International Journal of Qualitative Studies in Education* 37, no. 3 (2022): 767–84.
Dunbar, Robin. *Friends: Understanding the Power of Our Most Important Relationships*. London: Abacus, 2021.
Dundes, Lauren, and Jeff Marx. "Balancing Work and Academics in College: Why Do Students Working 10 to 19 Hours per Week Excel?" *Journal of College Student Retention* 8, no. 1 (2006): 107–20.
Durkheim, Émile. *Suicide: A Study in Sociology*. edited by G. Simpson. London: Routledge & Kegan, 1952 [1897].
Emirbayer, Mustafa. "Manifesto for a Relational Sociology." *American Journal of Sociology* 103, no. 2 (1997): 281–317.
Erikson, Emily. "Formalist and Relationalist Theory in Social Network Analysis." *Sociological Theory* 31, no. 3 (2013): 219–42.
Feld, Scott. "The Focused Organization of Organizational Ties." *American Journal of Sociology* 86 (1981): 1015–35.
Felten, Peter, and Leo M. Lambert. *Relationship-Rich Education: How Human Connections Drive Success in College*. Baltimore: Johns Hopkins University Press, 2020.
Felten, Peter, Leo M. Lambert, Isis Artze-Vega, and Oscar R. Miranda Tapia. *Connections Are Everything: A College Student's Guide to Relationship-Rich Education*. Baltimore: Johns Hopkins University Press, 2023.
Ferguson, Sherelle, and Annette Lareau. "Hostile Ignorance, Class, and Same-Race Friendships: Perspectives of Working-Class College Students." *Socius* 7 (2021): 1–17.
Finn, Kristy. *Personal Life, Young Women and Higher Education: A Relational Approach to Student and Graduate Experiences*. New York: Palgrave Macmillan, 2015.

Fischer, Claude S. *To Dwell among Friends: Personal Networks in Town and City.* Chicago: University of Chicago Press, 1982.

Fischer, Mary J. "Does Campus Diversity Promote Friendship Diversity? A Look at Interracial Friendships in College." *Social Science Quarterly* 89 (2008): 631–55.

Flannery, Mary Ellen. "The Mental Health Crisis on College Campuses." NEA News, 2023. https://www.nea.org/nea-today/all-news-articles/mental-health-crisis-college-campuses.

Flashman, Jennifer. "Academic Achievement and Its Impact on Friend Dynamics." *Sociology of Education* 85 (2012): 61–80.

Flora, Carlin. *Friendfluence: The Surprising Ways Friends Make Us Who We Are.* New York: Doubleday, 2013.

Fox, Emily C. "Toward a Sociological Perspective on the Gender and Sexuality of Friendship." *Sociology Compass* 18 (2024): e13263.

Franco, Marisa G. *Platonic: How the Science of Attachment Can Help You Make—and Keep—Friends.* New York: G. P. Putnam's Sons, 2022.

Freeman, Linton C. "A Set of Measures of Centrality Based on Betweenness." *Sociometry* 40 (1977): 35–41.

Gilkes Borr, Tamara. "The Strategic Pursuit of Black Homophily on a Predominantly White Campus." *Journal of Higher Education* 90, no. 2 (2019): 322–46.

Ginsburg, David. "Strategic Group Selection—By Teachers, Not Students. *Education Week*, 2011. https://www.edweek.org/teaching-learning/opinion-strategic-group-selection-by-teachers-not-students/2011/11.

Glaser, Barney G., and Anselm L. Strauss. *The Discovery of Grounded Theory: Strategies for Qualitative Research.* Chicago: Aldine, 1967.

Goldfarb, Anna. *Modern Friendship: How to Nurture Our Most Valued Connections.* Boulder, CO: Sounds True, 2004.

Granovetter, Mark S. "The Strength of Weak Ties." *American Journal of Sociology* 78, no. 6 (1973): 1360–80.

Grant, Adam M., and Susan J. Ashford. "The Dynamics of Proactivity at Work." *Research in Organizational Behavior* 28 (2008): 3–34.

Hall, Jeffrey A. "How Many Hours Does It Take to Make a Friend?" *Journal of Social and Personal Relationships* 36, no. 4 (2019): 1278–96.

*The Healthy Minds Study: 2021 Winter/Spring Data Report.* https://healthymindsnetwork.org/wp-content/uploads/2022/01/HMS_nationalwinter2021_-update1.5.21.pdf.

Hextrum, Kirsten. "Segregation, Innocence, and Protection: The Institutional Conditions That Maintain Whiteness in College Sports." *Journal of Diversity in Higher Education* 13, no. 4 (2020): 384–95.

Hirsch, Jennifer S., and Shamus Khan. *Sexual Citizens: Sex, Power, and Assault on Campus.* New York: W. W. Norton, 2020.

Holt-Lunstad, Julianne, Timothy B. Smith, Mark Baker, Tyler Harris, and David Stephenson. "Loneliness and Social Isolation as Risk Factors for Mortality: A Meta-Analytic Review." *Perspectives on Psychological Science* 10 (2015): 227–37.

Holt-Lunstad, Julianne, Timothy B. Smith, and J. Bradley Layton. "Social Relationships and Mortality Risk: A Meta-analytic Review." *PLoS Med* 7, no. 7 (2010): e1000316.

Hu, Yifan. "Efficient and High Quality Force-Directed Graph Drawing." *Mathematica Journal* 10 (2005): 37–71.

Hudson, Tara D. "Random Roommates: Supporting Our Students in Developing Friendships across Difference. *About Campus* (July–August 2018): 13–22.

Hudson, Tara D., Alyssa N. Rockenbach, and Matthew J. Mayhew. "Campus Conditions and College Experiences That Facilitate Friendship across Worldview Differences." *Journal of Higher Education* 94, no. 2 (2023): 227–55.

Hussey, Samantha. "A System for All? An Examination of Social Hierarchy, Power and Identity within Dartmouth's Greek Life." BA thesis, Dartmouth College, 2020.

Inkelas, Karen Kurotsuchi, Mimi Benjamin, and Jody E. Jessup-Anger. *Living-Learning Communities in Practice: A Guide for Creating, Maintaining, and Sustaining Effective Programs in Higher Education.* New York: Routledge, 2024.

Ispa-Landa, Simone, and Sara E. Thomas. "Navigating the Risks of Party Rape in Historically White Greek Life at an Elite College." *Sociology of Education* 96, no. 3 (2023): 169–83.

Jack, Anthony Abraham. *Class Dismissed: When Colleges Ignore Inequality and Students Pay the Price.* Princeton: Princeton University Press, 2024.

———. *The Privileged Poor: How Elite Colleges Are Failing Disadvantaged Students.* Cambridge, MA: Harvard University Press, 2019.

Jackson, Brandon. *Brotherhood University: Black Men's Friendships and the Transition to Adulthood.* New Brunswick, NJ: Rutgers University Press, 2024.

Johnson, Anthony M. "Collaborating in Class: Social Class Context and Peer Help-seeking and Help-giving in an Elite Engineering School." *American Sociological Review* 87, no. 6 (2022): 981–1006.

———. "'I can turn it on when I need to': Pre-college Integration, Culture, and Peer Academic Engagement among Black and Latino/a Engineering Students." *Sociology of Education* 92, no. 1 (2019): 1–20.

Johnson, Kenneth M. "New Hampshire Demographic Trends in an Era of Economic Turbulence." *Carsey Research* [Carsey Institute, University of New Hampshire] 49 (2019): 1–10.

Karp, Melinda Mechur, Katherine L. Hughes, and Lauren O'Gara. "An Exploration of Tinto's Integration Framework for Community College Students." *Journal of College Student Retention* 12, no. 1 (2010): 69–86.

Katz, Roberta, Sarah Ogilvie, Jane Shaw, and Linda Woodhead. *Gen Z, Explained: The Art of Living in a Digital Age.* Chicago: University of Chicago Press, 2021.

Khan, Shamus. "Legacy Admissions Don't Work the Way You Think They Do." *New York Times,* July 7, 2023.

King, Marissa. *Social Chemistry: Decoding the Patterns of Human Connection.* New York: Dutton, 2021.

Kristof, Nicholas. "We Know the Cure for Loneliness. So Why Do We Suffer?" *New York Times,* September 6, 2023.

Kuh, George D., Jillian Kinzie, John H. Schuh, Elizabeth J. Whitt & Associates. *Student Success in College: Creating Conditions That Matter.* San Francisco: Jossey-Bass, 2005.

Kuwabara, Ko, Jiao Luo, and Oliver Sheldon. "Multiplex Exchange Relations." In *Advances in Group Processes, Volume 27,* edited by Shane R. Thye and Edward J. Lawler. Bellevue, WA: Emerald, 2010.

Labaree, David F. "A System without a Plan: Emergence of an American System of Higher Education in the Twentieth Century." *Bildungsgeschichte: International Journal for the Historiography of Education* 3, no. 1 (2013): 46–59.

Lambert, Leo M., Jason Husser, and Peter Felten. "Mentors Play Critical Role in Quality of College Experience, New Poll Suggests." *The Conversation,* 2018. https://theconversation.com/mentors-play-critical-role-in-quality-of-college-experience-new-poll-suggests-101861.

Lareau, Annette. *Listening to People: A Practical Guide to Interviewing, Participant-Observation, Data Analysis, and Writing It All Up*. Chicago: University of Chicago Press, 2021.

Lazarsfeld, Paul F., and Robert K. Merton. "Friendship As Social Process: A Substantive and Methodological Analysis." In *Freedom and Control in Modern Society*, edited by Morroe Berger. Toronto: D. Van Nostrand, 1954.

Leath, Seanna, Lauren Mims, Khrysta A. Evans, Ti-Asia Parker, and Janelle T. Billingsley. "'I can be unapologetically who I am': A Study of Friendship among Black Undergraduate Women at PWIs." *Emerging Adulthood* 10, no. 4 (2022): 837–51.

Leath, Seanna, Taina Quiles, Meron Samuel, Uche Chima, and Tabbye Chavous. "'Our community is so small': Considering Intraracial Peer Networks in Black Student Adjustment and Belonging at PWIs." *American Educational Research Journal* 59, no. 4 (2022): 752–87.

Lee, Elizabeth M. *Class and Campus Life: Managing and Experiencing Inequality at an Elite College*. Ithaca, NY: Cornell University Press, 2016.

Lee, Jennifer J., and Janice M. McCabe. "Who Speaks and Who Listens: Revisiting the Chilly Climate in College Classrooms." *Gender & Society* 35, no. 1 (2021): 32–60.

Liming, Sheila. *Hanging Out: The Radical Power of Killing Time*. Brooklyn: Melville House, 2023.

Lu, Adrienne. "Everyone Is Talking about 'Belonging': What Does it Really Mean?" *Chronicle of Higher Education*, 2023. https://www.chronicle.com/article/everyone-is-talking-about-belonging.

Ma, Yingyi. *Ambitious and Anxious: How Chinese College Students Succeed and Struggle in American Higher Education*. New York: Columbia University Press, 2020.

Marín, Estéfani, and Janice McCabe. "Is Belonging What You Do, Who You're With, or Who You Are? Three Pathways of Belonging among Latina/o Co-Ethnics at a Predominantly White Institution." *Journal of Latinos and Education* (2024): 1–13.

Marmaros, David, and Bruce Sacerdote. "How Do Friendships Form?" *Quarterly Journal of Economics* 121, no. 1 (2006): 79–119.

Marsden, Peter V. "Network Data and Measurement." *Annual Review of Sociology* 16 (1990): 435–63.

Martinez Alemán, Ana M. "College Women's Friendships: The Longitudinal View." *Journal of Higher Education* 81, no. 5 (2010): 553–82.

———. "Race Talks: Undergraduate Women of Color and Female Friendships." *Review of Higher Education* 23 (2000): 133–52.

———. "Understanding and Investigating Female Friendship's Educative Value." *Journal of Higher Education* 68 (1997): 119–59.

McCabe, Janice M. *Connecting in College: How Friendship Networks Matter for Academic and Social Success*. Chicago: University of Chicago Press, 2016.

———. "Doing Multiculturalism: An Interactionist Analysis of the Practices of a Multicultural Sorority." *Journal of Contemporary Ethnography* 40 (2011): 521–49.

———. "Racial and Gender Microaggressions on a Predominantly-White Campus: Experiences of Black, Latina/o and White Undergraduates." *Race, Gender & Class* 16, no. 1 (2009): 133–51.

———. "'That's what makes our friendships stronger': Supportive Friendships Based on Racial Solidarity and Racial Diversity." In *Sharing Space, Negotiating Difference: Contemporary Ethnographies of Power and Marginality on Campus*, edited by Elizabeth M. Lee and Chaise LaDousa, 64–79. New York: Routledge, 2015.

———. "Why Study with Friends? A Relational Analysis of Students' Strategies to Integrate Social and Academic Life." In *Relational Sociology and Research on Schools, Colleges, and Universities*, edited by William G. Tierney and Suneal Kolluri, 135–56. Albany: SUNY Press, 2020.

McPherson, Miller, Lynn Smith-Lovin, and James M. Cook. "Birds of a Feather: Homophily in Social Networks." *Annual Review of Sociology* 27 (2001): 415–44.

Mead, George Herbert. *Mind, Self and Society*. Chicago: University of Chicago Press, 1934.

Moffatt, Michael. *Coming of Age in New Jersey: College and American Culture*. New Brunswick, NJ: Rutgers University Press, 1989.

Mullen, Ann L. *Degrees of Inequality: Culture, Class, and Gender in American Higher Education*. Baltimore: Johns Hopkins University Press, 2010.

Nathan, Rebekah (Cathy Small). *My Freshman Year: What A Professor Learned by Becoming a Student*. Ithaca, NY: Cornell University Press, 2005.

NCES (National Center for Education Statistics). *Digest of Education Statistics*. Washington, DC: US Department of Education Institute of Education Sciences, 2014.

Nelson, Ingrid A., Hannah J. Graham, and Natalie L. Rudin. "Saving Face While (Not) Talking about Race: How Undergraduates Inhabit Racialized Structures at an Elite and Predominantly White College." *Social Problems* 70 (2023): 456–73.

Nenga, Sandi K., Guillermo A. Alvarado, and Claire S. Blyth. "'I kind of found my people': Latino/a College Students' Search for Social Integration on Campus." In *Sharing Space, Negotiating Difference: Contemporary Ethnographies of Power and Marginality on Campus*, edited by Elizabeth M. Lee and Chaise LaDousa, 37–53. New York: Routledge, 2015.

Newcomb, Theodore M. *The Acquaintance Process*. New York: Holt, Rinehart & Winston, 1961.

Newman, M. E. J. "Modularity and Community Structure in Networks." *PNAS* 103 (2006): 8577–82.

Newport, Cal. *Deep Work: Rules for Focused Success in a Distracted World*. New York: Grand Central Publishing, 2016.

Nielsen, Kelly. "'Fake it 'til you make it': Why Community College Students' Aspirations 'Hold Steady.'" *Sociology of Education* 88, no. 4 (2015): 265–83.

Nunn, Lisa M. *College Belonging: How First-year and First-generation Students Navigate Campus Life*. New Brunswick, NJ: Rutgers University Press, 2021.

Obama, Michelle. *The Light We Carry: Overcoming Uncertain Times*. New York: Crown Random House, 2022.

Office of the Surgeon General. *Our Epidemic of Loneliness and Isolation: The U.S. Surgeon General's Advisory on the Healing Effects of Social Connection and Community*. Washington, DC: US Department of Health and Human Services, 2023.

O'Hara, Robert J. "How to Build a Residential College." *Planning for Higher Education* 30, no. 2 (2001): 52–57.

Opportunity Insights. "Mobility Report Cards." 2017. https://www.nytimes.com/interactive/2017/01/18/upshot/some-colleges-have-more-students-from-the-top-1-percent-than-the-bottom-60.html.

Pahl, Ray. *On Friendship*. New York: Polity, 2000.

Park, Julie J. "Clubs and the Campus Racial Climate: Student Organizations and Interracial Friendship in College." *Journal of College Student Development* 55 (2014): 641–60.

Park, Julie J., and Young K. Kim. "Interracial Friendship and Structural Diversity: Trends for Greek, Religious and Ethnic Student Organizations." *Review of Higher Education* 37, no. 1 (2013): 1–24.

Pascarella, Ernest T., and Patrick T. Terenzini. *How College Affects Students: Volume 2: A Third Decade of Research*. San Francisco: Jossey-Bass, 2005.

Paul, Pamela. "What is Lost When Freshmen Choose Their Roommates." *The New York Times*, April 18, 2024. https://www.nytimes.com/2024/04/18/opinion/roommates-college-strangers.html.

Portes, Alejandro. "Social Capital: Its Origins and Applications in Modern Sociology." *Annual Review of Sociology* 24 (1998): 1–24.

Putnam, Robert D. *Bowling Alone: The Collapse and Revival of American Community*. New York: Simon & Schuster, 2000.

Ray, Rashawn, and Jason A. Rosow. "Two Different Worlds of Black and White Fraternity Men: Visibility and Accountability as Mechanisms of Privilege." *Journal of Contemporary Ethnography* 41 (2012): 66–95.

Reeder, Heidi M. "The Effect of Gender Role Orientation on Same- and Cross-Sex Friendship Formation." *Sex Roles* 49 (2003): 143–52.

Reitman, Janet. "Confessions of an Ivy League Frat Boy: Inside Dartmouth's Hazing Abuses." *Rolling Stone*, March 28, 2012. https://www.rollingstone.com/feature/confessions-of-an-ivy-league-frat-boy-inside-dartmouths-hazing-abuses-238604/.

Reyes, Daisy Verduzco. *Learning to Be Latino: How Colleges Shape Identity Politics*. New Brunswick, NJ: Rutgers University Press, 2018.

Ridgeway, Cecilia L. *Framed by Gender: How Gender Inequality Persists in the Modern World*. New York: Oxford University Press, 2011.

Ridgeway, Cecilia L., and Shelley J. Correll. "Unpacking the Gender System: A Theoretical Perspective on Cultural Beliefs in Social Relations." *Gender & Society* 18, no. 4 (2004): 510–31.

Risman, David, Nathan Glazer, and Reuel Denney. *The Lonely Crowd: A Study of the Changing American Character*. New Haven: Yale University Press, 1950.

Rojas, Arizbeth. "Student Workers Find Community Within On- and Off-Campus Jobs." *The Dartmouth*, August 31, 2022. https://www.thedartmouth.com/article/2022/08/student-workers-find-community-within-on-and-off-campus-jobs.

Sacerdote, Bruce. "Peer Effects with Random Assignment: Results for Dartmouth Roommates." *Quarterly Journal of Economics* 116 (2001): 681–704.

Sanchez, Olivia. "The Worst of the Pandemic Is Behind Us: College Students' Mental Health Needs Are Not." *Hechinger Report*, February 9, 2024. https://hechingerreport.org/the-worst-of-the-pandemic-is-behind-us-college-students-mental-health-needs-are-not/.

Sandelson, Jasmin. *My Girls: The Power of Friendship in a Poor Neighborhood*. Berkeley: University of California Press, 2023.

Schnall, Simone, Kent D. Harber, Jeanine K. Stefanucci, and Dennis R. Proffitt. "Social Support and the Perception of Geographical Slant." *Journal of Experimental Social Psychology* 44 (2008): 1246–55.

Schudde, Lauren, and Sara Goldrick-Rab. "On Second Chances and Stratification: How Sociologists Think about Community Colleges." *Community College Review* 43 (2015): 27–45.

Schwartz, Seth J., Byron L. Zamboanga, Koen Luyckx, Alan Meca, and Rachel A. Ritchie. "Identity in Emerging Adulthood: Reviewing the Field and Looking Forward." *Emerging Adulthood* 1, no. 2 (2013): 96–113.

Senior, Jennifer. "It's Your Friends Who Break Your Heart." *The Atlantic*, March 2022, 32–44.

Shovestul, Bridget, Jiayin Han, Laura Germine, and David Dodell-Feder. "Risk Factors for Loneliness: The High Relative Importance of Age versus Other Factors." *PLoS ONE* 15, no. 2 (2020): e0229087.

Silver, Blake R. *The Cost of Inclusion: How Student Conformity Leads to Inequality on College Campuses*. Chicago: University of Chicago Press, 2020.

———. "Inequality in the Extracurriculum: How Class, Race, and Gender Shape College Involvement." *Sociological Forum* 35 (2020): 1290–1314.

———. "On the Margins of College Life: The Experiences of Racial and Ethnic Minority Men in the Extracurriculum." *Journal of Contemporary Ethnography* 49 (2020): 147–75.

Simmel, Georg. *Conflict* and *The Web of Group-Affiliations*. New York: Free Press, 1955.

Small, Mario. "'How many cases do I need?' On Science and the Logic of Case Selection in Field-Based Research." *Ethnography* 10 (2009): 5–38.

———. *Someone to Talk To: How Networks Matter in Practice*. New York: Oxford University Press, 2019.

———. *Unanticipated Gains: Origins of Network Inequality in Everyday Life*. New York: Oxford University Press, 2009.

Smith, Rachel A. "Magnets and Seekers: A Network Perspective on Academic Integration inside Two Residential Communities." *The Journal of Higher Education* 86, no. 6 (2015): 893–922.

Smith, Rachel A., Michael G. Brown, Kevin A. Grady, Stephanie Sowl, and Jessica M. Schulz. "Patterns of Undergraduate Student Interpersonal Interaction Network Change during the COVID-19 Pandemic." *AERA Open* 8, no. 1 (2022): 1–17.

Smith, Rachel A., Michael G. Brown, James J. Schiltz, Stephanie Sowl, Jessica M. Schulz, and Kevin A. Grady. "The Value of Interpersonal Network Continuity for College Students in Disruptive Times." *Innovative Higher Education* 48 (2023): 719–38.

Smith, Rachel A., and Christina Vonhoff. "Problematizing Community: A Network Approach to Conceptualizing Campus Communities." *Journal of College Student Development* 60, no. 3 (2019): 255–70.

Solórzano, Daniel G., Miguel Ceja, and Tara Yosso. "Critical Race Theory, Racial Microaggressions, and Campus Racial Climate: The Experiences of African American College Students." *Journal of Negro Education* 69 (2000): 60–73.

Sow, Aminatou, and Ann Friedman. *Big Friendship: How We Keep Each Other Close*. New York: Simon & Schuster, 2021.

Stearns, Elizabeth, Claudia Buchmann, and Kara Bonneau. "Interracial Friendships in the Transition to College: Do Birds of a Feather Flock Together Once They Leave the Nest?" *Sociology of Education* 82 (2009): 173–95.

Stevens, Mitchell L., Elizabeth A. Armstrong, and Richard Arum. "Sieve, Incubator, Temple, Hub: Empirical and Theoretical Advances in the Sociology of Higher Education." *Annual Review of Sociology* 34 (2008): 127–51.

Strange, C. Carney, and James H. Banning. *Designing for Learning: Creating Campus Environments for Student Success*. 2nd ed. San Francisco: Jossey-Bass, 2015.

Strayhorn, Terrell L. *College Students' Sense of Belonging: A Key to Educational Success for All Students*. New York: Routledge, 2018.

Stuber, Jenny M. *Inside the College Gates: How Class and Culture Matter in Higher Education*. Lanham, MD: Lexington, 2011.

Szell, Michael, and Stefan Thurner. "How Women Organize Social Networks Different from Men." *Scientific Reports* 3 (2013): 1214.

Tatum, Beverly Daniel. *"Why Are All the Black Kids Sitting Together in the Cafeteria?" And Other Conversations about Race*. New York: Basic, 1997.

Thomas, Scott L. "Ties That Bind: A Social Network Approach to Understanding Student Integration and Persistence." *Journal of Higher Education* 71, no. 5 (2000): 591–615.

Thornton, Jack. "Lucky Me: Acknowledging Class Privilege on an Elite College Campus." *Socius* 9 (2023): 1–15.

Tichavakunda, Antar A. *Black Campus Life: The Worlds Black Students Make at a Historically White Institution*. Albany: SUNY Press, 2021.

Tichavakunda, Antar. "Black Joy on White Campuses: Exploring Black Students' Recreation and Celebration at a Historically White Institution." *Review of Higher Education* 44, no. 3 (2021): 297–324.

Tinto, Vincent. *Leaving College: Rethinking the Causes and Cures of Student Attrition*, 2nd ed. Chicago: University of Chicago Press, 1993.

Uppaluri, Jayanth. "Quality over Quantity: A Senior Reflects on Lasting Friendships." *The Dartmouth*, February 7, 2024. https://www.thedartmouth.com/article/2024/02/quality-over-quantity-a-senior-reflects-on-lasting-friendships-65c2ddbd072c4.

Verbrugge, Lois M. "Multiplexity in Adult Friendships." *Social Forces* 57, no. 4 (1979): 1286–1309.

Villalpando, Octavio. "Self-Segregation or Self-Preservation? A Critical Race Theory and Latina/o Critical Theory Analysis of a Study of Chicana/o College Students." *Qualitative Studies in Education* 16 (2003): 619–46.

Wade, Lisa. *American Hookup: The New Culture of Sex on Campus*. New York: W. W. Norton, 2017.

Waldinger, Robert, and Marc Schulz. *The Good Life: Lessons from the World's Longest Scientific Study of Happiness*. New York: Simon & Schuster, 2023.

Way, Niobe. *Deep Secrets: Boys' Friendships and the Crisis of Connection*. Cambridge, MA: Harvard University Press, 2013.

Winkle-Wagner, Rachelle, Carmen M. McCallum, Courtney Luedke, and Brittany Ota-Malloy. "Instrumental or Meaningful Friendships: Black Alumnae Perspectives on Peer Relationships during College." *Journal of Women and Gender in Higher Education* 12, no. 3 (2019): 283–98.

Wood, Joanie. "Dark Side or Light Side?" *The Dartmouth*, February 14, 2024. https://www.thedartmouth.com/article/2024/02/dark-side-or-light-side-deconstructing-the-athlete-and-narp-divide.

Yin, Robert K. *Case Study Research and Applications: Design and Methods*. Thousand Oaks, CA: Sage, 2018.

Zúñiga, Ximena. "Bridging Differences through Dialogue." *About Campus* 7, no. 6 (2003): 8–16.

# Index

Page numbers followed by *f* and *t* refer to figures and tables, respectively.

academic outcomes, 6–7, 201, 242n40, 252n13
academic support: compartmentalized networks and, 103; keeping friends for, 86–87, 90, 165; multiplex ties and, 80, 103, 165, 179; same-race friendships and, 6, 179, 182; studying with friends as, 86, 108–9, 146, 165, 244n22; tight-knit networks and, 179, 182, 249n17; women's same-gender friendships and, 195
academic-social balance, 156, 162, 165–68, 227t
African American students. *See* Black students
agency, 10, 169, 206, 238n49
alcohol use, 10, 71, 122, 194, 195, 216
anomie, 162
Anthony, Amanda Koontz, 119
anxiety, 3, 90
Arizona State University, 157, 246n13
Asian and Asian American students: clubs and organizations for, 56; density of friendship networks, 189, 250nn30–31; graduation rate for, 9, 237n39; same-race friendships among, 8, 107–9, 185–86
assault. *See* sexual assault
Astin, Alexander, 7
athletics. *See* sports teams
attraction relationships, 240n18

belonging: academic, 247n15; campus-community, 162, 247n15; creation and negotiation of, 217, 248n3; dynamic nature of, 249n25; facilitation of, 46, 216; friendships and, 3, 6, 68, 109, 183, 185, 199, 208; Greek organizations and, 163, 173; homophily and, 198; identity development and, 9; lack of, 1, 20, 160, 166, 177, 184, 205; marginalized groups and, 20, 179, 186, 205; realms of, 247n15, 252n10; secondary friendship markets and, 51, 56; social, 51, 163, 247n15, 252n10; sources of, 20, 179, 199
betterment distancing, 119–20, 125
betweenness centrality of friendship networks, 141, 141t, 223–24, 225t, 236n12, 254n21
bias. *See* discrimination
Binder, Amy, 217
Black students: Black joy, 249n16; clubs and organizations for, 46, 55, 182; compartmentalized networks and, 91; density of friendship networks, 189, 197, 250nn30–31; graduation rate for, 9, 237n39; interracial friendships, 186–87, 189; on multiplex ties, 80; same-race friendships, 7–8, 36–40, 45–46, 183, 185, 236n23, 249n19; secondary friendship markets and, 4, 6; tight-knit networks and, 1, 37, 182

bonding social capital: characteristics of, 206–7, 243n61; development of, 201, 203; homophily and, 40, 179–84; marginalized groups and, 20, 190, 198; support through, 167–68, 185
boundary work, 248n3
Bowdoin College, 10, 168, 242n46, 249n12
boyd, danah, 237n32
bridging social capital: academic outcomes and, 252n13; characteristics of, 207, 243n61; class-based similarities and, 190; development of, 201, 203; marginalized groups and, 20, 184–86, 198; network types and, 184; orientation programs and, 207; resource access and, 168; weak tie friendships and, 62, 144, 246n6 (chap. 4)

Chambliss, Daniel, 79
class. *See* social class
clubs and organizations: barriers to participation in, 45, 149–51; at Dartmouth, 25, 29–30, 44–45, 56–58, 169, 240n9; as "foci" in network terms, 236n24; homophily in, 4, 6, 45–46, 56; as initial friendship markets, 34, 36, 43–46, 65, 158; at MCC, 6, 43–45, 144–45, 149–53, 188; parental support for participation in, 68; propinquity in, 4, 6, 7, 41, 69, 116, 149; race- or ethnicity-based, 45–46, 55–56, 100, 108–9, 182, 205, 248n3; as secondary friendship markets, 4, 6, 32, 49, 51, 56–58, 171, 204–5; as social capital, 56, 67, 242n52; spending time with friends in, 73, 75–76, 102; tight-knit networks and, 46, 169; at UNH, 4, 44–46, 56–57, 154, 169, 204. *See also* Greek letter organizations; sports teams
collaborations, 59, 67–69, 171, 191, 205, 243n55
colleges and universities: alcohol use at, 10, 71, 122, 194, 195, 216; cross-campus comparisons of, 11, 208, 216–17, 238n53; ethnographic accounts of, 9, 42, 56, 241n37, 250n42; experiential core of, 11, 238n52; feeling "at home" at, 7; graduation rates of, 9, 237n39; mental health crisis at, 3; number of students attending, 10–11; paradox involving, 3; racism at, 10, 157, 186–87; sexual assault at, 10, 216, 240nn10–11; structural diversity of, 8; student support for making, keeping, and losing friends, 68–69, 105–6, 132–33; transition to, 9, 35, 46, 68, 83, 201, 239n3. *See also* community colleges; residential campuses; *and specific institutions*
Columbia University, 240n10
common spaces, 10, 13–14, 40–41, 42, 51, 67, 68, 105, 143–44, 204, 220
communication. *See* conversation
community colleges: age diversity of, 6, 152; benefits of relationships, 153–54; homophily and, 206; making friends at, 6, 19–20, 141–49, 152; propinquity and, 141, 143, 147, 206; social and academic integration of, 237n44; social mobility through, 9; time spent with friends at, 74; as understudied, 10, 216, 237n42; weak tie friendships and, 63, 144, 206. *See also* Manchester Community College (MCC)
companionship, 90, 91
compartmentalized networks: academic support and, 103; betweenness centrality and, 223, 236n12, 254n21; challenges associated with, 91–93, 103; characteristics of, 4, 17; at Dartmouth, 16, 16t, 48, 91–101, 94t, 113, 129–30, 139–40, 140t, 168–69; density and, 4, 223, 236n12; emotional support and, 189; friendship expansion and, 98–101; friendship funneling and, 95–96; homophily and, 184; keeping friends and, 73, 91–93, 103; losing friends from, 113, 129–33; at MCC, 16, 16t, 139, 140t, 148; meaningful friendships and, 18; modularity and, 224, 236n12, 254n23; points of intervention, 205–6; social support and, 103; sociograms of, 4, 5f; at UNH, 16, 16t, 91–93, 139, 140t, 160

*Connecting in College* (McCabe): on academic-social balance, 156; data collection and analysis, 222–23, 239n65, 254n21, 254n23; on friendship networks, 16–17, 16t, 249n17; institutional factors proposed by, 94; Midwestern university as site of study, 7, 216; mom-like friendships of women in, 250n29; typology of friendship developed in, 8, 215

conversation: on disagreements and differences, 77–80, 103, 106; intergroup dialogue, 252n5; keeping friends and, 73, 76–80, 103–6, 243–44n4; making friends and, 41, 42, 51, 59, 60, 67; in meaningful friendships, 18, 77; opportunities to engage in, 202; strategies for starting, 240n17; striving episodes, 243n4; women and, 192–94

Cooley, Charles Horton, 246n7 (chap. 3)

COVID-19 pandemic: lessons learned from, 9, 208; loneliness and isolation during, 3, 66; propinquity changes during, 50, 116–17, 128; reevaluation of friendships during, 128; research projects interrupted by, 222, 238n58; social experiences impacted by, 253n6; suicide and suicidal ideation during, 162; technology during, 3, 83–84, 116

Cuba, Lee, 32–33

cultural diversity. *See* race and ethnicity

culture shock, 172, 248n1

Dartmouth College: academic-social balance at, 156, 162, 165–68, 227t; admitted students day, 39, 43, 61, 179, 241n38; alcohol use at, 216; betweenness centrality of friendship networks, 141, 141t, 225t; campus access for case study, 217; case study design, 11–12, 218–22, 238n58, 245n31; case study participant characteristics, 226–27t, 230–33t; clubs and organizations, 25, 29–30, 44–45, 56–58, 169, 240n9; compartmentalized networks, 16, 16t, 48, 91–101, 94t, 113, 129–30, 139–40, 140t, 168–69; culture shock at, 172, 248n1; density of friendship networks, 16t, 141, 141t, 189, 225t; description of, 14–15, 161–62, 228–29t, 238n60, 247n17; dining halls, 15, 48, 76, 174, 252n8; dorms and roommate selection, 1, 25, 26, 41–43, 137, 168, 201; emotional distress of students, 166, 247n22; faculty teaching schedules, 253n14; friendship markets, 20, 32, 35–60, 162, 167, 172, 248n4; Greek organizations, 1, 25–30, 53–55, 163, 166–67, 173–75, 215, 239n4, 240n11, 242n51, 247n27, 248n6, 253n1; house communities, 204, 216, 247n21, 253n6; modularity of friendship networks, 141, 141t, 225t; motto of, 162, 247n18; "Moving Dartmouth Forward" plan, 216; multiplex ties, 80–81, 165, 179–80; in national rankings, 161, 247n16; Novack Café on campus of, 109, 245n2; orientation and pre-orientation programs, 25–26, 36–40, 45, 64, 107, 169, 203, 239n3, 240–41nn21–24; racial diversity, 11, 174, 216; same-gender friendships, 251n47; sampler networks, 16, 16t, 94, 94t, 99–100, 140, 140t, 168–69; selection for case study, 11, 12, 216; sexual assault at, 216, 240n11; size of friendship networks, 16t, 140, 141t, 225t; sociograms of students, 28–29f, 37, 38f, 54f, 96–101f, 108–9f, 176–77f, 180–81f, 182; sophomore summer at, 29, 137, 163, 173, 215, 238n58, 248n6; sports teams, 46–48, 139, 167, 172–73, 242n45, 247n27; study abroad programs, 14, 52, 119, 164; tight-knit networks, 16, 16t, 28–30, 62, 94–95, 94t, 98–99, 102, 140, 140t, 169; time spent with friends at, 73, 75, 77, 143; undergraduate enrollment, 215; weak tie friendships and, 62, 144, 167, 178, 206. *See also* D-Plan schedule (Dartmouth College)

Denney, Reuel, 236n8

density of friendship networks: compartmentalized, 4, 223, 236n12; at Dartmouth, 16t, 141, 141t, 189, 225t;

density of friendship networks (*cont.*)
  gender and, 189, 197, 250n31, 251n52;
  at MCC, 16t, 140, 141, 141t, 145, 225t;
  racial and ethnic differences in, 189,
  250nn30–31; sampler, 4, 169, 223,
  236n12; social support and, 245n28;
  tight-knit, 4, 223, 236n12, 249n21; at
  UNH, 16t, 141, 141t, 225t, 251n52
depression, 3, 78, 90, 235n2
Desmond, Matt, 245n4
dining halls: at Dartmouth, 15, 48, 76,
  174, 252n8; at MCC, 143–44, 145,
  219; student interactions in, 3, 15, 61,
  68, 76, 204; at UNH, 15, 51, 57, 58,
  72, 75
discrimination: gender stereotypes, 193,
  198, 199; in Greek organizations, 160;
  microaggressions, 20, 60, 183–87,
  198, 199, 201, 250n26; racism, 10, 157,
  186–87. *See also* segregation
disposable ties, 245n4
diversity. *See* race and ethnicity
dorms: attraction relationships in, 240n18;
  at Dartmouth College, 1, 25, 26, 41–43,
  168; first-year, 1, 31, 32, 40–43, 46, 49,
  137, 159; initial friendship markets
  and, 32, 34, 36, 40–43, 46–48, 64, 67,
  158–59; mixed-year, 20, 49, 159, 171;
  percentage of close friends met in,
  243n54; physical layout of, 40, 41, 68;
  propinquity in, 32–33, 41–42, 54, 159,
  168, 241n34; requirements for living in,
  9; resident advisors in, 40, 43, 46, 69,
  91, 242n39; single-occupancy rooms
  in, 159; spending time with friends
  in, 73; terminology considerations,
  239n2; at UNH, 20, 41–43, 159. *See
  also* roommates
D-Plan schedule (Dartmouth College):
  compartmentalized networks and,
  139, 168; description of, 6, 240n19,
  245n33, 246n1; friendship markets
  and, 35, 49, 162, 167; keeping friends
  and, 6, 96, 162, 165, 215; off-campus
  activities during, 249n10; propinquity
  and, 137–38, 162–65
drinking. *See* alcohol use
Dunbar, Robin, 17, 239n67
Durkheim, Émile, 162, 235n8

education: identity development and,
  89; relationship- and resource-rich, 7,
  80, 153, 154; sociology of, 200, 206–9,
  215, 238n52. *See also* colleges and
  universities; *and specific institutions*
egocentric network data, 11, 221, 223
emotional labor, 194, 196, 197–99
emotional support: compartmentalized
  networks and, 189; Greek
  organizations and, 54; keeping friends
  for, 19, 84–86, 90; losing friends and,
  133; mom-like friendships and, 188,
  194, 251n42; multiplex ties and, 72,
  80; in one-sided friendships, 126;
  propinquity and, 245n4; same-race
  friendships and, 7, 109, 181, 187;
  tight-knit networks and, 208
ethnicity. *See* race and ethnicity
extracurricular activities. *See* clubs and
  organizations; sports teams

Facebook, 41, 81, 168, 201, 241n35
fear of missing out (FOMO), 81
females. *See* women
Ferguson, Sherelle, 186, 190, 217,
  250n26
First Year Summer Enrichment Program
  (FYSEP), 36–37, 45, 240n23
first-generation college students:
  belonging created by, 217; friendship
  fade-aways and, 113; making and
  keeping friends, 66, 79, 86, 94, 99–
  100; orientation programs for, 36–37,
  45, 182, 203, 240n23
Florida State University, 215–16, 238n59,
  253n2
FOMO (fear of missing out), 81
fraternities. *See* Greek letter organizations
friendship markets, 31–65; buyers and
  sellers in, 18, 31, 33, 42; at Dartmouth,
  20, 32, 35–60, 162, 167, 172, 248n4;
  loneliness and isolation in, 35, 64–65;
  at MCC, 6, 32, 35–36, 43–45, 49,
  51, 59–61; at UNH, 4, 6, 31–36, 39,
  41–46, 49–59, 61, 140, 158–60, 182,
  248n30; weak tie friendships and, 62–
  63, 67–68. *See also* initial friendship
  markets; secondary friendship
  markets

friendship networks: access to campuses for study of, 217–18; analysis of, 8–10, 18, 208, 223–24, 252n13; betweenness centrality of, 141, 141t, 223–24, 225t, 236n12, 254n21; campus structure and, 11–12, 19–20, 139–43, 169–70, 206, 208–9; case study design, 11–12, 208, 218–22, 253n15; case study participant characteristics, 226–27t, 230–33t; friends from home in, 16t, 17–18, 34, 37, 61, 95, 143, 160, 225t, 239n68; future research needs, 208; gender and, 189, 196–98, 250n31, 251nn50–52; identities and, 3–4, 6, 9, 20, 89, 179–89; institutional approach to, 3, 10, 208; loneliness spread within, 236n11; modularity of, 141, 141t, 223–24, 225t, 236n12, 254n23; origins of project for study of, 215–17; points of intervention, 21, 201–6, 202t; size of, 16t, 17, 140–41, 141t, 197, 225t, 239n66, 251n51, 253n15. *See also* compartmentalized networks; density of friendship networks; sampler networks; sociograms; tight-knit networks

friendships: adult, 3, 240n17, 243n62; belonging and, 3, 6, 68, 109, 183, 185, 199, 208; cross-class, 191; cross-gender, 195–96, 251n45; deepening, 19, 69, 74, 77–80, 91, 97, 102–6, 164, 204; Dunbar's circles of friendship, 17, 239n67; expansion of, 19, 73, 98–102, 104, 122, 164, 223; funneling of, 19, 73, 94–99, 104, 223; happiness and, 2, 55, 80, 165, 235n2; health and well-being impacted by, 2, 80, 90, 110, 235nn2–3; interracial, 8, 46, 174, 183, 185–89, 242n43; literature review, 6–10, 236n18; mom-like, 188, 192, 194, 250n29, 250n42; one-sided, 85, 125–26, 244n18; perceptions of, 4, 35, 94, 244n5; reciprocity in, 59, 85, 125–26, 187, 246n9 (chap. 3); same-gender, 27, 32, 194–96, 225t, 236n23, 251nn47–49; same-race, 7–8, 32, 36–40, 45–46, 107–9, 179–89, 217, 225t, 236n23, 249n19; social capital and, 7, 21, 87, 126; sociology of education and, 206–9; trapped in, 30, 32, 93, 131–33; valuing, 52, 64–66, 69; vulnerability in, 31, 67, 78, 194, 196; weak tie, 62–63, 67–69, 144, 167, 178, 206, 243n60, 246n6 (chap. 4); in young adulthood, 3, 89, 235n4. *See also* keeping friends; losing friends; making friends; meaningful friendships

FYSEP (First Year Summer Enrichment Program), 36–37, 45, 240n23

gender: in case study design, 11, 226t; classroom behavior and, 251n44; cross-gender friendships, 195–96, 251n45; friendship networks and, 189, 196–98, 250n31, 251nn50–52; inequality and, 197–98, 250n39; partitioning strategy and, 248n5; same-gender friendships, 27, 32, 194–96, 225t, 236n23, 251nn47–49; schemas related to, 194; segregation based on, 192, 196, 242n47; sports teams and, 47, 242n47; stereotypes related to, 193, 198, 199. *See also* men; women

Gilkes Borr, Tamara, 46
Glazer, Nathan, 236n8
Goldfarb, Anna, 240n17
Granovetter, Mark, 243n60
Greek letter organizations: belonging and, 163, 173; at Dartmouth, 1, 25–30, 53–55, 163, 166–67, 173–75, 215, 239n4, 240n11, 242n51, 247n27, 248n6, 253n1; discrimination in, 160; emotional support and, 54; gender segregation and, 196; identity mismatches with, 119; loneliness and isolation caused by, 163, 205; losing friends after joining, 55, 74, 118, 130; propinquity and, 7, 54, 159, 163, 191; reevaluation of, 126, 139; roommates and, 201, 252n2; rush process for, 1, 27, 55, 74, 166–67, 173, 175; secondary friendship markets and, 32, 49, 51, 53–55, 205; social capital and, 173, 175; social class and, 173, 198; social hierarchy among, 173, 239n4; at UNH, 53–55, 158–60, 242n51

group chats, 18, 81–82, 91, 102, 129, 130

Hall, Jeffrey A., 243n4
happiness, 2, 55, 80, 165, 235n2
Harvard Study of Adult Development, 235n2
health and well-being, 2–3, 66, 77, 80, 90, 110, 235nn2–3
heteronormativity, 196
higher education. *See* colleges and universities; *and specific institutions*
Hirsch, Jennifer, 240n10
Hispanic students. *See* Latinx students
homophily: belonging and, 198; bonding social capital and, 40, 179–84; in clubs and organizations, 4, 6, 45–46, 56; community colleges and, 206; compartmentalized networks and, 184; identity-based, 32, 37–39, 120, 157, 183–84, 203–4; initial friendship markets and, 37–41, 45–48, 203–4; interest-based, 32, 47–48, 56, 120, 157, 183–84, 203–4; in keeping friends, 19, 70, 79; orientation programs and, 37–39; roommate selection and, 168, 171, 201; same-gender friendships, 27, 32, 194–96, 225t, 236n23, 251nn47–49; same-race friendships, 7–8, 32, 36–40, 45–46, 107–9, 179–89, 217, 225t, 236n23, 249n19; secondary friendship markets and, 4, 6, 51, 56, 60; sports teams and, 47–48, 242n47; tight-knit networks and, 179
hostile ignorance, 21, 179, 186–89, 198, 199, 250n26
house communities, 204, 216, 247n21, 253n6
housing. *See* dorms
Hudson, Tara, 201–2, 252n3
Hussey, Sam, 239n4

identities: cookie-cutter, 9, 126, 250n39; development of, 9, 89–90, 118–19, 131, 246n7 (chap. 3); exploration of, 118, 246n6 (chap. 3); friendship networks and, 3–4, 6, 9, 20, 89, 179–89; homophily based on, 32, 37–39, 120, 157, 183–84, 203–4; intersectional, 20, 178, 186, 198, 199; keeping friends and, 19, 20, 88–91; living-learning communities and, 43; losing friends and, 20, 109–11, 113, 118–21, 131–32; making friends and, 20, 25–27; marginalized, 6, 20, 166, 179, 182, 186, 204; mismatch of, 118–21, 131; multiplex ties and, 80, 179–80; orientation programs based on, 36–39; racial and ethnic, 155, 178, 198, 217, 249n16; sexual, 6, 251n55; shared, 6, 27; social, 9
identity work: betterment distancing, 119–20, 125; friendship breakups and fade-aways and, 111, 119; friendship talk as, 90, 119, 155, 245n26; keeping friends and, 19, 91; reevaluating friendships and, 130
ignorance. *See* hostile ignorance
Indiana University–Bloomington, 215–16, 238n59, 253n2
inequalities: gender, 197–98, 250n39; racial and ethnic, 9; social class, 9, 174, 191, 248n8; structurally-based, 10; student experiences of, 207
initial friendship markets, 32–49; clubs and organizations, 34, 36, 43–46, 65, 158; at Dartmouth, 20, 32, 35–48; dorms, 32, 34, 36, 40–43, 46–48, 64, 67, 158–59; failure to make friends during, 4, 49, 64–65, 69; homophily and, 37–41, 45–48, 203–4; intensity of, 35, 43; loneliness and isolation in, 35, 64–65; at MCC, 35–36, 43–45; openness of, 34–36, 40–43, 48–49; orientation and pre-orientation programs, 32–40, 46, 67, 68, 158–59, 182, 203; points of intervention, 202t, 203; prevalence of, 18, 31; propinquity and, 33, 38–42, 47–48, 204; sports teams, 46–48; at UNH, 31–36, 39, 41–46, 140, 158–60, 182; weak tie friendships and, 62, 68
Institutional Review Boards (IRBs), 218
International Student Pre-Orientation Program (ISPOP), 36, 241n24
international students, 36, 37, 56, 80, 169, 185, 241n24
intersectional identities, 20, 178, 186, 198, 199
isolation. *See* loneliness and isolation

Jack, Anthony Abraham, 241n25, 248n1
Johnson, Anthony, 59, 243n55

keeping friends, 70–106; for academic support and motivation, 86–87, 90, 165; for companionship, 90, 91; compartmentalized networks and, 73, 91–93, 103; conversation and, 73, 76–80, 103–6, 243n4; deepening ties and, 19, 69, 74, 77–80, 91, 97, 102–6; D-Plan schedule and, 6, 96, 162, 165, 215; for emotional and social support, 19, 84–86, 90, 244n13; friendship expansion and, 19, 73, 98–102, 104; friendship funneling and, 19, 73, 94–99, 104; for fun and enjoyment, 19, 87–88, 90–91, 165, 244n24; homophily in, 19, 70, 79; identity and, 19, 20, 88–91; intentionality and, 70–72, 74–75, 82–84, 89, 103, 106, 115; meaningful, 77–80, 84–85, 95–96, 98, 208; multiplex ties and, 72, 80–81, 103; propinquity in, 7, 19, 70–76, 82, 84, 137–38, 158, 162, 171; sampler networks and, 73, 92, 93, 104; shared activities and, 70–77, 102, 104–6; spending time together and, 70–77, 84, 91, 102–6; takeaways for students, parents, and colleges, 102–6; technology and, 18, 81–84, 91, 102, 177, 244n12; tight-knit networks and, 70, 73, 91–93, 103, 245n28
Khan, Shamus, 240n10

Lareau, Annette, 186, 190, 217, 250n26
Latinx students: barriers to friendship, 174; boundary work by, 248n3; clubs and organizations for, 45, 100, 175, 182; culture shock experienced by, 172; on deepening friendship ties, 79; density of friendship networks, 189, 197, 250nn30–31; dorm experiences of, 42–43; graduation rate for, 9, 237n39; Greek organizations and, 173–75; identities and campus structure, 217; interracial friendships, 174; on making friends at community colleges, 141; multiplex ties and, 179–80; same-race friendships, 8, 179–82, 185; terminology considerations, 248n2
Lazarsfeld, Paul, 38
living-learning communities (LLCs), 43, 203, 252n6, 252n12
loneliness and isolation: anomie and, 162; betweenness centrality and, 254n21; in classrooms, 60; combating, 3–4, 21, 200, 206, 207; in COVID-19 pandemic, 3, 66; epidemic of, 3, 21, 110, 198, 200–201, 208–9, 235n7; Greek organizations causing, 163, 205; health and well-being impacted by, 3, 66, 90; historical concerns with, 235n8; initial friendship markets and, 35, 64–65; of marginalized groups, 20, 179, 183; meaningful friendships as protection from, 3, 18, 209; in mixed-year dorms, 159; negative consequences of, 243n63; sampler networks and, 63–65, 104, 176–78, 184; social media and, 8, 81; spread within friendship networks, 236n11; tight-knit networks and, 62; in young adulthood, 3, 235n5
losing friends, 107–33; breakups, 99, 110–13, 118, 120–24, 129–31, 239nn7–8; from compartmentalized networks, 113, 129–33; disposable ties compared to, 245n4; fadeaways, 19, 107–21, 123–24, 126, 128–31, 137; Greek organizations and, 55, 74, 118, 130; identity and, 20, 109–11, 113, 118–21, 131–32; prevalence among students, 107; propinquity and, 109, 115–18, 131, 162–63; reevaluation of friendships, 124–28, 130; romantic relationships and, 113, 121–23, 131; from sampler networks, 129, 131–33; social space changes due to, 123, 138; takeaways for students, parents, and colleges, 131–33; from tight-knit networks, 93, 113, 130–33
low-income students, 36–37, 45, 56, 87, 182, 190–91, 241n25

Ma, Yingyi, 185
maintaining friends. *See* keeping friends
making friends, 25–69; age diversity and, 6, 152; barriers to, 15, 18, 46, 49, 63–66, 69, 144, 152, 174; at community colleges, 6, 19–20, 141–49, 152; conversation and, 41, 42, 51, 59, 60, 67; dimensions of, 31–32; identity and, 20, 25–27; intentionality and, 30–31, 34, 46, 49–52, 58, 66–67, 69; practice, 64, 65, 69; propinquity in, 4, 6, 33, 38–42, 47–48, 51–52, 58–60, 158, 245n4; on residential campuses, 9, 15, 20, 31, 143, 157–60; takeaways for students, parents, and colleges, 67–69; technology and, 81; temporal patterns of, 32–33, 240n15; tight-knit networks and, 28–30; weak tie friendships, 62–63, 67–69. *See also* initial friendship markets; secondary friendship markets
Manchester Community College (MCC): academic programs, 145–49; academic-social balance at, 156, 227t; age diversity on campus, 6, 152; benefits of relationships and, 153–54; betweenness centrality of friendship networks, 141, 141t, 225t; campus access for case study, 218; case study design, 11–12, 218–22, 238n58, 253n11, 253n13, 253n17; case study participant characteristics, 226–27t, 230–33t; clubs and organizations, 6, 43–45, 144–45, 149–53, 188; compartmentalized networks, 16, 16t, 139, 140t, 148; density of friendship networks, 16t, 140, 141, 141t, 145, 225t; description of, 12–13, 15, 143–44, 228–29t, 238n61; friendship markets, 6, 32, 35–36, 43–45, 49, 51, 59–61; modularity of friendship networks, 141, 141t, 225t; multiplex ties and, 81, 165; reasons for attending, 141–42; same-gender friendships and, 251n47; sampler networks, 16, 16t, 129, 140, 140t, 143; selection for case study, 11, 12, 216; size of friendship networks, 16t, 140, 141t, 225t; sociograms of students, 148, 148f, 188, 188f; staff characteristics, 144–45, 153; tight-knit networks, 16, 16t, 140, 140t, 145, 148; time spent with friends at, 74, 75, 144; transfer partners, 142, 246n3; weak tie friendships and, 62, 144

Martinez Alemán, Ana, 27, 195
MCC. *See* Manchester Community College (MCC)
Mead, George Herbert, 246n7 (chap. 3)
meaningful friendships: barriers to, 18, 63–66, 69; belonging and, 162; benefits of, 2, 3, 18, 85, 209; in classrooms, 205; at community colleges, 153; conversation in, 18, 77–78; developing, 26, 30–31, 52, 67–68, 132, 147, 171; D-Plan schedule and, 163; embedded within networks, 4, 18, 209; identity work and, 155; interracial, 183; keeping, 77–80, 84–85, 95–96, 98, 208; lack of, 51, 63–66, 69; living-learning communities and, 203; multiplex ties and, 80, 103; network type and, 4, 18, 103–4; parental support for, 68; points of intervention, 201; reevaluation of, 106, 124, 128; secondary friendship markets and, 204, 205; as "worth the work," 19, 84, 131
men: cultural frames regarding, 192–93; density of friendship networks, 197, 251n52; same-gender friendships, 194, 196, 251nn47–49; social spaces dominated by, 27, 195; tight-knit networks and, 197. *See also* gender
mental health, 3, 77, 80, 235n2
Merton, Robert, 38
microaggressions, 20, 60, 183–87, 198, 199, 201, 250n26
Miller, Chris, 253n1
minorities. *See* race and ethnicity
modularity of friendship networks, 141, 141t, 223–24, 225t, 236n12, 254n23
mom-like friendships, 188, 192, 194, 250n29, 250n42
motivation, 2, 72, 86–87, 90, 109, 147, 165
Mullen, Ann, 216–17, 238n53
multiplex ties, 72, 80–81, 103, 165, 179–80

*National Lampoon's Animal House* (film), 215, 253n1
Native American students: at Dartmouth, 11; density of friendship networks, 189, 250nn30–31; graduation rate for, 9, 237n39; at MCC, 219
Nelson, Ingrid, 248n9, 249n12
network diagrams. *See* sociograms
Newport, Cal, 79
nonresidential campuses. *See* community colleges
Novack Café (Dartmouth College), 109, 182, 245n2
Nunn, Lisa, 51, 217, 247n15

Obama, Michelle, 244n18
one-sided friendships, 85, 125–26, 244n18
organizations. *See* clubs and organizations
orientation and pre-orientation programs: bridging social capital and, 207; at Dartmouth, 25–26, 36–40, 45, 64, 107, 169, 203, 239n3, 240–41nn21–24; for first-generation college students, 36–37, 45, 182, 240n23; homophily and, 37–39; identity-based, 36–39; initial friendship markets and, 32–40, 46, 67, 68, 158–59, 182, 203; interest-based, 36, 39; for international students, 36, 37, 241n24; for low-income students, 36–37; objectives of, 9, 31, 36, 68, 239n3; propinquity and, 38, 39, 241n28; at UNH, 32, 36, 39, 158, 182, 203, 240n22

parental support, 68, 104, 132, 170, 199
partitioning strategy, 248n5
prejudice. *See* discrimination
pre-orientation programs. *See* orientation and pre-orientation programs
Princeton University, 247n16
propinquity: in clubs and organizations, 4, 6, 7, 41, 69, 116, 149; community colleges and, 141, 143, 147, 206; COVID-19 pandemic and, 50, 116–17, 128; in dorms, 32–33, 41–42, 54, 159, 168, 241n34; D-Plan schedule and, 137–38, 162–65; emotional support and, 245n4; friendship expansion and, 102, 122, 164; Greek organizations and, 7, 54, 159, 163, 191; initial friendship markets and, 33, 38–42, 47–48, 204; in keeping friends, 7, 19, 70–76, 82, 84, 137–38, 158, 162, 171; losing friends and, 109, 115–18, 131, 162–63; in making friends, 4, 6, 33, 38–42, 47–48, 51–52, 58–60, 158, 245n4; orientation programs and, 38, 39, 241n28; roommates and, 41, 168, 171, 241n34; secondary friendship markets and, 4, 6, 51–52, 58–60, 170; sports teams and, 4, 6, 47–48, 116, 191; study abroad programs and, 52, 164
Putnam, Robert, 207, 243n61

race and ethnicity: as barriers to friendship, 174; in case study design, 11, 219, 226t; clubs and organizations based on, 45–46, 55–56, 100, 108–9, 182, 205, 248n3; at Dartmouth, 11, 174, 216; density of friendship networks and, 189, 250nn30–31; hostile ignorance and, 186–87; identities based on, 155, 178, 198, 217, 249n16; inequality and, 9; interracial friendships, 8, 46, 174, 183, 185–89, 242n43; marginalization based on, 177; multiracial students, 2, 6; partitioning strategy and, 248n5; same-race friendships, 7–8, 32, 36–40, 45–46, 107–9, 179–89, 217, 225t, 236n23, 249n19; self-segregation by, 38, 183; sports teams and, 47, 242n47. *See also specific racial and ethnic groups*
racism, 10, 157, 186–87
reciprocity, 59, 85, 125–26, 187, 246n9 (chap. 3)
relational sociology, 169, 206, 238n49
relationship-rich education, 7, 80
residence halls. *See* dorms
resident advisors (RAs), 40, 43, 46, 69, 91, 242n39

residential campuses: academic-social balance on, 156; friendship markets on, 35, 36, 41; making friends on, 9, 15, 20, 31, 143, 157–60; orientation programs on, 9, 31, 36; peer-centered environment of, 15, 238n62; social and academic integration on, 237n44; student affairs departments on, 9, 15; time spent with friends on, 73, 144. *See also* dorms; *and specific institutions*
residential college system. *See* house communities
Reyes, Daisy, 217, 238n53
Ridgeway, Cecilia, 197
Risman, David, 236n8
romantic relationships, 84, 110, 112, 113, 121–23, 131
roommates: attraction relationships among, 240n18; challenges involving, 1, 64, 117, 126–27, 154–55, 241n35; Greek organizations and, 201, 252n2; initial friendship markets and, 40–43, 64; institutional decisions involving, 10, 208; points of intervention, 201, 202t; propinquity and, 41, 168, 171, 241n34; selection of, 41, 154, 168, 171, 201, 202t, 241n35. *See also* dorms

Sacerdote, Bruce, 252n2
sampler networks: activity types for, 105; betweenness centrality and, 223, 236n12, 254n21; challenges associated with, 104; characteristics of, 4, 16–17; at Dartmouth, 16, 16t, 94, 94t, 99–100, 140, 140t, 168–69; density and, 4, 169, 223, 236n12; friendship expansion and, 99–100; keeping friends and, 73, 92, 93, 104; loneliness and isolation in, 63–65, 104, 176–78, 184; losing friends from, 129, 131–33; at MCC, 16, 16t, 129, 140, 140t, 143; meaningful friendships and, 18; modularity and, 224, 236n12, 254n23; points of intervention, 205–6; social capital and, 184; social support and, 63, 104, 160, 178, 179; sociograms of, 4, 5f; at UNH, 16, 16t, 93, 140, 140t, 160, 247n15; women and, 196–97

Sandelson, Jasmin, 244n24
secondary friendship markets, 49–62; belonging and, 51, 56; classes, 49–51, 58–61, 67, 68, 205, 243n54; clubs and organizations, 4, 6, 32, 49, 51, 56–58, 171, 204–5; at Dartmouth, 32, 35, 49–60, 172, 248n4; failure to make friends in, 51, 54–55; friends of friends, 61, 243n59; Greek organizations, 32, 49, 51, 53–55, 205; homophily and, 4, 6, 51, 56, 60; at MCC, 6, 49, 51, 59–61; points of intervention, 202t, 204–5; prevalence of, 18–19, 31; propinquity and, 4, 6, 51–52, 58–60, 170; study abroad and off-campus programs, 32, 49, 51–52; at UNH, 4, 6, 50–59, 61, 160, 182, 248n30; weak tie friendships and, 62, 67
segregation: gender-based, 192, 196, 242n47; Greek organizations and, 196; residential, 248n29, 249n12; self-segregation, 38, 183, 199; social experiences and, 248n9; sports teams and, 242n47
sexual assault, 10, 27, 216, 240nn10–11
sexual geographies, 10, 240n10
shared spaces. *See* common spaces
shine theory, 85
Silver, Blake, 56, 126, 248n5, 250n39, 250n42
Simmel, Georg, 235n8
Small, Mario, 207, 243n60
smartphones, 8, 17–18, 81
Smith, Rachel A., 252n12, 254n21
Snapchat, 82, 172
social capital: clubs and organizations as, 56, 67, 242n52; defined, 236n21; friendships and, 7, 21, 87, 126; Greek organizations and, 173, 175; sampler networks and, 184; tight-knit networks and, 184, 185. *See also* bonding social capital; bridging social capital
social class: as barrier to friendship, 174, 190; in case study design, 11, 226t; comfort in academic spaces and, 59; cross-campus comparisons and, 216–17; cross-class friendships, 191; Greek

organizations and, 173, 198; hostile ignorance and, 186, 189; inequalities related to, 9, 174, 191, 248n8; low-income students, 36–37, 45, 56, 87, 182, 190–91, 241n25; markers of, 174, 198, 251n56; partitioning strategy and, 248n5; sports teams and, 47, 242n47

social media: advice for quitting, 79; challenges and opportunities of, 3, 237n32; keeping friends and, 18, 81, 177; loneliness and isolation caused by, 8, 81; roommate selection through, 41, 168, 201, 241n35; social comparison through, 81, 166. *See also specific platforms*

social spaces: alternative, 29, 30, 204, 240n9; in classroom settings, 59; credentials in, 249n12; losing friends and changes in, 123, 138; male-dominated, 27, 195; social class and comfort in, 191

social support: compartmentalized networks and, 103; density of friendship networks and, 245n28; keeping friends for, 84–86, 90, 244n13; losing friends and loss of, 118; multiplex ties and, 72, 103, 179; same-race friendships and, 6, 179, 181, 183, 185; sampler networks and, 63, 104, 160, 178, 179; tight-knit networks and, 103, 131, 160, 177–79; women's same-gender friendships and, 195

socioeconomic status. *See* social class

sociograms: color as utilized in, 254n25; of compartmentalized networks, 4, 5f; of Dartmouth students, 28–29f, 37, 38f, 54f, 96–101f, 108–9f, 176–77f, 180–81f, 182; Gephi software for generation of, 223; of MCC students, 148, 148f, 188, 188f; node size in, 224, 249n15; of sampler networks, 4, 5f; of tight-knit networks, 4, 5f, 28–29f; of UNH students, 34f, 40f, 71f, 92f, 155f, 161f

sociology: of education, 200, 206–9, 215, 238n52; relational, 169, 206, 238n49

sororities. *See* Greek letter organizations

spaces: academic, 59, 191; common, 10, 13–14, 40–41, 42, 51, 67, 68, 105, 143–44, 204, 220; exclusive, 7, 55; Greek, 176, 178; green, 13, 14; minority, 172; owned, 30, 204–5; physical, 10, 19, 158, 178; public, 12, 219; racialized, 38, 174, 178; safe, 27, 195; sexual geographies and, 10, 240n10. *See also* social spaces

sports teams: at Dartmouth, 46–48, 139, 167, 172–73, 242n45, 247n27; homophily and, 47–48, 242n47; initial friendship markets and, 46–48; percentage of students on, 47, 242nn45–46; propinquity and, 4, 6, 47–48, 116, 191; segregation and, 242n47; at UNH, 4, 6, 13, 46, 139, 238n59, 242n45

stereotypes. *See* discrimination

striving episodes, 243n4

strong tie friendships. *See* meaningful friendships

Stuber, Jenny, 216–17, 238n53

study abroad programs, 13–14, 32, 49, 51–52, 100, 119, 129, 164

suicide and suicidal ideation, 3, 78, 162

Takacs, Christopher, 79

talking. *See* conversation

technology: in COVID-19 pandemic, 3, 83–84, 116; group chats, 18, 81–82, 91, 102, 129, 130; in making and keeping friends, 18, 81–84, 91, 102, 177, 244n12; smartphones, 8, 17–18, 81. *See also* social media

Thomas, Scott, 252n13

tight-knit networks: academic support and, 179, 182, 249n17; activity types for, 105; betweenness centrality and, 223, 236n12, 254n21; Black students and, 1, 37, 182; challenges associated with, 93, 103; characteristics of, 4, 16; in clubs and organizations, 46, 169; at Dartmouth, 16, 16t, 28–30, 62, 94–95, 94t, 98–99, 102, 140, 140t, 169; density and, 4, 223, 236n12, 249n21; emotional support and, 208;

tight-knit networks (*cont.*)
friendship expansion and, 98–99, 102; friendship funneling and, 95; homophily and, 179; keeping friends and, 70, 73, 91–93, 103, 245n28; loneliness and isolation in, 62; losing friends from, 93, 113, 130–33; making friends and, 28–30; at MCC, 16, 16t, 140, 140t, 145, 148; meaningful friendships and, 18; men and, 197; modularity and, 224, 236n12, 254n23; points of intervention, 205–6; social capital and, 184, 185; social support and, 103, 131, 160, 177–79; sociograms of, 4, 5f, 28–29f; trapped in friendships of, 30, 32, 93, 131–33; at UNH, 1, 16, 16t, 37, 70, 130, 139–40, 140t, 155, 160, 169; weak tie friendships and, 62

Trips (orientation program), 25–26, 36, 39, 64, 107, 169, 240nn21–22

Tulane University, 216

universities. *See* colleges and universities; *and specific institutions*

University of Central Florida, 246n13

University of Michigan, 240n18

University of New Hampshire (UNH): academic-social balance at, 156, 227t; betweenness centrality of friendship networks, 141, 141t, 225t; campus access for case study, 217–18; case study design, 11–12, 218–22, 238n58; case study participant characteristics, 226–27t, 230–33t; clubs and organizations, 4, 44–46, 56–57, 154, 169, 204; compartmentalized networks, 16, 16t, 91–93, 139, 140t, 160; density of friendship networks, 16t, 141, 141t, 225t, 251n52; description of, 13–15, 154, 228–29t, 246n10 (chap. 4); dining halls, 15, 51, 57, 58, 72, 75; dorms and roommate selection, 20, 41–43, 154–55, 159, 201; friendship markets, 4, 6, 31–36, 39, 41–46, 49–59, 61, 140, 158–60, 182, 248n30; Greek organizations, 53–55, 158–60, 242n51; modularity of friendship networks, 141, 141t, 225t; multiplex ties, 72, 81, 165; orientation and pre-orientation programs, 32, 36, 39, 158, 182, 203, 240n22; same-gender friendships and, 251n47; sampler networks, 16, 16t, 93, 140, 140t, 160, 247n15; selection for case study, 11, 12, 216; size of friendship networks, 16t, 140, 141t, 225t; sociograms of students, 34f, 40f, 71f, 92f, 155f, 161f; sports teams, 4, 6, 13, 46, 139, 238n59, 242n45; study abroad programs, 13, 52; tight-knit networks, 1, 16, 16t, 37, 70, 130, 139–40, 140t, 155, 160, 169; time spent with friends at, 70–77, 143; undergraduate enrollment, 157, 246n13; weak tie friendships and, 62, 206

unstructured interactions, 204, 206, 236n10

Vonhoff, Christina, 252n12, 254n21

vulnerability, 31, 67, 78, 194, 196

weak tie friendships, 62–63, 67–69, 144, 167, 178, 206, 243n60, 246n6 (chap. 4)

well-being. *See* health and well-being

White students: density of friendship networks, 189, 250n30; graduation rate for, 9, 237n39; in high status social spaces, 249n12; homophilous friendship bonds among, 179; interracial friendships, 174, 185–87, 189; microaggressions from, 185; same-race friendships, 8

White supremacy, 10

women: academic and social support among, 195; communication skills of, 192–94, 250n40; cultural frames regarding, 192–93, 221; density of friendship networks, 189, 250n31, 251n52; emotional labor of, 194, 196, 197–99; mom-like friendships of, 188, 192, 194, 250n29, 250n42; same-gender friendships of, 27, 194–96, 236n23, 251nn47–48; sampler networks and, 196–97. *See also* gender

Wood, Kate, 217